PERGAMON INTERNATIONA
of Science, Technology, Engineerin
*The 1000-volume original paperback libi
industrial training and the enjoyment of leisure*
Publisher: Robert Maxwell, M.C.

GROUP THEORY FOR
SOCIAL WORKERS

An Introduction

SOCIAL WORK SERIES

General Editor: Mrs Jean P Nursten

Other titles in the series

Other titles of interest

GROUP THEORY
FOR SOCIAL WORKERS
An Introduction

by

KEN HEAP

PERGAMON PRESS

OXFORD · NEW YORK · TORONTO · SYDNEY
PARIS · FRANKFURT

U.K.	Pergamon Press Ltd., Headington Hill Hall, Oxford OX3 0BW, England
U.S.A.	Pergamon Press Inc., Maxwell House, Fairview Park, Elmsford, New York 10523, U.S.A.
CANADA	Pergamon of Canada Ltd., 75 The East Mall, Toronto, Ontario, Canada
AUSTRALIA	Pergamon Press (Aust.) Pty. Ltd., P.O. Box 544, Potts Point, N,S.W. 2011, Australia
FRANCE	Pergamon Press SARL, 24 rue des Ecoles, 75240 Paris, Cedex 05, France
FEDERAL REPUBLIC OF GERMANY	Pergamon Press GmbH, 6242 Kronberg-Taunus, Pferdstrasse 1, Federal Republic of Germany

First English edition 1977
Reprinted 1978

Library of Congress Cataloging in Publication Data

Heap, Ken, 1929-
Group theory for social workers.

Translation of Gruppeteori for sosialairbeidere.
Bibliography: p.
Includes index.
1. Social groups. 2. Small groups. 3. Social group work. I. Title.
HM131.H3713   1976   301.18′5   76-12521
ISBN 0-08-018956-3 (Hardcover)
ISBN 0-08-018955-5 (Flexicover)

Printed in Great Britain by The Aberdeen University Press.

Contents

Foreword

This is not a book about *how* to conduct social work with groups. Its aim is rather to introduce some of the facts, concepts and propositions about behaviour in small groups, which social workers need to know about in order to understand how problems, needs and feelings are exhibited or aroused in groups. It is an introduction to background group theory, rather than to group work practice.

There is an extensive and growing literature on group theory, to which several disciplines have contributed, each with its own purpose, frame of reference and terminology. Some group theory is generated by clinical practice or by intuitive and sensitive observation of life situations. Much of it is a product of rigorous and sophisticated laboratory experiment. Some is addressed to apparently peripheral fragments of group life or to seemingly academic questions. The methodology of small-group research is often very technical and its language rather specialised.

These and other factors imbue the subject with a daunting and distant quality for many practitioners, who—quite appropriately—are more concerned with utility. The social workers, teachers, psychiatrists, nurses, milieu therapists, residential workers and many others whose professional life is spent in group situations often ignore or retreat from this abundance of obstruse technicality. It seems so far removed from the urgent realities and crises with which they must daily deal in the groups they serve. ... This is regrettable, for the group theory already developed contains a wealth of material with important implications for group treatment. Further, the current trend in group dynamics is markedly in the direction of treatment-orientated and action-orientated research. We have entered an era where the social worker and others in clinical and educational practice have available an increasing and valuable aid to group work in their various fields.

I hope that this book will encourage the reader to make a preliminary approach to this material. It is intended primarily for social work students and practising social workers who are extending their practice to include work with groups. My experience in teaching, supervising and planning group work programmes in recent years has revealed the need for an introduction to the study of group dynamics which emphasises its relevance to social work, and which makes its concepts more meaningful and accessible to colleagues and students about to enter this field. This purpose is reflected in the concepts chosen for discussion, in the occasional discussion of their possible treatment implications, and in the illustrative case material.

Since the book is so specifically addressed to social workers and students, knowledge of the aims and principles of social work is assumed, as is a certain familiarity with the concepts of the behavioural sciences basic to social work. Despite this emphasis, however, the findings, propositions and ways of observing and thinking about groups which are the core of the book have much wider relevance.

Group processes are a part of life. They are not the private possession of any profession. Other professional people who work in group settings may recognise the notions discussed here as representing group processes relevant also for their fields. But the implications for their professional functions would be different in many cases, and other examples than mine would be more appropriate. However, the phenomena of group interaction, the ordering of group life and its components of change, growth or resistance are not essentially different simply because a group is in a classroom or hospital ward rather than an office in a social work agency. I hope therefore that colleagues in other fields than social work will also find the book relevant and will seek analogies between the social work examples included here and experiences in their own settings.

The material in this volume is adapted from a brief sequence of lectures and exercises given during the course of a three-year course in social work. Our intention is to disseminate selected basic knowledge, rather than to present a large number of facts and findings which can already be found in many excellent books. I have only included those facts and findings which I regard as the minimum essential background knowledge for the student of social group work method. I hope this will help the student to observe and reflect about group phenomena on the basis of increased interest and awareness, and perhaps to seek further knowledge of this important subject. I have provided numerous references with this in mind.

There are notes at the end of most chapters—recommended reading, associations to the main material or explanations of terms which may be unfamiliar; anything whose inclusion in the body of the book might have distracted attention from the main material.

In the book I use the "we" form. This is not a royal kind of "we", but an ambivalent and rather troubled kind; an attempt to avoid both the self-assertive "I" and the impersonal and uncommitted "one".... But "we" don't really like it.

In reading books by other people, I confess that I usually hop over that part of the foreword where thanks and acknowledgements are made to all kinds of people. I shall never do so again. I now realise the extent of their contribution.

Whatever merit this book may have is due in large measure to the helpful criticism and suggestions made by a number of colleagues and friends. I am profoundly grateful to them for their criticism and encouragement, their perception and their generosity with hard-pressed time. These colleagues, to whom I am so indebted, are Elizabeth Irvine, formerly of York University and the Tavistock Clinic, Wallace McCulloch of Bradford University, Siegi Hirsch of Brussels, Inger-Fi Skar of Nic Waal's Child Psychiatric Institute, Oslo, and my wife Kari Killén Heap, of the Aarhus School of Social Work, Denmark, and formerly of the Norwegian State School of Social Work, Oslo. I am aware of weaknesses, which probably have a great deal to do with the advice I chose not to accept. The responsibility for these is of course entirely my own.

I am also deeply indebted to the colleagues in Norwegian, Danish and British agencies who have made their case material available to me, and generously consented to its inclusion here. The locations, identifying information and agencies have all been disguised in the usual ways in order to protect the confidentiality and private concerns of the clients and other people involved, and I am therefore unfortunately not able here to thank by name these contributors who have provided so much of the material of the book. I most warmly thank these necessarily anonymous friends.

I wish also to thank the publishers and individual authors who have kindly given permission to quote material to which they hold copyright. These include Penguin Books, for the passages from Storr's *Human Aggression* and from Foulkes and Anthony's *Group Psychotherapy* on pages 75 and 39 respectively; Harper and Row, for the passages from Sherif and Sherif's *Reference Groups* appearing on pages 48, 57 and 68; Mohr Books, for the passage from le Carré's *The Spy Who Came in from the Cold* on page 110; Knopf, for the passage from Redl's "Group emotion and leadership" on page 150; the *Journal of Social Issues* for the extracts from Benne and Sheats' "Functional roles of group members" appearing on pages 144 to 147; and the Family Service Association of America for the passage from Wasser's *Creative Approaches in Casework with the Aging* which appears on page 198.

Wm. Fawcett Hill of California, Miss E. M. Goldberg of London, Richard Lake of Idaho, David Macarov of Jerusalem, Henry Maier of Washington, Robert Bales of Harvard, Rosemary Sarri of Michigan, and Ralph Kolodny of Boston have all kindly given permission to quote from their publications. Several of these colleagues have also been willing to enter into correspondence about their current work, which has both enriched the book and greatly eased the task of writing it.

Gwenneth Bellerby, away in the Midlands of England, has with patient skill transformed my collection of handwritten notes, Scotch tape and pencilled arrows into a readable manuscript and has safely shuttled the various bits and pieces through the postal strikes and services of three countries. Blessings upon you, Gwenneth!

Finally I wish to express my profound gratitude and admiration for those many clients and students who daily continue to teach me that most valuable of all lessons—how very much more there is to learn.

Aarhus, 1975   KEN HEAP

CHAPTER 1

Introduction

Groups and the Social Worker

The social worker is concerned with many kinds of groups, whether as leader or member, as insider or outsider. In this book we shall have much to say about behaviour in groups and the vicissitudes of group process, its value and its problems. But first we must discuss the varieties of group with which the social worker is concerned, and his role in each kind.

Social workers increasingly work not only with groups of clients, but also in interdisciplinary groups with colleagues. We work with, for, and—occasionally—in opposition to groups of elected or appointed officials who have administrative responsibility for various social services. These different group settings will be introduced briefly and separately.

GROUPS OF CLIENTS

Social workers provide preventive, treatment and rehabilitive service to groups whose members have certain psycho-social problems or disadvantages in common. Such activity is usually called either *social group work* or *social work with groups*. We are discussing groups whose members are "clients" and whose formal "leaders" are social workers, who have both professional responsibility for and professional relationships with the former. While social group work is less well established in Europe than in North America, we are now developing an increasing interest in the method and it is being adopted into the service and practice of a growing number of social agencies in European countries.

Social work with groups is a manifold activity, which embraces numerous techniques. Its objectives are many and diverse. Its sphere of application includes the whole range of existing social work services. The organisational and political trend in the profession's present development suggests, further, that it will play an increasingly important role in tomorrow's social work.

The method involves a purposive and sensitive use of the worker's relationship with the group members. This leads to many different kinds of verbal and active intervention by the worker, as well as to the demonstration of certain attitudes. The use of the relationship may be supportive, stimulating, confrontive, informative, limiting, reflective, or have many other qualities. In some situations the worker will also decide to be inactive in the interests of the group's need to develop its own resources and ways of working.

This latter point is important. The worker is rarely the *main* agent of change. This is a function of the group itself. Fundamental to the group work method is the liberation and mobilisation of members' own ability to help themselves and each other through participation in the group. To this end they co-operate in discussing common problems. They share in relevant and rewarding activities. They are democratically and responsibly involved in the life and growth of their groups. Through a very wide range of styles and foci of activity, social work groups help themselves, and are helped by the social worker, to reach an equally wide range of objectives.

Activities, therapeutic discussion and involvement in the ordinary processes of social living are present in all social work groups, but which of these receives most emphasis is determined by the *aims* of the group concerned. These in their turn depend upon the needs, problems and resources of the members.

We shall discuss this question of the aims of social work with groups further. A well-known definition of social-group work (Konopka, 1964) refers to its objectives of ".... enchancing social functioning" and aiding members to "... cope more effectively with their personal, group or community problems". These "personal, group or community problems" may be manifested in many different ways, so the broad aim of "enchancing social functioning" embraces in practice a wide spectrum of more specific objectives.

We shall not attempt an exhaustive and systematic classification of these, but we shall indicate some of the most common aims in order to provide a preliminary orientation in the field. In relation to each aim we shall refer to pertinent case accounts and discussions in the literature, selected for both variety and brevity, to serve the purpose of orientation. (In subsequent chapters we shall not use case material from the literature, but illustrate instead with unpublished material from current North European practice.)

Some social work groups aim primarily at *alleviating social isolation.* Such groups have the preventive function of reducing the debilitating effects of isolation, as well as the more creative purposes of life-enrichment and increasing self-esteem. This is a common aim of work with the aged and infirm, with the severely handicapped and with many former psychiatric patients. The literature has examples of social group work with patients suffering from muscular dystrophy (Eisenstein, 1959), with deaf-blind adults (Verstrate, 1959), with mentally-ill people living in the community (O'Connor, 1970; Riehman and O'Brien, 1973), with adult male exhibitionists (Freese, 1972), and with young unmarried mothers (Barclay, 1969).

Another aim is that of *orientating and preparing* people for new experiences which may arouse uncertainty, disorientation, or fear. While this usually involves giving information, its inclusion in the social work function assumes that working through feelings precipitated by the new experience is also necessary. Cases in point are pre-discharge groups of prison-inmates or psychiatric patients, intake groups in mental hospitals and children's hospitals, groups of prospective adoptive parents, and so on. Germane case reports, typical of this application of social group work, are those by Saul *et al.* (1962) on an admission group for new residents in an old people's home, Eisen (1958) on group work with newly admitted psychiatric patients, and Champion *et al.* (1963) who describe group work with single mothers about to enter or re-enter full-time employment. Knapp and Hansen (1973) describe an extensive programme of group work with parents whose children are dying of leukemia, where support in the important process of "anticipatory mourning" was a main function of the groups reported.

Other groups are mainly intended to contribute to the *social learning and maturation* of people who encounter obstacles to normal social growth and development. Such groups are often conceived as a kind of "mini-society", where social skills may be tested and developed, in the hope that they may be generalised into more mature and satisfying social behaviour in the wider society outside the group. Members are accorded the greatest possible opportunities for taking decisions, accepting responsibility, working through conflicts of interests, and experimenting with forms of co-operation. Varied activities enable different styles of contact and self-presentation. Group response to these is an important developmental influence on the individual members.

This kind of social work group is most often found in the youth service. Clubs for young people at risk, settlements and adventure projects are common examples. Treatment homes and hostels for maladjusted children and young people provide rich opportunities in the daily life of the agency for such experiental social learning. Currently, some agencies for young misusers of drugs also offer this kind of treatment. Many youth-work agencies also provide a base for so-called "unattached" group workers, who contact young people at risk in their own milieux—street-corners, derelict housing, empty warehouses, the docks, and so on. Also many adults' social problems have their roots in immaturity, and can be relieved by this kind of group work. Groups of neglectful mothers, homeless hostel dwellers, prison inmates, over-protected young deaf adults and many others have been reported in the literature or observed.

The literature on group work aiming at social and emotional maturation is very extensive indeed, so any attempt to suggest "representative" or "most rewarding" papers on this subject involves a large element of chance and subjectivity. With this reservation, we suggest that the following papers may provide an informative cross-section.

Matthews (1964) attempts in a brief note to define the contribution of this kind of social work to youth services. (This note was later elaborated and included in a book on group work with young people (Matthews, 1966)). Matsuschima (1962), in the context of residential treatment of disturbed and aggressive boys in early puberty, describes the impact of group living on these clients and its potential as a therapeutic resource. These themes of group and community treatment of youth problems are taken up at a more general level by Konopka (1970) in a clear and thoughtful paper. Books by both Spergel (1966) and Goetschius and Tash (1967) discuss group work with unattached youth engaged in or susceptible to criminality, while Ackley and Fliegel (1960) offer in a brief article a more readily available impression of this kind of "street-corner" group work. Euster (1972) argues for an expansion of the school social worker's role and shows how social-group work may be used to further social learning in the school situation. Richards and Lee (1972) sketch the use of group process in an imaginative and systematic approach to furthering maturation in six different groups of young retarded adults who were in training in sheltered workshops. Group work aimed at the social and emotional growth of immature adults is reported by Walker and Irvine (1968), who describe and discuss the patient and sensitive process of helping nine problem-family mothers to achieve some incease in their self-esteem, their capacity to relate to others, and their ability to use their skills and resources. Shapiro (1971) describes group work in the setting of a slum "hotel", whose reduced and alienated tenants included the chronically and mentally ill, hard-drug addicts, alcoholics, old people, jobless migrants and petty thieves. All of these were near-destitute, and received subsistence payments from official welfare sources. Shapiro's work was aimed at mobilising the latent resources of this profoundly dependent and passive group, and increasing their mutual helpfulness, as well as their ability to use existing medical and welfare facilities.

Another important aim of social work with groups is that of *solving problems*. One might well say that this is the aim of all social work, including the ventures mentioned above, but we are thinking of problem-solving in a more focused and circumscribed sense. Rather than such general aims as preventing isolation or aiding social growth, we are concerned here with the needs of some clients to take decisions, to work through feelings, to ventilate and to solve—wholly or partially—a specific problem in some area of life. "I am a discharged prisoner. No job. No digs. They said you would help me. ... " " We have just got our first child. He's a mongol. We know someone who would take him, but ... ". "We think our 12-year-old is beginning sniffing or something. But he just won't talk to us anymore."

The social worker's clients do not come to him, as to an analyst, and say, "I don't know what is the matter with me. I get nothing out of life. I'm so depressed . . . but I don't know why . . .", or "I am chronically unhappy and tense; diffusely but continually anxious. Please help me", or other messages which say, in effect, "Change me". Nor do they come, as to the revolutionary leader, and say "Change the world around me". The social worker's client typically presents circumscribed and fairly well-defined problems, or clusters of inter-related problems, such as those quoted earlier above. Social work treatment is focused upon and limited to these. Other issues such as underlying feelings, attitudes and environmental factors are brought into treatment only to the extent that they facilitate a clarification of the problem with which the client is faced, and help him to act, or to make decisions or develop attitudes and behaviour which relate to his needs and to the realities of his situation.

This is all familiar to the caseworker or casework student, but many such problems are also dealt with today by clients working together in groups. The student will find that this kind of social work is often referred to in the literature as group counselling, or even as casework in groups. Perhaps because it often involves sitting in a circle and talking about shared problems and feelings, it is also sometimes called group therapy. This is certainly one area where the competence and functions of the social worker and the clinical psychologist may overlap. How-ever, we will not in this book clarify further this rather complex question of the designation of treatment methods and its relationship to aims, competence and required knowledge. Our present purpose may be adequately served by illustration, without entering further into problems of definition and classification. The following papers provide typical case reports and discussions.

A timely report by Strickler and Allgeyer (1967), which uses the concepts of crisis theory and intervention, describes the use of short-term problem-solving groups in an adult "walk-in" clinic. Lavan (1970) reports simultaneous group treatment of mothers and their behaviourally disturbed children attending a child guidance clinic. As social worker she was one of the two leaders of the mother's group, which was intended to achieve greater understanding and some modification of attitudes towards the children and their problems, so as to be able to handle them more appropriately in the home situation.

Goldner and Kyle (1960) report a group of patients with cardiac illness, which was formed during the members' post-crisis hospitalisation. The aim of the group was to offer support and information and to stimulate contributions from "experienced" members, to help these patients avoid such common, but self-destructive, "solutions" to cardiac illness as excessive invalidism or denial of the problem. Many other comparable uses of problem-solving groups in hospitals are described in the literature. For example, Abramson (1975) reports the use of group work in helping the families of burn-injured patients: Singler (1975) describes group work with hospitalised stroke patients. Frey and Pizzitola (1973), in another setting, show how experience in groups of concrete problem-solving with attainable problems may also serve wider and more long-term goals, for instance as a feature of the treatment of schizophrenia. Fenton and Wiltse (1963) have prepared a collection of brief case reports of group counselling in American welfare agencies. Many of these concern "problem-solving" groups in the sense in which we have used the term, including work with adoptive parents, foster parents, alcoholic clients seeking financial aid, newly divorced mothers, elderly people attempting to find work, and others.

We have already indicated that clarification of feelings is a common feature of practice in such problem-solving groups. As in casework, this may sometimes involve the exploration of feelings which are not immediately accessible since they lie at a preconscious level. Social work at this depth may be said to have the aim of *achieving insight*. For example, our client is an immigrant worker who is unable to keep a job, and the problem is to help him find a job which he is able to keep. In order to do this, however, the social worker may have to help him to examine the ways in which he ensures his own repeated dismissal. The reasons for his doing so may also be brought into treatment, for instance the client's wish to provide a situation in which "circumstances" compel him to return to his home country. He may be destroying his chances here in order to resolve his ambivalence about the initial decision to leave home. Problem-solving in this case necessitates gaining insight into the preconscious motivation of behaviour. This type and level of practice is familiar from casework. Social group work aimed at gaining insight, or whose aims presuppose insight, is also quite well represented in the literature.

Hallowitz and Stephens (1959) describe a group of fathers of behaviourally disturbed children, in which the alleviation and articulation of repressed conflicts and feelings of failure played a central role in treatment. Green (1970) briefly reports a group of unemployed negro men, ghetto dwellers in an American city. Subject all their lives to multiple disadvantages, they had also developed self-defeating ways of dealing with some of their problems, which were conducive to their own continued recapture in the familiar net of discrimination, manipulation and failure. One aim of this group was to "gain insight into behaviour and attitudes that inhibit(ed) effective functioning". Sanges (1962) describes a group of chronically ill geriatric patients who were unresponsive or subtly hostile to all attempts to help them to use the hospital facilities better and to derive greater satisfaction from the social life of the ward. A counselling group was formed with the aim of gaining insight into the defensive and inhibiting nature of their withdrawal, and of the sources of their irrational distrust and suspicion.

The problem-solving groups mentioned above, whether or not their aims necessitate the exploration of feelings and attitudes, are concerned with the problems of the *members* themselves. Focus is upon the clients' needs, conflicts and resources. However, like all social-work problems, these include environmental elements. Indeed some problems are primarily the results of environmental rather than personal conditions. Many features of current social and economic change compel people into situations where they need help. The rapidity of technological development, the demand for mobility, the pervading fear of widespread unemployment, rising costs, increasing bureaucratic power, the emphasis on educational achievement and productive performance, the population explosion and the resultant gap between services needed and services available—all place an increasing number of people in the client role.

Skilled treatment may alleviate the results of some of these induced problems. Social workers are, however, increasingly participating in ventures whose aim is to prevent the need for such treatment occurring. This preventive activity covers a spectrum including direct personal engagement in political life, and increasing professional involvement in social planning and administration. More social workers also contribute to social debate in the mass media. But this part of social work also includes work with *groups* of citizens aiming at *solving specific environmental problems* which affect them. Such organisation is further intended to decrease the feelings of impotence, futility and alienation which are concomitants of many of these problems. This kind of problem-solving group work provides the area of social work in which client-treatment and community work overlap. It is sometimes contended—in our view quite wrongly—that a dichotomy exists between these two kinds of activity. The use of groups we have just mentioned shows how far common principles, values and aims underlie these closely related methods. An introductory impression of this important area of social work may be gained from Benington (1970), who describes a community development project in Coventry, England, carried out in a heavily populated district faced with problems of poverty, slum clearance, high-rise development, increased concentration of immigrants, and the burdens of a "slum" tradition and reputation. This project was conducted at several levels, with a team of three social workers in different roles. One of them was exclusively occupied in direct group work with the local tenants, establishing and developing many different kinds of interest groups, activity groups and action groups. Purcell and Specht (1965) describe a contrasting case in which the tenants of one single tenement house, neglected by landlord and public services alike, were helped to organise effective action to achieve improvement in their living conditions. Of many papers dealing with the social-worker's role as "mediator" between client groups and organisations which provide inadequate welfare services, we recommend Heymann (1971) who shows, with brief case illustration, how the social worker in the American anti-poverty campaign has in fact two sets of clients and roles. He must help the poor to demand badly needed services, but must also help the social services concerned to co-ordinate and focus their fragmented, ineffective and ambivalent provision of service. In the same publication, Weiner (1971) discusses an experiment in group work with trade union representatives, which aimed at achieving better integration into the work situation of mentally impaired employees. (It should be mentioned that group work addressed to problems arising in the clients' environment—either locally or on a wider scale—has only slowly become established in practice. An American study on the "misuse of groups" (Levinson, 1973) indicates a marked tendency to use groups for "changing individual behaviour" even where "collective effort for changing the clients' environment is clearly needed").

We have briefly indicated some common aims of social work with groups of clients. It is important to note that these are not mutually exclusive. Some groups, certainly, have only one of the aims mentioned, but some have two or even more simultaneously. Yet other groups first achieve one aim and then embark upon work directed to a subsequent aim. All of these alternatives are represented in the case reports and other articles which we have recommended. For example, Freese's (*op. cit.*) group of exhibitionists and voyeurs, through its success in the aim of furthering relationships between these very isolated men, was able to go further and facilitate both some problem-solving and the gaining of insight. Knapp and Hansen's *(op. cit.)* groups of parents of leukemia sufferers were intended to reduce isolation and to aid anticipatory mourning, but many concrete problems were also worked on and the parents' relationships with other persons and agencies in their environment were also clarified and improved.

We shall now remind the reader of other group situations, where the social worker is rarely the leader, but participates as colleague, employee or advocate. In spite of his very different role in such groups, knowledge of group dynamics is equally relevant and useful.

ADMINISTRATIVE GROUPS

Publicly elected or appointed bodies of many kinds proliferate in the administration of social services. Most of these were originally formed by the same waves of social legislation and energetic philanthropic initiative which led to the growth of modern social work.

Such bodies control or influence the policies of most major social agencies. Many both determine and scrutinise the detailed activities and dispositions of agencies, even at the level of the individual client. Their mandate, their wisdom or lack of it, and the way in which they use their power are often of critical importance for the work of the agency.

Most such bodies establish some kind of formal group structure with which social workers and others have contact. Common examples of this kind of group are child care committees, probation committees, social service councils, boards of managers or governors of diverse institutions, benches of lay magistrates and so on. It is not the concern of this book to discuss the contribution which such groups make to the social services. But clearly it would be as naîve to contend that the system always brings forth well-functioning groups of wise, humane, intuitive and informed members as to contend that it never does so. Even in our own necessarily limited experience, we have experienced wide variations in such bodies, owing to differences in composition, in styles of leadership and in the prevailing priorities, values and attitudes of members. However that may be, social workers are in frequent—sometimes daily— contact with such groups.

Some workers act as secretaries to these groups, perhaps performing both administrative and field-work functions. Many are appointed and employed by such groups, accepting the treatment or preventive tasks which the group determines, and being accountable to the group for the quality of job-performance. Some social workers also function as advisers to such groups. In this role they may collect information, suggest plans and dispositions, and may submit for committee approval a wide range of both proposals for future service and solutions to current problems. Some workers play all of these roles at the same time.

The degree of skill with which these complex and delicate role-situations are handled is often quite decisive for the quality and relevance of the help which the individual client receives, or sometimes for whether he receives any help at all.

GROUPS IN PROFESSIONAL CO-OPERATION

Many kinds of public service increasingly necessitate inter-professional co-operation.

Loeb (1960) succinctly explains this trend while indicating some problems. Skills are increasingly specialised, and the knowledge base of each profession becomes both more extensive and esoteric. This leads to mutual dependence between the professions, since each possesses fragments of the total skills and knowledge required for the solution of complex problems. Increased awareness of the complexity of human problems therefore increases this mutual dependence. However, each profession spends progressively more time in training, often in specialised institutions, and develops attitudes, behaviour, values and even language peculiar to its specialisation. Thus, the necessity for inter-professional co-operation increases simultaneously with difficulties in inter-professional communication. We would add to Loeb's analysis that emerging professions, of which the twentieth century has seen several, are inevitably somewhat defensive, and tend to be either too assertive or too self-effacing in co-operation with others.

Social workers are involved in a great deal of inter-professional co-operation. Their work brings them into contact with architects, clergymen, civil servants, doctors, employers, health visitors, residential workers, lawyers, nurses, police, psychiatrists, psychologists, teachers and others. Much of this co-operation consists of spontaneous inter-agency contact in connection with specific problems which arise. However, much also occurs in planned and comparatively structured group situations which it is relevant to mention here.

There is the *staff group* of *traditionally organised institutions* in which social work is a secondary function. A hospital, a prison, a magistrate's court, or a large school are cases in point. Most such institutions are hierarchies, where relative status is defined by both regulation and tradition. Tasks (which do not necessarily coincide with areas of competence) are also usually distributed by directives from higher-status members of the staff. The extent to which a social worker in such a setting is able to serve the interests of the clients effectively is therefore determined by the flexibility of the system, the possibilities of communication both upwards and downwards in the hierarchy, the worker's ability to demonstrate and explain his function, and the other members' ability to understand and accept this explanation.

Such hierarchies contrast somewhat with another kind of staff group, namely the *"team"*. The team approach has become increasingly common during the past two decades, particularly in psychiatry, family counselling, rehabilitation and more recently in social planning. While teams must also have some kind of formal organisation in order to function, they are based on a more egalitarian philosophy. The team principle assumes the equal value and authority of all relevant contributions, and encourages joint participation in problem-solving. Members' contributions to the group are assumed to be derived from their special knowledge and competence. The efficiency of such teams seems to be closely related to the members' ability to limit their activity in this way, while the atmosphere, relationships and effectiveness of the group are also influenced by members' ability to accept that some knowledge, skills and functions must be common.

The staff team is not unlike another kind of group, namely the *Case Conference or Committee,* in which social workers and perhaps others from a number of agencies combine their observations and experiences in order to resolve common problems, or to give more effective help to a particular family or client with whom several agencies have contact.

Our final example of an inter-professional group is that formed for the purpose of *group consultation,* which refers to consultation as defined by Caplan (1959, 1961 and 1970). Both in order to engage clinical workers in preventive functions, as well as to utilise clinical resources economically, Caplan and his colleagues developed the method of "mental health consultation". A number of "key persons"—family doctors, nursery school teachers, club leaders, health visitors and others—have contact with children and families at a period when incipient problems may be both recognised and treated. Their own professional skills do not necessarily equip them for this function. Mental health consultation was developed as a means of helping such key people to understand and deal with these problems. This is not only a method of prevention, however, but has also been extended to enable treatment homes, special schools and the like to improve the quality of their service by the use of expertise from "outside". Psychiatrists, psychologists and social workers have all been involved in giving such consultation. It may occur either on a one-to-one basis or in a group led by one consultant.

This method has been remarkably well formulated and systematised. It is an economical, difficult and highly productive use of groups. An interesting example can be found in the companion presentations of Brown (1960) and Docker-Drysdale (1960). Mrs. Docker-Drysdale, the leader of a residential treatment and educational home for disturbed children, describes the experience of receiving consultation.

Miss Brown, the agency's consultant, describes the social-worker's procedures and observations in that particular instance of group consultation.

We have drawn attention to some of the group situations in which social workers are engaged. We have especially emphasised their work with groups of clients and have sketched a number of common aims of such social group work. It is this aspect of group experiences with which social workers are currently most concerned. At the same time, we have found it appropriate to remind briefly of certain other group experiences, concerned respectively with the administrative or elected groups under whose aegis many social workers serve, and with different kinds of groups established for the purpose of co-operation.

It will already have become clear both that social workers have many different functions in groups, and that some of the group settings in which they function are very complex. In all of these settings it is therefore desirable for social workers to understand as much as possible about group behaviour. This is particularly true where work with groups of clients is concerned, since most group-work method is based on understanding ("social diagnosis") of the needs which are manifested by group behaviour. What the worker does is determined by what he hopes to achieve. This in its turn is related to members' needs and problems. His main guide to these is his understanding of the members' behaviour in the group itself. The social worker's role in the administrative and co-operative groups we have mentioned is very different from that in such client groups. We suggest, however, that here also his possibilities for effective contribution depend upon his taking into account the various influences of the group situation on both the other members and himself.

In short, today's social worker must know something about group dynamics.

The Field of Group Dynamics

Group dynamics, group processes, group theory. These are alternative terms for the study of human behaviour in groups. Some readers may disagree, contending that they are discrete terms. There is, however, no wide consensus on differentiated usage of these expressions. Indeed, the term "group dynamics" alone is used in no less than four quite distinct ways (Knowles and Knowles, 1959).

We do not propose to discuss terminology. We merely wish to emphasise that *our subject is human group behaviour,* and to note that we will, with a happy disregard for semantics, use these terms alternatively to denote that subject.

Group dynamics is a very extensive study. Research and theory have been stimulated by a wide variety of interests, including industry, education, warfare, criminology, penology, social planning, therapy of various kinds, academic curiosity and others. Moreover, investigators of group behaviour represent several disciplines. Prominent among these are social and clinical psychology, small-group sociology, cultural anthropology, inter-personal psychiatry, organisation theory and social work. We should also remind ourselves that over the centuries philosophers, dramatists, authors, poets and political innovators have also enriched our insight into group experiences.

Because of the many sources of its concepts and propositions group theory is a difficult field in which to orientate oneself initially. It is poorly co-ordinated, terminology is inconsistent, and investigation is conducted within many frames of reference, which also often overlap.

There are no organised and exclusive schools of group dynamics. However, investigators reflect a variety of orientations and parent disciplines, both in the phenomena which engage their interest and in their approach to understanding them. Knowles and Knowles *(op.cit.),* in a useful primer, distinguish between the approaches of Field Theory, Factor Analysis, Formal Organisation, Sociometry, Interaction Process Analysis, Psycho-analysis and Social group Work. While these do in fact represent approaches which have their special characteristics and which have all generated theory, there are few investigators today who would identify themselves exclusively with any one of these schools. Overlapping between these and other orientations characterises modern group dynamic investigation.

In our proposal for advanced social work training we have indicated another possible parameter of differentiation between approaches (Heap and Killén-Heap, 1969). We distinguish there between group

theoreticians who are predominantly sociological or social-psycholog-
ical in orientation, and those who are mainly influenced by psycho-
analytic thinking, or by other clinical approaches. Among the former,
Lewin, Lippitt, Bales, Jennings, Mills and the Sherif's come readily to
mind. The latter may be represented by, among others, Redl, Bion,
Scheidlinger, Durkin, Ezriel, Rogers, Perls and Stock-Whitaker.
(These names, with references, will occur later in this text.) Again,
however, our cautious use of such terms as "predominantly" and
"mainly" reflects our hesitation about ascribing rigid commitment on the
part of the writers named to these orientations and parent disciplines. The
trend in modern group investigation is away from exclusivity and
towards a gradual integration of complementary perspectives.

Individual studies, however, continue in various degrees at least to
emphasise some kind of favoured orientation, some particular type of
problem, or some parent discipline. This is an inevitable concomitant
of research, since it is in the nature of research method for single
variables or small clusters of variables to become the foci of study.
Other aspects of group life are either stabilised by some research
procedure or consciously excluded from study. The researcher selects,
and in doing so he reflects his preoccupations.

Unlike research, practice with groups—as in social work—does not
allow such narrowing of focus. The group worker in any field is faced
with the total group experience, and cannot isolate aspects of it.
Whether in school, psychotherapy, residential care, or social work,
group members are present in order to manifest and meet their own
needs; they need a leader or facilitator, not a researcher. Thus they
demonstrate both individually and as a group a myriad complex forms
of behaviour which the worker must understand and to which he must
respond. They react on the basis of their own needs and personalities
to the group situation, to the worker, to their problems, to each other
and to the environment in which the group takes place. Clearly, no
single approach to group dynamics, no single behavioural science,
can provide a frame of reference enabling the worker to understand so
many different interacting variables. But he must attempt, as far as
humanly possible, to gain such understanding. In the continuing, and
perhaps inevitable, absence of a synthesis of the various approaches,
the social worker must therefore attempt to acquire useful insights

from all those aspects of group dynamics which have potential relevance for his particular work. All approaches contribute something to an understanding of the total group experience. The social worker must therefore become sufficiently familiar with them to enable him to observe, to understand and participate as appropriately as possible.

The student may well become engrossed in a particular approach. The satisfying precisions of small-group sociology and the exciting speculations of psychodynamics, for instance, appeal to different people. But it is important to avoid total commitment to any one approach to group processes. Such commitment would involve setting up what Deasy (1964) has called "conceptual screens" which cut the worker off from other dimensions of understanding. Thus, for instance, a number of studies cited in this book combine sociometric measurement with interaction process analysis. They would be either impossible or impoverished without such combination. Similarly, in our introduction to communication theory it will be seen that we also find it necessary to use psycho-analytical concepts (defence mechanisms) in order to interpret the case material more fully.

In brief, the social worker's approach to group theory must be *eclectic*. But, because of the sheer mass of material, a life-long study in itself, the social worker also has to be very *selective*.

We suggest that concepts should be selected for study on the basis of the *utilitarian* questions; "What, of all this, seems particularly relevant to the behaviour, problems and needs of social work groups? What is there here which may cast light on the ways in which clients must use the group situation and in which the social worker may participate and contribute?"

These are the considerations which have guided the selection of the material presented in the following chapters.

We include research findings, group dynamic models used in both research and practice, and observations from treatment and other practice situations. We also include more discursive and speculative comment about group behaviour in everyday life, in the hope that this will stimulate interest, discussion and association.

Finally, we will remind the reader that the book is intended as a minimal introduction to the field, and as a guide to further study. The further reading to which we refer consists in the main either of central formulations in the general study of groups, or of material which may take us further in focusing aspects of group theory onto social work situations.

CHAPTER 2

Some Purposes and Types of Groups

In this chapter we briefly introduce some important features of the relationship between individuals and the groups to which they belong. This is seen mainly in terms of the purposes of group membership. We also note some attempts which have been made to order such observations into group typologies. Some of the points raised here will be more extensively discussed in later chapters.

The Proliferation of Group Experiences

Group behaviour is as old as mankind. In his well-known evolutionary study of man, the zoologist Morris (1967) discusses how the "naked apes" were able to survive their descent from the safety of the trees and to gain supremacy over rival species. He proposes that their success in these encounters and their ability subsequently to exploit the environment more efficiently was a result not merely of greater brain size, but perhaps primarily of their ability to use resources in co-operative endeavour. Had man not developed skill in efficient social organisation, the vulnerable naked ape might have been yet another of the many species which did not survive at all.

Since man first existed, individuals have formed family groups and hunting groups. These in their turn have formed communities in order most effectively to meet common needs and to promote the integration and exploitation of the specialised skills of individual members. The earliest records we have of human activity—the paleolithic cave-drawings of Southern Europe—depict hunting, an organised group pursuit. Warfare, an equally ancient human institution, is in its very nature a group and inter-group activity. This is also true of social protest. The abused peasant of the Middle Ages, the American Negro of today, has had no possibility through individual action of improving his situation. It is only when such individuals have combined in groups that they have had sufficient impact on their surroundings to achieve meaningful and effective demand for change. The remarkable technological advances made during the twentieth century, no matter how ambivalently we may currently regard them, would have been entirely unattainable without highly organised and differentiated co-operative effort. These random examples show us that men throughout history have drawn together in groups of various kinds to meet the most vital of their needs—for production of food and implements, for emotional and physical warmth, for defence, shelter, protest and learning.

The individual is, then, to a large extent dependent for his physical and emotional survival upon the groups to which he belongs. If we may for the time being accept the notion of the group as an entity, we may also say that it is in its turn dependent upon its individual members for its own survival, and upon their individual contributions for achieving its objectives. Thus there exists a situation of mutual dependence between the individual and the group, which has its roots in the human condition. It exists in all cultures and at all times.

Certain features of contemporary Western society, however, demand of the individual that he experience membership of a steadily increasing number of groups in his daily life. Such factors as the increased complexity of production processes, population redistribution, the separation of labour from the home and of education from both, the fragmention of the family, the organisation of leisure, and the growth of bureaucracy, of organisations and of institutional social provisions, all conduce in various ways to increasing the number and variety of group experiences to which each individual is exposed.

For example, there are usually at least two family groups in which we live during our lifetime. Often more, with the increasing incidence of divorce and remarriage. There are many groups in which we learn, train or study at various levels. There is the group with whom we work in our own speciality or production unit. There are other specialised groups with whom we have tangential or interlocking contact in our work situation. There is the group with whom we travel to work or study. There is the group with whom we retrain to keep pace with developments in our field, or to acquire skills in yet new fields, that we may survive the processes of industrial change and re-location dictated by the interests of capital. There are the groups with whom we pursue our political, organisational and religious interests. There is the group with whom we perform our military service or declare our conscientious objection. There is the neighbourhood group, either meeting informally while clipping their lawns, or organising purposefully to demand that a pavement be built on the children's road to school. There is the group with whom we get away from it all, be that at the pub, on the football field, shooting small birds, or in the tranquility of a pot party. There is the T-group where we try to equip ourselves better for living, by increasing our sensitivity to self and others. There is the group where the repair job is attempted, in psychotherapy or social work. And many more. And there is the geriatric ward at the end of it all.

Types of Groups

This profusion and diversity of groups in modern life has inevitably challenged group theorists and practitioners to seek conceptual order by classification into types of groups.

One important distinction is that between *primary* and *secondary* groups. Curiously, this distinction seems to elude satisfactory definition. Many different formulations have been proposed since Cooley introduced these concepts in 1909. The main features, however, are these. Where groups are small enough to allow face-to-face contact, where this contact continues over sufficient time for relationships to be formed, and where these relationships generate mutual identification and influence, we may speak of a *primary* group. The family is the classical example of this intimate and dynamic type of group. Other small groups of people living together or undergoing meaningful experiences together over a period of time may also be described as primary groups. These may be exemplified by continuing peer groups through childhood and adolescence, by the inmates of an old people's home, by some treatment groups, by today's "communes", and the like.

Meanwhile we also use the term "group" to refer to larger and less intimate associations where individuals experience a degree of identification with others although they do not necessarily meet or even know these others. Some subjectively important characteristic or interest provides the common bond which is recognised by members. This may or may not give rise to formal organisation. Such associations are referred to as *secondary* groups. These may be exemplified by political parties, nations, people with a common handicap, interest or life-situation, supporters of a team, members of a profession, etc. Secondary groups lack the immediacy of primary groups, and membership will not normally exercise so great a degree of influence upon members. However, the influence of secondary group membership may at once be more intense and pervasive when the group is subjected to pressure or engaged in struggle, thereby intensifying the awareness and implications of "belonging". "I am a Jew", "I am a Black Panther", or "I am a homosexual", is a declaration of membership of a secondary group which is a vital determinant of one's identity feelings and life-style, and which draws its great strength, perhaps paradoxically, from exposure of the group to sustained persecution and humiliation. (One writer suggests that this process—which may lead to what he calls "ethnic affirmation"—provides resources, hitherto little used, which offer through political coalitions possibilities for effecting major social change (Vigilante, 1972). He points out a role for the social worker in such a development.)

The social worker is professionally engaged in both primary and secondary groups. At the risk of over-generalisation, we could say that work with primary groups is exemplified by such uses of the group as have traditionally been referred to as "group counselling", "social group work", "mental health consultation", "social group treatment", and the like, i.e. direct work with small client groups over a period of time. But those areas of social work usually referred to as "community work", "social action", "social planning" and "social administration" contribute to the prevention and solution of problems at the secondary group level. Some of this work is addressed directly to the secondary group by such means as publicising needs through communication media, political activity and stimulating organisation. But some may again involve direct work with face-to-face groups in neighbourhoods, committees, etc., at the so-called "grass roots" level.

While this book is mainly concerned with the small primary-type group it will from time-to-time be appropriate to associate from this material to the secondary group. It is sometimes rewarding to illuminate small-group dynamics by analogy with comparable secondary group phenomena. But caution must be exercised in doing so, since the differences between these types of group inevitably cause some important differences in the ways in which they function. For instance, while the dynamics of scapegoating in small groups are clearly relevant to discrimination against minorities in the wider society, the processes of communication or of decision-taking in primary and secondary groups are very different from each other.

The distinction between *psyche groups* and *socio groups* is also commonly made. These concepts were introduced by Jennings (1950). They build upon the observation that certain groups—usually informal and rather homogeneous—come into being in order to provide emotional satisfactions for members. Others—usually more formally constituted and relatively heterogenous—come together in order to pursue explicit goals. The former are called psyche groups and the latter are socio groups. The success of these groups may be registered respectively by how enjoyable are the former and how effective are the latter. But clearly this is an over-simplification. Jennings uses these concepts mainly to refer to complementary dimensions of group life, since most groups will demonstrate both psyche and socio attributes. One feature will, however, usually be dominant, and the other recessive. Thus, in a group which is predominantly psyche-orientated, the socio dimension is also necessary to give some direction and stability, and perhaps to provide a framework enabling the psyche dimension to flourish and enrich the group members.

Example 1. Among the groups meeting at the after-care unit of a large psychiatri: hospital is a knitting and crochet circle. The 11 women in the group, all former patients, live alone. They are middle-aged and elderly. Few are in employment. The group is not there primarily to knit: the knitting (socio-dimension) provides a focus and *raison d'être* for the formation of a group whose main functions (psyche-dimension) are to stimulate relationships, to counteract social isolation and to increase feelings of self-esteem.

Conversely, a group which is mainly characterised by socio attributes usually needs the psyche dimension in order that relationships may develop together with an emotional atmosphere favourable to co-operation in completion of the task.

Example 2. Members of a youth club call an extraordinary general meeting to clarify their attitudes and to formulate related and acceptable rules about the use and distribution of cannabis in the club. This is work—the socio dimension. But without the psyche dimension of emotional involvement, mutual identification, and enjoyment of the club, the task would be neither meaningful nor possible.

Many further suggestions for differential definition of group types exist, which build upon other attributes than the primary-secondary and the psyche-socio distinctions. A useful overview of such typologies has been compiled by Macarov (1964). Although this is by no means exhaustive, the author includes eighteen different classifications of group types based on the various criteria which have appeared pre-eminent to particular observers within each their frame of reference. Thus, in addition to the distinctions discussed above, Macarov reminds us of other relevant bases of categorisation such as group size, duration of group life, exclusivity of membership, method of formation, focus of activity, and others. We shall later, in other contexts, discuss the relevance of some of these features of group life, but will not at this point extend the list of classifications beyond those already mentioned.

While these typologies draw our attention to the diversity of factors which give shape and life to groups, it is important to note that they do not represent mutually exlusive categories. Thus, a primary group may also be a psyche group. In fact it usually will be. It may also be a "reference group", a "natural group" and a "peer group", to use terms which we will define later and which are also included in Macarov's tabulation. Group life is so manifold and complex that a high number of overlapping parameters of classification are necessary to embrace the whole. No "category" may be devised which will exhaustively describe the nature of any particular group.

The distinctions between the aspects of groups to which we have drawn especial attention seem to us to be particularly relevant to social work.

Implications of Common Purpose

At this point it is profitable to return to a more basic point which has earlier been made. Whatever the nuances of motivation underlying group formation, however many "types" of groups we may be able to identify, there remains the central fact that group members come together, or are brought together, on account of some kind of common purposes, interests, or needs. These may be more or less conscious. They may lend themselves more or less readily to clear articulation by members. They may emerge and establish themselves rapidly or very slowly. They may for various reasons be concealed behind a screen of other rationalised explanations for the group's existence. But within every group there exists somewhere an area of common purpose or need which in our view provides the most important reference point for any discussion of that group's behaviour, life and development.

The notion of common purpose has a number of important implications. It provides a reason for the members' investment in the group, a motivation for interacting and for encouraging each other, and it increases the sense of unity. This "we" feeling, or *group bond*, is also an important basis of the personal relationships which develop between group members. This is a reciprocal phenomenon, since mutual liking also intensifies the sense of identification with the group. An individual's needs bring him into the group. Once provisionally accepted he contributes what he can to group life, in pursuit both of his own satisfactions and the group's goals. During this process he becomes known and valued for his contribution. Being valued, he in turn values the others. The group is not only a useful place to be but also a "good" one. It has become "his" group, "their" group, and members are partly differentiated from non-members in that their feelings of identity embrace the shared emotional experience of "belonging" to that particular group. Thus purposive activity, inter-personal relationships and the development of group bond go hand-in-hand.

For example, a group of mothers of mentally defective children, who co-operate in running a mutual child-minding service, interact with each other because of their common aims and problems. On this basis they also identify with each other. They gradually supplement and refine their knowledge of each other and develop relationships. Similarly, a number of slum-dwellers organising in protest against the property owners about their living conditions, interact intensely with each other because strategy must be worked out and because their demands must be carefully formulated. Common interest in reaching their objectives cuts across many differences and provides an emotional bond. Their anxiety, both about their own aggression and its possible consequences, also causes an intensification of their contact with each other. All this increases both intimacy and self-respect, which one expects in its turn to enrich relationships within this community.

Common purpose thus leads to interaction and relationships, while interaction and mutual identification in turn result in the discovery or development of common purpose. The balance and sequence varies, of course, from one group situation to another. Distinctions between group "types" have been made on this basis also, but this seems to us primarily a question of alternative emphases rather than mutually exclusive patterns of establishing group life. Wherever the main emphasis may lie, however, it is important to be aware that individual and group purposes are rarely identical. Further, we must remind ourselves that individual identity includes indentification with given groups, but also has many other components. Thus the relationship between individual and group which we here have touched upon always poses a number of problems. We shall return to these in Chapter 4. Before doing so, it is necessary to look more closely at the ways in which groups come into being and to discuss some of their implications, both in general terms and in the context of social work.

CHAPTER 3

Group Formation

The purposes for which groups come into being were briefly discussed in the preceding chapter. We shall now discuss the ways in which they do so. This is referred to as *group formation*. Some of the implications of group formation for the practice of social work with groups will also be indicated. (The closely related subject of *group composition*, i.e. how criteria for membership are established, will not be discussed here. In the context of social work, composition is usually a feature of the planning of treatment and therefore belongs in a book on treatment method rather than group theory. Meanwhile, Douglas (1970) is warmly recommended for an instructive review of formulations on criteria for group composition in social work and other treatment methods).

Types of Group Formation

It is common to refer to three main types of group formation, according to the degree of volition on the part of members.

Thus, many groups are *compulsory*. Some agency, external to the group, forms a group by the exercise of authority. For example, school entrants are required to commence attendance, whereupon they are placed in classes A, B and C on the basis of certain criteria which the school administration considers appropriate. A platoon of soldiers is formed on some arbitrary basis such as age, size, district of origin or alphabetical position, without allowing the members any choice at all. Many alcoholic and drug-treatment institutions and an increasing number of mental hospitals require patients or inmates to attend group treatment sessions of various kinds, regardless of their wishes.

It should be noted that compulsory membership does not rule out common purpose. In our examples, the patients have the common purpose of cure, the pupils of learning and the soldiers of survival. We shall see that compulsion may in fact sometimes even intensify the experience of common purpose.

Other groups may be referred to as *formed* groups. Whilst these too are frequently formed by external initiative, the members have more choice. In a sense they select themselves, since they may accept or refuse the invitation of the sponsor. Some ministerial secretary, perceiving the need for expert guidance on proposed legislation, offers membership of an advisory committee to a number of people with more or less appropriate qualifications. A sufficient number choose to accept this offer, and a viable group is formed. Or a social worker, concerned with the problems of mentally defective children and their families, believes that certain parents would be able to help each other to work through some of their problems, feelings and decisions. He writes or visits them to offer group service. They choose to enter the group situation or not.

Another kind of group formation is that of the *natural* group. These groups arise spontaneously. Without external initiative or compulsion, the members simply "come together" through circumstances which often seem to involve a large element of chance. Children in the same street play together as toddlers, attend the same schools, fight the same fights, and often through many years retain a high degree of group feeling, of belongingness. At what point the group came into being, and "who started it" no one can say. Or a group of teenagers, whether shoplifting to finance amphetamine purchase, or organising paper salvage to help finance a new church steeple, will also have come into being in this same diffuse and spontaneous manner, in response to factors of chance, propinquity and shared interests or needs.

Implications for Social Work

These kinds of group formation have relevance to the practice of social work with groups. According to the social work agency concerned, one or other of these three types of formation will be represented. Experience suggests that the conditions of formation exert substantial influence on the members' attitudes to the group, on their readiness to identify with its objectives and with each other, and not least on their attitudes to the agency and the worker.

Compulsion always evokes some aggression and often also dependence. (There is no paradox here, since dependence and aggression tend to go hand-in-hand.) This also applies to compulsorily formed groups, no matter how well feelings may be repressed by the members. Thus the social worker leading a group which has been compelled into being will not be of very much assistance to the members unless he is able to help them express this aggression and deal with it in some appropriate way. Of the many examples which could be given, the following case extract is selected since it indicates how rapidly the worker and the group may enter into meaningful communication, even in a forced group, when the worker is able to recognise the feelings and problems which are precipitated by the group situation, including the circumstances of its formation, as well as by the members' more clearly defined "presenting problem".

Example 3. During the late 1950s and the 1960s many penal institutions in Europe were beginning to clothe the infantilising and repressive nature of their administration with a respectable veneer of "treatment". This usually consisted of no more than a single session of group discussion each week. Occasionally, these were led by staff with training in some relevant therapeutic profession, but usually, not. Otherwise, life in the institution went on as before, "curing" as the saying goes, "nothing but heterosexuality".

A social work student was placed during field-work practice in one such institution, where young men in their late teens and early twenties were imprisoned. He was pleased when given the opportunity to lead a group, looking forward to wrapping the meat of practice around the fragile bones of his social school theory.

The first meeting was a tense and painful experience. Members were either totally silent or replied very briefly to direct questions. The student—anxious not least about his own performance—dealt with this by repeated and unsuccessful attempts to find some subject which would engage the group's interest. By the end of the meeting he was talking almost continually himself. He made a "mistake" with the time, and finished 15 minutes earlier than intended.

Mature enough to bring his problems to supervision, and fortunate in his supervisor, the student was enabled to understand what had happened and to prepare appropriately for the second meeting.

At the beginning of the second meeting he invited the group to bring up whatever they had uppermost in their thoughts. This was met with expected passivity. After a period of silence, the student carefully said, "This is like last time, isn't it?. .Your silence bothered me. I felt hopeless. . So I talked twenty to the dozen. Which I guess helped neither you nor me. So I've talked with Mrs. X (prison social worker and supervisor) about it, as I told you I would discuss things with her. . . . The more I've thought about it—and it's already the same this time—the more I feel that there's a lot of anger around which neither you nor I felt that we could talk about. . "He had the group's attention. Their silent but intense engagement encouraged him to take the next step . . "I think you really want to tell me to stuff the group, don't you?"

Wry grins from some members. Comments from some, such as, "Well, you said it, staff", and "They're your words mate". . . . Then, "We didn't *ask* for this bloody group, you know". . . The student picked up this last comment—"That's it, isn't it? . . . It's been pushed onto you." Looked around group, "Isn't that the trouble? . . . What do you others say?"

One member slowly and emphatically replied, "Do you think that somebody, someday, in this place will—just once—*ask* us to do something? Fair enough that we're made to work. Fair enough that we're shoved in the Peter (isolation) now and then. Fair enough that we're made to have Lights Out at 10 o'clock like good little boys. . . . But do you really think that you can make us come into this group and talk about our "problems"— which half of us haven't got, and the other half want to keep to themselves? . . . Why should we? We've never done it before. We don't know whether we can trust you. We don't even know whether we can trust each other! . . ."

From this point on the group was working. The student's interpretation of the group's silence as aggression and his enabling the group to express their anger at being compelled into this situation had brought central feelings and problems into the open. These included anger at manipulation; resentment about the extension of acceptable control into a humiliating deprivation of rights; the existence or nature of life problems underlying their criminality, the question of whom, if anyone, can be trusted, and their relationship to authority figures. On his part, the student had demonstrated his concern for and wish to understand the group, had shown acceptance of attitudes not normally encouraged in such institutions, and by exposing his own earlier helplessness had shown that it was possible to express feelings and acknowledge problems in the group.[1]

The aggression aroused by compulsion may of course be expressed in other ways than unco-operative silence. It may simply come directly into the open. It may also lead to indirect forms of sabotage such as low or late attendance ostensibly caused by sickness, or by other duties or by "forgetting". A more subtle and common form of sabotage is that of apparent but very superficial co-operation. Groups in penal and alcoholic institutions seem often to enter into the "game"[2] of group treatment. They talk much and fill the time because the leader—who has Power—is "pleased" by this. But they may in fact remain very well defended. Such games will continue unless the worker at an early stage takes up the basic here-and-now problem of the group's anger at having been manipulated. His attempts to create openness about feelings and to demonstrate his understanding seem hollow to the group when they are preoccupied with aggression about compulsion, which he does not take up, either because he is too ambivalently involved in it to be able to take it up, or not sufficiently insightful to register it as a problem.

Sarri and Galinsky (1964) suggest another consequence of compulsory formation, but with this we are only partly in agreement. In such groups " ... dependence upon the professional worker can be expected to last longer and, therefore, the leadership structure within the group might be expected to develop more slowly." While this is certainly true of many compulsorily formed groups, there are also many exceptions. Our impression is that in problem-centred groups where aggressive feelings are present it only applies to leadership sympathetic to the objectives of the agency. Indigenous leadership hostile to the agency and the worker may in fact be very quick to develop in such groups. This is, of course, consistent with what we know about reactions to force. Furthermore, such mobilisation of aggression is in our view desirable, both in terms of the mental health of the group members and of the therapeutic advantage which a clear statement of group feelings offers.

The *formed* group, which is much more typical in social work, presents other characteristics. That members have chosen to join implies more positive attitudes towards other members, the agency and the worker, as well as higher motivation for the group's proposed goals and some responsibility for helping to attain them. Further, there is more likelihood of positive relationships developing between members. Positive relationships are of course by no means excluded in groups formed by compulsion, since shared aggressive feelings or shared dependence upon authority may also lead to feelings of close association. The relationships in formed groups are, however, more likely to have therapeutic potential.

Example 4. At a child psychiatric clinic the children were treated individually by a clinical psychologist or psychiatrist. The parents received parallel supportive treatment from the social worker. Five such parental couples, whose children had newly commenced psychotherapy, were offered the opportunity of forming a group under the social worker's leadership. It was suggested that they could "discuss common problems and solutions, and help each other in clarifying some of their thoughts and feelings". Four couples accepted. They quickly became acquainted with each other. At their own suggestion they used the first meeting to tell each other about their problems as they saw them, and tentatively to indicate their expectations of the group. Their positive and hopeful attitude seemed clearly to embrace not only the group, but also the social worker, the agency and its resources.

It is important, however, not to idealize this kind of group formation. It, too, has its problems. Whilst natural groups arise spontaneously out of existent relationships and merely strengthen existing identification by organisation, formed groups are artificially created, with no more than a reasonable hope that a similar bond will arise from the discovery of common problems, needs and purposes. But it is by no means certain that this will occur. The varying ability of members to accept themselves and others may severely hinder this process. Unforeseeable negative responses to others, and the numerous intangible obstacles to interaction are more likely to manifest themselves in formed than in natural groups. The formed group assumes that bonds will develop on the basis of certain similarities beween members. It may be, however, that members attach more importance to observed differences (of speech, social class, etc.) than to the attributes they have in common. In such a case they will resist involvement in the group.

Nor does the decision to join rule out ambivalance about doing so. Feelings about the group may perhaps never be entirely positive. Resistance and defence are inescapable components of all therapeutic processes and are not eradicated simply because members have chosen to enter treatment, rather than being compelled. Initial motivation may arise from various perceived needs and stresses, but at times the stresses of group life and relationships will outweigh these. Motivation for participation may then temporarily decrease or disappear. Further, it may frequently be found that solving problems is a more painful process than members anticipated. Changes in life-situation which are not immediately acceptable may be incurred. Disturbing feelings or guilt-laden attitudes which have earlier been denied or projected elsewhere may have to be examined. Hidden satisfactions which were concomitants of the problem may have to be given up, and this may sometimes be so difficult that the client will prefer to keep the problem and withdraw from the group. This latter situation is repeatedly encountered in social group work as in other forms of therapy.

Other problems in formed groups may arise from the group's feelings about the agency or worker on whose initiative the group was formed. Assumptions made about the leadership function and expertise of the initiator often seem to imply a readiness to take a receptive and subordinate position. The worker is then expected to take a correspondingly authoritarian position as "expert" leader. This is no doubt due partly to earlier role models—teacher, doctor, parent, etc. Whatever the cause, however, there can be elements of manipulation of the worker, of regressive abrogation of responsibility for self, but also of quite rational expectation that the initiator has notions about appropriate ways of using the group. This common feature of formed groups is described here as a "problem" since it represents dependence upon the social worker and therefore militates against interaction between group members. The whole purpose of working with clients in groups is thus undermined, since the main resource of group treatment lies dormant. (This is particularly problematical for the worker or student with authority problems, who may very easily be seduced into playing some kind of omniscient and directive role.)

The *natural* group is of increasing interest to the social worker, who is moving more and more into organisational functions at the neighbourhood level and who is carrying out detached work in the cafés, derelict houses, street-corners and dockyards haunted by groups of young people in need of preventive or crisis treatment services. These and other such natural groups present their own strengths and their own difficulties. The social worker here meets a group which is already in existence, and which may in fact have existed for a long time. Group interaction, structure and bonds have already developed or may readily be helped to do so. Group objectives may also already be very clear for the members. In community work at the neighbourhood level, such objectives imply for the social worker a clarifying and mobilizing function. He is usually identified with the group's objectives and lends himself to them as a resource person. He provides relevant information about existing social provisions or the structural aspects of social services; or perhaps he is initially most active in helping the group to find an effective organisational form and to develop a strategy.

But in other natural groups—a group of pre-puberty glue-sniffers, for example—the social worker's difficulties will arise precisely from his oppostion[3] to the group's objectives. The natural group has already established a norm system related to their objectives before meeting the worker. These aims and ways of behaving may be a source of identity and unity for any such group. However, they raise a problem for newcomers, since any newcomer is a potential threat to the established culture of the group. Where the newcomer is demonstrably "different", and seems likely to represent objectives and values contrary to those already established by the group (as may be the case with the social worker), this problem will be intensified. Here, it is the social worker who is at a disadvantage, where acceptance by the group is concerned. This is the central problem of detached social work, particularly while establishing initial contact.

Overlapping of Types of Formation

Group formation cannot always be easily classified in this way, however, since overlapping occurs between the proposed types. We have seen earlier that this problem recurs in most attempts to categorise attributes of groups. A natural group, for example a street-corner gang which accepts an offer of group-work service, is still a natural group, technically speaking, but it now also presents some of the properties, potentials and problems of a formed group.

A particular case of such overlapping is of special interest. The group which is "formed" may sometimes have a somewhat spurious voluntarism. Alternatives to membership may be so unattractive that the group might in fact more honestly be said to be formed, if not by force, at least by manipulation. Many closed institutions, which do not actually compel participation, make it known that participation is regarded with approval. Such groups may also offer the only alternatives to empty hours, or to attendance at largely irrelevant classes forming part of an unplanned educational programme—killing time. The expression "pseudo-voluntary" groups has been used in this context.

Even in groups which are initially formed in a voluntary and democratic manner, and which meet the motivation of the members at the time of formation, the worker may later in subtle ways compel and manipulate. In a discussion of small groups and political behaviour, Verba (1961) describes some common forms of pseudo-democracy in which members' apparent participation in leadership is in fact an exposure to subtle forms of persuasion and control rather than a genuine involvement in decision making. While Verba's concern with this phenomenon is with its appearance in the realms of politics and industrial leadership, we are forcefully reminded of the common practice in institutions and other groups of apparently offering a choice, while in effect imposing one's will, either by limiting alternatives or by indicating which choices would meet with most approval. This kind of concealed compulsion may well be expected, once it has become recognised, to arouse at least as much hostility as overt compulsion.

It could perhaps be argued that some degree of compulsion exists in all groups, though not necessarily imposed by external authority. We saw in the previous chapter how groups come into being to meet a wide variety of economic, political, social and emotional needs. One cannot play football, build a ship, exert political influence, enjoy amateur dramatics, raise a family, receive group-work treatment, alone. The individual's satisfaction in such activities is conditional upon participation in groups where other individuals are also seeking satisfactions. Our personal needs compel us into "voluntary" group membership and therefore into situations necessitating compromise between private and shared goals. It may be that this is a partial explanation of the periodical conflict and aggressivity manifested even in many groups where harmony and friendship might most be expected.

For example, the belief that sport aids human relations has long been cherished. It is odd that the violent conflicts which we so frequently witness between both members and supporters of various teams have not long ago dispelled this myth, at least as far as inter-group relationships are concerned. But of more relevance to our theme is the difficulty we have in acknowledging the frequency with which rivalry, envy and recrimination arise also between members of the same team or club. Many individual sportsmen are probably orientated towards self-fulfilment and display. The condition that this must occur within a framework of group activity and co-operation builds dependency, frustration and therefore some degree of resentment into the team situation. To pass the ball to the inside-right who is more favourably placed, instead of taking a chancier shot at goal oneself, is an exercise in group discipline and in sacrifice of personal satisfactions to others. This is advanced social behaviour. It would be strange indeed if no ambivalence were involved. Similarly, a group of homeless alcoholics meet each night at the railway sidings or in packing-cases at the docks. Here they sleep, and they share the spirits which one member has earned by casual labour that day, as well as the tobacco and food which others have begged, stolen or picked up. They do not necessarily relish their inter-dependence. They certainly do not like giving up these precious commodities. But such groups are necessary organisational forms ensuring for each giver that he himself may also continue to be a receiver. We suggest that the extreme lability of these groups, swinging as they do from warm comradeship to a sometimes murderous violence, has its roots in the complex of needs/dependency/compulsion/ aggression now under discussion.

Again, this is analogous to the social-group work situation. Each member of a group of clients is primarily motivated towards help for himself. It is purely his own problems which first bring him to the agency. His acceptance of the condition of treatment as a group activity does not mean that he contentedly accepts the apparent risk of diluted investment of therapeutic resources in himself and his specific problems. But, once he is a group member, as with the football player and the alcoholic vagrants above, a compromise has to be found between his wish for personal satisfaction and the necessity of being accepted by the group. This compromise becomes possible through his growing awareness that his own satisfactions may be derived in such a situation only through participation in the work of the group, that is by helping others also to meet their needs. But even though a commonality of needs and problems may thereby emerge, this situation of dependence and concealed compulsion brings ambivalence, competition and resentment into the group. Thus, the group which made progress this week in approaching the clarification of common problems may surprise the social worker next week with their passivity or with their overt and inexplicable conflict.

This ambivalence about sharing pervades life. Learning to deal with it is a part of the socialization process which only the exceptionally mature ever work through entirely.

This is a recurrent, almost fugue-like theme in any treatment group, whatever the presenting problems may be. In analytical group psychotherapy it may frequently be taken up in terms of its transference components. The competition for the therapist's individual attention may be interpreted as a re-activation of earlier sibling rivalry, and the attempted seduction of the therapist into an exclusive intimacy as a re-enactment of earlier Oedipal struggles. In social work it is less often appropriate to interpret transference phenomena.[4] The social worker is more likely to deal with this aspect of ambivalence and rivalry in a manner which by-passes transference implications and by helping the group to focus on current realities. He may, for instance, reject members' fantasies about his own omnipotence and reflect the problem back to the group. He thereby draws attention to their own resources, demonstrates his own recognition of them, and both mobilises and reinforces the existing ego-strengths in the group.

Example 5. A group of foster-parents, caring for children with considerable behavioural problems, was formed in a rather inaccessible district of scattered hill-farms. Members, acutely aware of their need for supportive help, initially requested the social worker repeatedly for authoritative advice about their individual problems. They vied somewhat with each other in presenting their particular foster-child's behaviour for analysis and solution.

During the first two meetings the worker repeatedly had to make such comments as... "You know, you are the real experts here, not me. Everyone here has one or more foster-children living with them 24 hours per day. Some of you over several years ... I haven't .... I think I can help by leading the discussion a bit, and by coming in when I think my more theoretical knowledge and things I have seen elsewhere can help us to understand some things better. But mostly I think you will gain by talking to each other. The problem one has, the others have, or have had. Some of you have already found the understanding or solutions that others are looking for.... Ask each other.... Talk to each other.... That's why you've come together here. ... And for my part I'll come in when I think I have anything useful to add...."

This kind of response was consistent with the short-term objectives of stimulating interaction and mutual identification, and also with the longer-term objectives of improving the foster-parents' understanding and treatment of the children in their care. These long-term aims subsumed other aims of establishing a more open and co-operative relationship with the Child Care Authority and reducing to a more reasonable level the demands which the foster-parents made upon themselves where criteria for "successful" care were concerned. A more interpretive response to the group's expectations, drawing attention to their dependence, rivalry, ambivalence and transference might have been frightfully clever, but would have been quite irrelevant to the needs, aims and motivation of the group.*

These basic group problems concerning formation, dependence and ambivalence may find expression in many other ways. The social worker will also deal differently with them from one situation to another. He will be guided by the manner in which the problem is

*Extracted from published report (Heap and Tredt, 1971).

manifested, by the needs and motivation of the group concerned, and by the nature of the treatment agreement or "contract" which has been established. We will not exemplify further, however, since this would involve us more deeply in social work method than is intended here. Our present purpose is to draw attention to types of group formation and their consequences, and to show that these consequences are relevant to social work group situations.

A Note on Commonality

The common needs which provide the basis of group formation, particularly those of a social and emotional nature, may often be neither particularly conscious nor explicit. This is perhaps especially true of natural groups, where intangible needs such as those of friendship, belonging, reassurance, support, or being valued by someone may supply the formative force. In such groups, mutual identification is often more at a level of diffuse feeling than of sharing clearly perceived goals. But groups formed around clear and tangible goals also develop their emotional aspects, so that there is a constant interplay between common feelings and shared activity—between the psyche- and socio-dimensions—whatever the starting point may be.

Often the common formative factor is not so much a manifest need as a feeling about something, such as loyalty to an ideal, which, once it has been recognised and articulated, seeks expression in activity. Whether this activity is communal worship or throwing open paint-tins into the foreign embassy of one's choice, the mechanism is the same. "We are together because we feel or believe 'X', and our belief in 'X' makes this kind of collective behaviour appropriate." Similarly, individuals may be drawn together because of common feelings about a person. The person may or may not be present in the group, and the feelings may be either negative or positive, but they cause the members to feel drawn to each other. This may simply be because of the charisma of the person about whom feelings are shared—as in a fan-club, for example. It may also be, however, that he or she represents ideas and values which are both common and important to the group members. For example, a group of students meeting to discuss the thoughts of some political exemplar—whether of Mao Tse-Tung or of Enoch Powell—may, though they have never met before, have reasonable expectations of forming a viable group. They will meet others who, through their engagement in the same political figure, may be expected to share not only feelings about him, but also value systems, social attitudes, objectives and to some extent life-styles.[5] On the basis of these shared feelings, beliefs and activities the members identify with each other, and a group is in being. It is a sequence of discovery of commonality, affirmation of commonality, and mutual identification.

This issue of commonality seems to have great importance in determining the success of social intercourse, much of which is concerned with the question, "How much like me are you?" Any group of people meeting in an unstructured situation, compelled by the proprieties to get along with each other, seem to enter first into an exploratory process aimed at discovering common ground. "Are you from...?", "do you know...?", "have you read...?", "what do you think about...?", are asked and established until common acquaintances, origins, viewpoints, experiences and expectations are located. These provide a focus for at least initial contact and often for subsequent interaction. The absence of common ground is an embarrassment and usually leads to withdrawal if this is possible.

When a newcomer enters an established group, both he and the group are involved in mutual testing of commonality. Once he and the group are reassured and he is accepted as a member, he becomes a part of the group which subjects the next newcomer to examination. Foulkes and Anthony (1965) observe:

> In most ...individuals, one can discern the wish (to belong), which is tanta-mount to saying that, fundamentally, man is a group animal. The stranger in the human group feels the rub of strangeness until he finds acceptance and can blend with his surroundings. The next newcomer reactivates the past uneasiness and challenges the present familiarity with his obtrusive strangeness. It is disturbing to the self-satisfaction of the group, and they must deal with it either by assimilation or extrusion. The persistence of strangeness is intolerable to the group.

There is something almost atavistic about this feeling-out process, a kind of social sniffing of each other, establishing that "we are the same sort". Despite the potential enrichment of life by intercourse with people unlike oneself, the tendency is—once commonalities are discovered—to gather into clusters of similar people. The artist associates with other artists. The social-work student—that budding expert in human relations—tends to do the same. Packard (1959) tells of the widespread practice in the American real-estate market whereby speculative builders recommend the suitability of their housing projects to potential purchasers of given race, religion, income-bracket and range of professional interests. This is by no means an exclusively American phenomenon. We could insert the name of any random sub-cultural group in the following statement and confidently expect to hear it somewhere . . . "I've got nothing against black men/white men/Pakistanis/Irishmen/gypsies/catholics/the poor. It's just that I like to be among my own sort." This strong intrinsic tendency to insularity in human group life probably provides as serious a barrier to the development of more pluralistic societies as do the vested interests of the conflicting economic, political or religious groups. The vision of student-worker solidarity, for example. How rarely achieved!

It is, of course, neither surprising nor sinister that people of like interests and identifications wish to associate with each other. But the tendency to do so exclusively has two regrettable consequences. The first of these is that it favours the perpetuation of stereotype images of other groups of whom one has no knowledge but only opinions. The second is that it closes doors to alternative ways of life, to new attitudes, viewpoints and pursuits. Perhaps the latter point partly explains the pervasiveness of this tendency. If we never mix with people unlike ourselves we will never risk the accusation that we are "wrong", "bad", "inadequate", "mistaken", "crazy" or something equally painful.

This hypothesis explains our interest in the issue of commonality. The social worker's clients are very often people in situations which might be confidently expected to generate just such accusations. In consequence, clients commonly bring anxiety to the group situation. Are they going to be "accused" there, because they are chronically unemployable, unmarried mothers, delinquent, unsuccessful parents, mentally unstable, alcoholic, or whatever? Or is it true, as the social worker said, that the others who are coming are "like me"? And if they are, are they sufficiently "like me" to accept me without judgement, and to enable me to feel comfortable and safe with them? And what about the social worker himself, who manifestly is not "like us"? What kind of thoughts and feelings about people like us does he really have?

To what extent dare I show what people in our situation sometimes feel and think and wish? How will he react if I do?

Thus the social worker experiences that most formed groups need to go through an initial exploratory process in which the answer to these questions is sought. This may be brief or protracted, open or concealed, depending upon the extent of insecurity, conflict and guilt-feelings present, but it is always an intense and anxious process. Its successful completion is a necessary condition for establishing mutual identification and the development of a group which is sufficiently cohesive to meet members' needs. Clearly, the process will also commonly include some testing out of the social worker.

(A model of group development is summarised in Chapter 8 in which this process is reported as a recurring feature of social work groups. It is referred to as the "Search for Commonality", and it is suggested that an important part of the social worker's function is to aid this process.)

Notes on Chapter 3

1. In the journal extract quoted, the student's helpful communication of personal feelings could well be seen in established casework terms as support enabling clarification of feelings, a concept adapted and applied to social work with groups by Frey (1962). An alternative perspective enables us to introduce some current and relevant group dynamics material. There has been much debate in recent years about the relative merits of a "blank screen" kind of therapeutic leadership and a leadership including "personal involvement" with the client. This debate has become increasingly and, in our view, artificially polarised as if there were one "correct" way of leading groups. The debate has been of particular concern to group psychotherapists, but also to social group workers and caseworkers.

   Empirical studies are now being addressed to this question. A key concept in these is that of "self-disclosure". Kangas (1967, 1971) studying treatment groups of different kinds in a variety of settings, found that the greater the number of self-disclosures by the group leader, the greater were the number of self-disclosures in his group ($r = 0.72$). He also verified that self-disclosure by members stimulates and enables self-disclosure by other members. Query (1964), also studying on-going treatment groups, found that the more a member self-disclosed in the group, the more he was attracted to and identified with the group. This series of studies exemplify the kind of applied research to which we referred earlier. It challenges, dismisses or confirms existing treatment assumptions. It also introduces fact and scientific rigour into professional discussion which is often as much coloured by fashion and faith as it is informed by tested fact and by objective observation. And, like most good research, it leaves the student with more new questions than answers.

2. The term "game" is used here in the sense introduced by Berne (1964). He perceives many interactions between persons as sequential steps in sterotypic interactions called "games". There are rules and expectations to be met. They involve ritual and pretence. Sometimes such "games" are meaningless non-communication, sometimes they are extremely manipulative and complex patterns serving such ends as social dominance, rationalisation of failure, maintenance of neurotic relationship patterns, etc.

3. The word "opposition" is used here advisedly. The social work principle of self-determination was never intended to be regarded as an absolute. It includes an evaluation of the client's ability to determine his own interests. Senility, mental defect, psychosis and immaturity exemplify conditions in which unmodified self-determination may lead the client unintentionally to self-destructive behaviour. But currently some tortuous argument is advanced extending this principle to include everyone's right to self-destruction. If the person concerned knows that his choice is self-destructive, and makes it rationally and unambivalently—agreed. If through defect, immaturity or other condition the ability to choose is in question, or the consequences of choice are not fully appreciated—we disagree. In such case we hold that the function of any responsible adult and of the social worker in particular is a protective and containing one. Thus we are, as a case in point, "in opposition" to the aims and norms of the group of children in our example who are slowly and painfully killing themselves by sniffing glue.

4. A particularly clear discussion on this question is to be found in Irvine (1956). The student is warmly recommended to this brief paper. While Mrs. Irvine discusses transference phenomena within a casework context, there is nothing there which might not equally well be applied to the group work situation.

5. This kind of group formation around a person about whom feelings are shared is the role phenomenon of the "central person". This is more extensively discussed in Chapter 7.

CHAPTER 4

Differentiation and Integration

In the literature of social work with groups and of group psychotherapy the term "group-as-a-whole" is frequently encountered. It is also used in this book, together with other expressions which imply that the group may be regarded as a unitary social organism. "Group needs", "group objectives" and "group motivation" are cases in point. But opinion differs as to how far we are justified in imputing to "the group" this kind of collective qualities.

One very productive approach to group dynamics research certainly does so. Cattell (1955) and his colleagues have introduced the concept of "syntality". This attribute in effect ascribes personality characteristics to groups, particularly those of energy and ability to use resources. Leary (1957) not only uses such terms as "personality of the group", but has moved towards expressing such concepts in operational terms. Using a classification of the personality characteristics of individuals based on interpersonal behaviour and attitudes, he is able to predict their resistive behaviour as group members. This work strongly suggests that the resistive behaviour of the group-as-a-whole may be similarly predicted. Le Bon (1895), writing many years ago about crowds, admittedly a special case, postulated the existence of a "group mind". This was seen as a collective perception and response apparatus, which both transcended and transformed the minds of the individual members.

> Whoever the individuals be ... however like or unlike ... (being) in a group puts them in a sort of collective mind which makes them feel, act and think in a manner quite different from that in which they would feel, think and act in a state of isolation. ... Isolated, a man may be a cultured individual ... in a crowd he is a barbarian. ...

Sprott (1958), however, rejects this concept and suggests a number of simpler explanations for the phenomena with which Le Bon was concerned. Some earlier writers have also felt it appropriate to use the concepts of psycho-analytic personality theory to refer to attributes of groups—such as group ego and group super-ego. However, while psychodynamics richly illuminate many aspects of group life, such direct transfer of personality concepts to the group "organism" is regarded by many as questionable. Indeed, while Freud himself was not unimpressed by Le Bon's group mind concept (1921), he cautioned elsewhere about the too facile translation of the concepts of individual psychology into collective psychology (1939)[1].

Nevertheless, we repeatedly meet life-situations in which groups behave in a manner of which the individual members are apparently incapable and in response to some kind of group expectations, impulses, or standards whose origins are not immediately apparent. Twenty frightened soldiers may as a group stand and fight, where they would individually have run away. Or they may collectively, in terror, panic and hate, slaughter a village of helpless civilians with whom each one, alone, might even have sought refuge. Eight men with a long history of alcoholism may, as members of an A.A. group, be able over several years to achieve a temperance and control which is probably quite impossible for them to sustain alone. Five teenage boys from solid middle-class families may commit damage and theft as a gang activity, although none of them individually have ever behaved anti-socially or shown any tendency to do so. Group behaviour may, clearly, be something very different from some kind of "average" of the individual members' habitual behaviour.

But the group is, after all, an aggregation of individual human beings, who each bring to it their particular needs, motivations and resources. The behaviour of the "group-as-a-whole" must therefore bear some kind of relation to these. Yet it can seldom occur, even in the most harmonious group, that individual members agree about every aspect of professedly common aims, or in their interpretation of any agreement which apparently exists. Equally rarely may we expect the behavioural standards of the individual to harmonise precisely with the behaviour expected of him by the group. Some kind of adjustment has to take place.

The group must mobilise to perform its function. The individual must be orientated towards performing his role as group member. But he continually meets situations where his own perceived needs and those of the group are somewhat at variance, or where the behaviour of the group-as-a-whole requires him to extend his own behavioural and attitudinal pattern in a manner which arouses his resistance. His resources and personality also limit the group demands to which he is in fact able to adjust. Thus, group life may be viewed as a continual process of discord and resolution between two sets of forces, those tending towards the *integration* of the individual into the group and those inclining him to *differentiate* himself from the group—towards an assertion of his autonomy and of his personal needs and limits. This dilemma is often referred to in the literature as that of being "together and apart". At the group level this dilemma is manifested in two simultaneous tendencies. These are, respectively, those of consolidation and dissolution. Thompson and Kahn (1970), making an interesting and appropriate use of an individual psychological concept, refer to this fundamental feature of social life as the "ambivalence of the group".

Some aspects of these processes will be discussed and exemplified in this chapter. Relevant concepts include those of norms, conformity, group cohesion and reference groups. The family as a group and the process of socialisation will also be briefly referred to in this context.

Approval and Disapproval

It has already been emphasised that the common purposes motivating members to participate in the group lead to mutual identification at varying levels—to the development of group bond and of relationships.

A further consequence of common purpose is group approval or disapproval of certain attitudes and forms of behaviour. Those which serve the aims of the group tend to be rewarded with support, encouragement and prestige. Contrary attitudes and behaviour tend to meet disapproval and may lead to isolation, rejection or even punishment.

We may clearly see this at a societal level in attitudes on the one hand to productive citizens and on the other to criminal or other deviant members of society.

Whether the rewards of productivity and conformity are an excessive share in affluence—the "3-car family"—or public acclaim as a Worker Hero is for the individual a matter of geographical chance. The group mechanisms involved are too fundamentally connected with basic social processes to be invalidated by political systems. This also applies to disapproval and punishment. San Quentin and the camps of Siberia may have very different regimes. They may exist for punishment or preventive isolation following contrasting types of offence. But they are identical in their basic purpose of reinforcing societal values and objectives, however these may differ from one society to another. The growing unease about the destructive competitiveness of the meritocracy and current attempts to find alternative systems meet major obstacles rooted in these basic and persisting group processes of rewarding group-approved performance and censuring group-disapproved performance.

These mechanisms are equally evident at the small-group level. Members of the school football team behave very differently towards the eager goal-scorer than towards the indifferent "passenger". The village chapel congregation regards its most pious member with reverence. But the teenage member who becomes pregnant is regarded with horror, and pays a high price for what is perceived as her rejection—and therefore undermining—of the group's value system.

We could endlessly exemplify this circular interplay between group aims and values, individual behaviour, group response to that behaviour, and the impact of that group response on the individual. It is relevant here to draw attention to this inter-play as the very nucleus of the social work process in group settings.

It is in this regard that group treatment is most clearly distinguished from individual forms of treatment. In social casework and other individual therapies, treatment occurs within a one-to-one relationship between the client and the worker. Whatever practical dispositions may be made or decisions taken, whatever feelings and problems may be clarified or solved, it is the special characteristics of the relationship between these two people which is the primary source of help. Work with groups contrasts somewhat with this. While the worker/client and worker/group relationship are also here of great importance, it is the relationships between the group members themselves and the mutual influence arising from their interaction which is the main resource in social growth, in problem-solving or whatever the aims of the group might be. Vinter (1967) states the following principle: "The group is not merely the context . . . but also the means of treatment." (This deceptively simple statement refers to a difficult and complex process. We have attempted to construct a learnable model of that process in a booklet on social group work method, Heap, 1974.)

This guided mobilisation of members' potential for self-help and mutual help is commonly referred to as "use of the group", or more appropriately, "use of the group process". Where this interplay of group needs and individual behaviour leads to approval and encouragement, we see the use of the group as a means of mutual *support*—a central feature of social work with groups.

Example 6. A group of long-term psychiatric patients was formed to work on problems relating to impending discharge from the hospital. These problems included, among others, acute separation anxiety, fear of inadequacy outside the hospital, and fear of being conspicuously "different" and therefore rejected. One very anxious member, Doris, reported back to the group after a surprisingly successful weekend with her family and in contact with earlier friends. The group found her experiences reassuring. They were thereby enabled both to ask many questions not previously raised and to give expression to feelings which they had hitherto repressed. Their interest in her experience and admiration for her performance were in their turn very positive experiences for this anxious and self-effacing woman and clearly increased the confidence with which she approached her problems and with which she performed in the group. Successful sorties by other members were for some weeks thereafter referred to as "Doing a Doris".

The interplay of group and individual aims and behaviour may well also lead to disapproval and the mobilisation of group *control*. Used appropriately, this is also an important resource in social work in group settings, not least in the institutional treatment of behavioural disorders.

Example 7. Among a probation officer's teenage clients were a number whose behaviour tended to be destructive, impulsive and markedly immature. Some were demonstratively "tough" and very self-centred. Seven of these accepted an invitation to spend 3 weeks jointly in an adventure exercise with two probation officers, both of whom were experienced climbers. They were to camp together in an isolated mountain area, to carry out climbing and training and survival exercises and to be entirely self-sufficient. In this situation of protracted intimacy and interdependence, their customary behaviour and attitudes would have placed work-burdens on their fellows and exposed them to both discomfort and hazard. Where individual members occasionally did behave with their usual self-centred and apparently cynical disregard for others, group interests caused an immediate negative response from the group—sometimes very strong indeed. Thus, members experienced group control from a number of similarly-situated peers which was strongly geared to responsible, democratic, other-directed behaviour. This was valuable experiential social learning. It also provided material of central relevance for therapeutic discussion, both in the group and in later casework treatment.

These forms of behaviour, in which so much interest is displayed by groups and which are the focus of so much approval, support, disapproval and control are the "norms" of the group. The reader may be familiar with the definition of norms as "the behavioural rules that are accepted by all or most members of a group" (Thibaut and Kelly, 1959). A more extensive definition by Sherif and Sherif (1964), takes us a little further.

> As members interact in joint activities with appeal value to them, they develop common practices, common evaluations, and shared tastes in addition to those which brought them together. They may develop nick-names for members, frequently epitomizing their roles in the group. ... Sometimes they adopt a name for the group.[2]
>
> They arrive at common definitions of what is good and desirable, how a "good" member should and should not treat his fellows and outsiders.
>
> Generically all such products of interaction may be called the *"norms"* of the group. The standardized practices and evaluations which are called norms need not, however, be identical with typical or statistically average behaviour in the group. They often embody conceptions of *expected* behaviour, of the goals or ideals for a "good member". This "ethical" or "moralistic" feature of norms can be detected in criticisms of behaviour or performance in the group, in praise of successful group or individual effort, and in the outrage which greets instances of deviation.

Thus the group bond involves more than mutual identification and a supportive experience of shared interests. It also includes an element of enforced subjugation, which we have referred to as group control. The conformity to group norms to which these combined influences of support and control give rise is thus a product of both individual volition and group pressure. The strength of these processes has been repeatedly demonstrated in observations and experiments in which participants have rejected, repressed or ignored objective evidence in order that their expressed judgement shall better conform to group norms (Asch, 1951; Bennett, 1955; Fendrich, 1967).

The question arises of why the individual not only submits to group pressure, but also as group member is himself a party to exerting such pressure upon his fellow members? The answer to this returns us yet again to the common purposes with which the group was formed.

We usually "need" the groups to which we belong. These needs may be at a very material level or of a more emotional nature. However that may be, we are at least to some extent agreed upon their objectives and have an investment in them. Thus we have on the whole a wish for group approval and are dismayed by disapproval, because the former strengthens and the latter threatens our position in the group, and thereby our possibilities for the satisfaction of our needs. The tendency thus has to be towards a certain conformity with our immediate groups.

The Family and Socialisation

While this last observation has wide validity, it particularly invites comment on *the family* in small-group perspective.

Virtually all existing models and theories of personality development postulate that each individual's major personality characteristics are formed by the kind of process under discussion. Interaction occurs between the needs of the new child, which are in part constitutionally determined, and the response they meet in the primary family group as it adjusts to the newcomer's presence and demands. This basic pattern is described in many different ways, and the nuances of the subsequent development are variously perceived. But the central features are always the growing child's problems in learning to modify or postpone his gratifications in order to win approval by conforming to family norms, the primary group's striving to encourage or to compel him to do so, and the lasting impact on the child's personality of the extent and ways in which this is achieved.

All families have certain common objectives, including economic survival, acceptance by the wider society, and emotional cohesion. Such objectives require certain forms of behaviour from family members and also imply values which growing members must in time come to share. But each family also has idiosyncratic aims and norms which reflect the special values, preoccupations and perhaps the problems of that particular family. These more esoteric norms might include such value-loaded aspects of behaviour as high achievement, extreme industriousness, repression of feelings, or denial of sexuality.[3]

The baby is helpless and totally dependent upon the parents for the satisfaction of his needs. Indeed he perceives the world as consisting only of his needs and their satisfaction or frustration. His mother's breast, the bottle, the parents' arms—are depersonalised objects which exist for his gratification. There is universal preparedness to accept the new child as being helpless. His dependence is a biological fact. But from the very beginning there are extensive differences in parents' views about the appropriate response to that helplessness. There is "demand-feeding" versus "the timetable", both persuasions resting on the arguments that the preferred method is best for both stomach and soul. There is "pick him up as soon as he is distressed", versus "it is good for his little lungs to cry a bit", and besides "he must not feel that he is Master". . . . And so on. The protracted and infinitely varied minuet has begun between, on the one hand, the needs, dependence and wish for approval of the individual, and on the other, the aims, values, feelings and power of the group. All family groups expect the new child to give up his extreme egocentricity and to become more able to wait, to consider others, to be "a member". But "how soon?", "to what extent?" and "how to achieve this?" are questions to which there are as many answers as there are families.

The answers are partly determined by cultural factors and partly by the psychodynamic configurations of each family. Within the permitted framework of the cultural pattern, wide variations exist due to the different degrees of maturity, rigidity, flexibility and sensitivity of the parents. These factors are in their turn related to the parents' own familial experiences in childhood, their present marital relationship and through these to their relationship to the child. These combined influences may enable the parents to perceive the child as a unique and separate individual with his own resources and right to self-realisation. Their needs may, however, be such that his attempted assertions of individuality are experienced as threatening to the existing family values and structure, and therefore to be blocked—by disapproval, coercion or manipulation.

This introduces a recurrent group dilemma. Group aims require that members conform to group norms. Members' needs for group approval conduce to conformity. But they also include self-assertion and therefore some degree of deviance. Whether this is permissible depends upon the rigidity of the group, and therefore its maturity and growth potential. For just as a certain degree of conformity is necessary, so also is some degree of deviance and experimentation in order that change and development may occur.

In family groups, this dilemma is brought into sharp focus when the child reaches adolescence. His former helplessness and dependence have given way to new strengths. He is physically stronger and is capable—at least potentially—of economic independence. His earlier emotional dependence upon the family group is subordinated to the intensity of new affiliations to peer groups and to his first sexual partners. These affiliations introduce him to new values, attitudes and behaviour and support him in experimentation. His assertion of differentiation and separateness from the family group is stronger than ever before.

At this point the maturity, relevance and flexibility of the family's norms is tried. If values and controls are so rigid that his experimentation is strongly experienced as rejection, the family will either in its turn reject him, punitively and self-defensively, or will intensify the attempt to control him. If the family's controls have been excessive and punitive, the child will have conformed out of fear rather than identification through love. In such cases his adolescent experimentation may be a rejection of the family group in fact as well as in their fantasy, in addition to whatever other import it may have.

Even where control has not been rigid and concern for the child has not been overridden by excessive concern for the maintenance of established norms, his behaviour at adolescence will be difficult to experience and adjust to. The family, particularly the parents, will inevitably to some extent experience it as rejection, but in such cases it is unlikely that they will meet it with corresponding rejection. Structural and value adjustments are inseparable from this phase of family development, but here they should lead to enabling the young person to experience increasing independence and autonomy. He still belongs to the primary group, without being constrained by it.

These family-group experiences are central to the process of *socialisation*. They are, however, by no means the only relevant experiences. From birth we all experience a widening circle of groups in which similar processes of assertion and adjustment occur. The family, the yard or street, kindergarten, school, perhaps university, workplace, clubs, neighbourhood groups, political and professional organisations all provide settings where we seek our own satisfactions but are exposed to group expectations, and are more or less dependent upon group approval for our continued membership.

The term "socialisation" is often interpreted as meaning "learning to conform" to society's prevailing norms and values. However, this is a restrictive view of socialisation and does not allow sufficiently for the need and right of the individual to develop his own unique capacities and life-style. Further, it implies a certainty about the validity of established values and behaviour which is both disturbingly authoritarian and culturally sterile. No matter how commonly held, this view cannot be acceptable to the social worker whose aims include furthering the individual's self-realisation and enhancing his self-respect, as well as contributing to the development of a more accepting society. We are concerned with a "socialisation" concept which embraces personal realisation at the individual level as well as adjustment to the reasonable and necessary expectations of the milieu.

This combination of personal freedom and conformity to the group implies a built-in conflict and continuous need for mutual adjustment, accommodation and compromise. This is a continual conflict for any small group, and indeed for any democratic society. It is one with which the social worker is very sharply confronted, since he functions in that marginal area where the needs and behaviour of unhappy, unproductive, disadvantaged and deviant individuals and groups meet the control apparatus of organised society. The apparatus consists not only of its courts, tribunals and penal institutions, but also of its school system, its psychiatric and alcoholic services, its offers or restrictions of employment and housing, and the often moralistic and manipulative bureaucracy of its "welfare" services. Conflict is inherent in the socialisation process. In any society it will inevitably give rise to some manifest maladjustment. In modern industrial society with its increasing emphasis on competition, aquisition, efficiency, mobility and rationalisation, and with the expedience and profit-driven nature of socio-economic development, it is not surprising that maladjustment and alienation are so prevalent. Perhaps we should rather be surprised that these conditions are not even more common, when we consider the enormity of the expectations and pressures on the individual human being. That they are not is in our view a demonstration of the extraordinary resilience and adaptive skill which have served man so well during his evolution. But the question increasingly poses itself of whether this adaptive skill is not currently being exploited to serve the short-term ends of manipulative and powerful minorities at the expense of the long-term interests—perhaps the very survival—of society itself.

The population at large accepts the gains and therefore does not protest the consequences of the prevailing abuses of technology and capital. The individual allows himself to be diminished to a mobile unit of production, who has little intrinsic value, and who is accurately expected to co-operate in polluting and exhausting his own living-space to the point of serious hazard. But he ambivalently colludes in this self-destructive process because he is persuaded that it accords with his own immediate interests, which are identified by exploiter and exploited alike as material affluence. On this issue group and individual aims converge. "Socialisation" thus becomes possible, even in what has been described as the anthropological paradox of a "Culture against Man" (Henry, 1963).

In introducing political and echological factors, we go outside the small-group focus of this book. We have, however, attempted to show how processes of integration and differentiation pervade all levels of group life and how they inevitably involve conflict and associated adjustments, either unilateral or mutual. That we have briefly touched upon a source of social problems in which the social worker has important preventive and treatment functions, so far sadly neglected, is self-evident.

Capacity for Change and Choice

The possible extent of self-assertion and the necessary degree of adjustment to the group have much to do with both the individual's and the group's capacity for change and choice. We have seen that all individuals achieve a great degree of change from the total self-centredness of infancy to varying degrees of integration into the family and other social groups. The qualitative aspect of such changes is determined by the norms and pressures of the family and the society in which it exists. These decide both which behaviour and impulses are deemed unacceptable and which directions of change are approved.

Many perfectly natural impulses of developing individuals are contrary to common standards in our culture. If allowed to come to unmodified expression they therefore threaten stability and satisfactions at both the societal and the small group level. The individual may deal with such impulses by repression and denial, a solution which in the long term may raise more problems than it solves. He may deal with them more maturely by a conscious postponement or relinquishment of satisfactions in order to serve the group or win its approval. Very commonly such impulses and feelings are sublimated and canalised into other activities which are socially acceptable. The tensions of anger and frustration may be released through work, construction, sport or relevant debate, instead of the more destructive aggressive activity common to earlier maturational stages. Envy, greed or the desire for power may first be acted out, but later be sublimated in administrative, business or political activity and thereby even confer social approval and success.

Such changes in individual behaviour are features of the integrative process on which we have so far tended to concentrate. We by no means wish to imply, however, that the individual is totally without other characteristics than those imposed upon him by his group associations and his search for group approval. He is able in most contexts to exercise some degree of choice about which groups he joins, so that his standards, needs, and personality are to some extent already mirrored in the group which he finds attractive. For example, the articulate radical student has an affinity with other articulate radical students. They have commonality, to use our earlier terminology. Similarly, one does not become a homeless meths-drinker simply by exposure to that milieu. The young discharged prisoner, who is rejected by his family, who is emotionally, intellectually and physically incapable of work, is already at risk when he enters the milieu. His quietly desperate, self-destructive flight from the world has already begun, and it harmonises with the culture[3] of the group into which "chance" brings him.

Further, just as the individual participates in maintaining the norms and values of his group, he may also participate in effecting at least some degree of change in them—within the limits imposed by the rigidity of the group's attitudes to its culture and objectives.

Every baby changes the family into which it comes. Every newcomer in some way changes the group he enters, however slightly. Once there, he may continue to do so, provided that the group is not rigidly bound by its established way of working or by an inflexible hierarchy of influence, and provided also that the group either finds the change advantageous or so trivial as to be unthreatening.

Where rigidity and flexibility of norms are concerned it is relevant to remember the general human tendency to resist change. This tendency exists in individuals, groups and societies. The more fundamental and rapid the change, the greater the resistance. But it is often an ambivalent resistance, since commitment to the *status quo* conflicts with a wish for progress, with development towards "having it better". Thus some change must be accepted by any group which is orientated towards growth or problem-solving. It must therefore be prepared to accept a certain degree of experimentation and deviance from its individual members, since only by these means may change and progress occur.

Colleagues and students with experience in the Peace Corps or other work in the developing countries will have been made sharply aware of this conflict between the conscious wish for progress and the less conscious resistance to the change which progress necessitates. Our impression is that it emerges there as a very central problem in community development, generating some of the ambivalence with which help is often met.

This is, however, a recurrent theme in all social work at the community, institution or small-group level. Repeatedly we see that one member, more mature and secure, or perhaps more in contact with his aggression and ambivalence than others, behaves or expresses attitudes at variance with the group norms so far established. But this behaviour may be more relevant to group aims than compliance with group norms. Accepting his behaviour would involve change—both in the group and in life outside it. It is therefore resisted. It may be ignored, rejected, ridiculed, or subjected to critical or moralistic discussion. But at some level of consciousness the group are aware of the advantages—the implications for progress—of the "deviant" be-

haviour. They may thus gradually extend the range of permitted behaviour and attitudes to include those originally defined as "deviant".
This process of working through their own resistance results in a much
more integrated acceptance of the change than would mere imitation,
or compliance with orders or advice.

Example 8. To return to the group of foster-parents in e.g. 5 (p. 37). A recurrent problem
of long-term foster-care is the relationship between the natural parents (or single mother)
and the foster-parents. Foster placement often occurs under circumstances in which the
natural parents are confronted with their inadequacy and failure. The distress which
this arouses is commonly defended against by projecting inadequacy onto the foster-
parents, of whom they may become highly critical. The foster-parents, particularly if
they are childless or have phantasies about adoption, may in their turn be envious of the
strong biological union between the child and the natural parents. They seem not
infrequently to enter into competition for affection and admiration, as if afraid of
"losing" the child if it goes on loving its own mother. This may come to expression
in open criticism of the parents to the child, perhaps both of their neglect of him and
their way of life, moral standards, etc. This places the child in an insoluble conflict
situation, to which he may only react in self-defeating ways. It also increases his already
substantial problems of security, identity and self-esteem.

The social worker hoped that the group could explore this question, among others, if
it were shown to be relevant for them.

Already at the first meeting, rejecting and highly condemnatory attitudes to the
natural parents were expressed (e.g. "Such people ought to be put in camps"). The group
were apparently unanimous on these attitudes. None of the members encouraged the
children to write or have other contact with the natural parents ("only bad could come
of it"). None encouraged visits by the natural parents to the foster home, but one foster-
father, Mr. Smith, "did not feel that he could stop" the child (aged 13 years) from going
into town to see his mother (divorced, deserted, convicted both for theft and prostitution),
"and was not sure that he wanted to stop him either". Consensus on the condemnation
of the natural parents, except for Mr. Smith's cautious reservation, was so strong and so
emotion-laden that the social worker did not find it appropriate to pursue this issue at a
first meeting, although it had arisen spontaneously. The meeting was taken up with
members' presentations of their foster-children's behavioural problems, their attempts—
successful and unsuccessful—to deal with these, and the needs which were possibly
signalled by such behaviour. Members were intensely engaged.

At the second meeting, 2 weeks later, the group continued the previous discussion. At
an early stage Mr. Smith (who contributed rarely, but with effect) said that he had been
preoccupied since the previous meeting with thoughts about the children's own parents.
"It bothers me. . . .We all agreed last time that the children ought not to be punished
for their bad behaviour, because it was caused by something. But we feel qualified to
blame their parents. . . . Isn't their behaviour caused by something too? . . . " This
was greeted initially by protest. " . . . . Yes, but they are adults. . . Old enough to know
better. . . . There are limits, you know. . . . " The group became somewhat defensive
when Mr. Smith wondered aloud "how we all would have been if we had had the same
chances (as the natural parents)". Mr. Smith's increasing concern with this issue was
clearly arousing guilt, and therefore increasing defence in the group, at this early
stage. Since this would tend to consolidate the norm of condemnatory rejection, the

worker introduced the less disturbing but related theme of how the children seemed to perceive their parents. This led into discussion of the children's need to hold tightly onto what was "good" about their parents. This was well perceived by the group, who gave many examples.

During the third meeting, Mr. and Mrs. Smith were asked about their foster-son's pilfering and bed-wetting, which had earlier been observed to coincide with episodic restlessness. They reported that following the previous group meeting they had decided to meet such restlessness by inviting the boy's mother to visit. Such an occasion arose. The mother had eagerly come, and a joint weekend had been an unqualified success. The boy was now calmer than at any time during the 1 ½ years of his placement with them. They had now decided, given the Child Care Committee's approval to maintain such contact.

This theme did not arise again until late in the fifth meeting when members expressed a confused and half-sympathetic ambivalence towards the parents, rather than rejection.

By the termination of the group at six months, three of six pairs of foster-parents had initiated either regular or periodic contact between the children and the natural parent(s). They agreed that "whatever we think about them" we should make "an honest effort" to help the children maintain as positive an image of their parents as if possible and realistic.

The above example illustrates the sequence of individual assertion, group resistance, group acceptance and normative change in relation to a single issue during a brief series of meetings. This kind of process will become very familiar to students as they expand their practical experience. A large part of the learning of social group work method consists in learning to take a professionally appropriate part in this process. It will probably be observed that the group's attitude to individual member's experimentation or deviance is affected by the extent to which the group members collude defensively against change, and by the appropriateness of the member's deviant behaviour in relation to group objectives.

A number of interesting observations were made by Sherif and Sherif (*op. cit.*) in their study of conformity and deviation among adolescents. Concerning the so-called "latitude of acceptance", they concluded:

> The more significant the activity for the identity and continued maintenance of the group and its central interests, the narrower the range of acceptable behaviours for all members, the latitude for the leader being narrowest. Conversely, the more incidental the activity to the foregoing concerns of the group, the broader the range of individual variation without the arousal of sanction, the latitude for the leader being greatest.

These findings confirm our impressions from practice, already indicated. Behaviour or attitudes tending in the direction of fundamental change (including maturation and problem-solving) is resisted. According to the group and the change concerned, this resistance may result in a constructive working through of a problem, leading to meaningful and accepted change, or in the consolidation of existing norms which have some social or therapeutic advantage, or in stagnation. Where the deviance relates to peripheral issues, there may be little resistance and therefore no group control. Such issues provide an area of freedom for individual members, which helps to prevent the restrictions and disadvantages of membership from outweighing the advantages.

The group "gives" a little. The individual must also "give", often rather more generously, and this process provides possibilities for change for both parts.

No one except the new-born baby ever enters or attempts to influence any group without having already acquired experience of group life. We are all in constant interaction with each other in some kind of group situation, participating continually in this process of mutual adjustment and infuence. We influence our groups and are influenced by them. The patterns of interaction vary, of course, from one culture, group and situation to another, but group experience is a constant factor in human life and it profoundly influences the way in which we perceive both our environment and ourselves, and in which we behave.

We have already drawn attention to the relationship between successful participation in this process and our self-image. This is a very important determinant of our behaviour. Success or failure in one group situation increases the likelihood of similar experiences in later ones. We bring into new groups our particular personalities, attitudes and self-images which are partly results of earlier group experiences. These greatly influence our behaviour in the new group and thus its response to us. The anguish of the shy and self-effacing wallflower and the polished ease of the silver-spooner predetermine the measures of success which they may expect in new social situations. Their behaviour is as much determined by their earlier group experiences as by the reality of their present situations. Similarly in social-group work, the ease with which both client and social worker enter the group will depend as much on their experiences in earlier groups as on the realities of the social-work situation.

It will already be clear, however, that this is not a static and unchangeable attribute. The fact that the individual may in various ways change as a result of new group experiences is indeed basic to social work with groups, as to other forms of group treatment. As group members, we are all exposed to the influence of new ideas, new attitudes and new relationships. The group may also support us in experimenting with new behaviour and attitudes, or earlier behaviour may be modified by group controls. Unexpected strengths may be discovered. Unconscious wishes may become both conscious and attainable. Courage, or something like it, may blossom under group control and support, or previously forbidden impulses may be acted out.

Scheidlinger (1952), within a psycho-analytic frame of reference, has described the processes of identification, introjection and contagion which occur within the group, showing how the "group is a potent influence system" where the individual's ego and super-ego functioning "are constantly open to change".

Dependence

How "potent" an influence system the group is and how "open to change" the individual, are highly variable factors. Very important determinants of this are the intensity of the group experience for the members and the degree of their dependence upon the group.

Some intensive and protracted group situations have been described and experienced in which major personality change has occurred. Bettelheim (1960) has movingly described the impact of the concentration camp experience on many prisoners. He shows how, through protracted subjugation to humiliating and value-effacing experiences, through gross unpredictability, through planned dissolution of the group bond, and through their own defensive indentification with the aggressor's evaluation of themselves as worthless, vast numbers of prisoners underwent major personality change. Bettelheim uses the term "extreme environmental condition" to describe milieu and group experiences at this level of intensity. Despite his own initial strong commitment to classical Freudian analysis as the agent of lasting personality change, he was able through these experiences to see that suitably adapted intensive group situations might also be used to contribute to such change in the treatment of mentally ill children. This provided the rationale for the therapeutic methods practised at his Orthogenic School in Chicago (1950, 1955). Other extreme environmental pressures on groups, as in protracted guerilla warfare or very lengthy imprisonment, may also be seen to lead to major change in members' ego and super-ego functioning. Some analytically orientated long-term psychotherapy groups, embodying both stimulation and interpretation of transference and other unconscious phenomena, also seem to aim at restructuring major elements in the patients' personality.

This degree of change may not occur through relatively superficial group experiences, however. While basic personality characteristics certainly are established through group process in childhood and adolescence, they are rarely more than modified and refined through later group experience. Later change, except under "extreme environmental conditions", is more at the level which we have indicated earlier, namely change in perception of self and others with accompanying attitudinal modification, and behavioural modifications resulting from changed ability to use existing resources. Since this is the level of change at which most social work aims, the group is a particularly appropriate context for social work treatment.

To indicate the role played by dependence upon the group in this kind of change, we shall compare the life-situations of two people. We see that their needs, their self-images, and their different degrees of dependence upon the groups in question, lead to substantial differences in their attitudes to group membership and to the accommodations they are prepared to make in the process of differentiation and integration.

Case 1

Our subject is a fisherman. His responses to such questions as, "Who are you?" or "What are you?" might include... "I am John Smith, husband and father. We are a happy family. ... I and my brothers had a good childhood, too. My parents still live just down the road. We all see a great deal of each other. ... I own my own trawler and have a crew of five. There have been hard times, but we have done very well these last years. ... When it becomes necessary we can reduce our catches without going broke. ... I am Chairman of the local branch of the Fishermen's Union. . . . I play the accordion at the Saturday-night folkdances when we are in port. Good fun. The family all come too. ... I, etc., etc. ... I have also been a member of the Child Care Committee this last year. I can't agree with their policies at all. They decide important things too quickly and then hurry off to the next committee, or whatever...."

Our subject derives his identity and self-esteem from both earlier and present group membership, and from the continuing responses which he receives to his self-presentation in his current groups, of which there are many. He successfully plays many roles, is well regarded, and fulfils himself.

The last group he mentions is going badly. His reaction to that situation is germane to our present point. Because of his concern for Child Care he may for a time attempt to influence the committee members' attitudes. When he fully realises that he is unable to do this, he may resign. It is important to note that this withdrawal/rejection affects neither his self-image nor his personal security. So many other group memberships give him satisfaction and positive response that he is unlikely to sacrifice his views and interests and to change his perceptions and attitudes, in order to conform with the group. The committee may go to pieces when he leaves, but he will not.

Case 2

Let us now consider a person in a contrasting social situation. A middle-aged, divorced woman, belongs to a group of discharged psychiatric patients. She does not possess the rich and varied sources of response and reassurance of our first example. Asked to describe herself, she might say, "Well ... I never knew my parents. I grew up in Homes. ... I married though, but my husband left me when I became ill. ...My children, now married are ashamed of me. I never see them. ...I can't work. People frighten me. ...I think I frighten them. ...But I am a member of this club. All the others are like me. We meet twice a week, talk together, make things, arrange trips, see films. I don't know what I would do without the group. I have no one else."

Clearly, this woman has very much more of herself invested in the ex-patients' club than our fisherman had in the Child Care Committee. Not only does she derive a great deal of satisfaction and pleasure from it, but it is essential that it continue in being if she is to be able to experience herself as a person of value and interest to others. She will, then, in common with the other members, invest a great deal in maintaining the group. She is motivated towards finding it satisfying, "approving" of the group, just as she seeks its approval of her. Threat of dissolution will arouse anxiety in her and her fellow members alike and will mobilize them to keep it together. Threat of withdrawal by one member will cause the others to exert pressures and persuasion to remain, not only because of interest in the person concerned but because of the importance to themselves of preserving the group.

It is precisely this high level of mutual dependence which enables group work with such patients to succeed, since the resulting group support and control strongly tend to hold the group together despite the recurrent crises and conflicts inseparable from work in the psychiatric sector. This is particularly pronounced when a member shows signs of an impending relapse. In such situations the group tends to mobilise an intensive support activity, both at practical and emotional levels. This is, of course, partly for the threatened member's own sake, but there is also self-interest here, since all withdrawal—including that into illness—is experienced as disintegrative and must be averted. (Clinical material suggests that the rate of relapse of such patients is lower than that of those who do not belong to such groups, although no research on this has come to our attention.)

Like such group concepts as conformity and cohesion, which are later discussed, dependence is a descriptive concept to which we readily ascribe value—in this case, a negative moral value. It is in some way "bad" to be dependent. But in the group briefly sketched in Case 2 above, mutual dependence was a source of strength and support for a number of highly disadvantaged women. These clients were continually at risk of re-hospitalisation, but they maintained a relatively high degree of autonomy out in the community by using the strength and resources gained and reinforced in the group. Clearly, the question is not simply whether certain individuals are highly dependent upon a given group, but what are the consequences of their dependence for their ability to use their social and emotional potential?

Above, we saw dependence paradoxically liberating such potential. In the following, we see how a very similar process may seriously inhibit the differentiated social and emotional development of individual members.

Example 9. An informal group of male East-European refugees drift from café to café during the greater part of most days, and the whole of every evening. Few work, most of them receiving National Assistance, or other forms of financial aid. Those who had been married are now divorced. Several of them live tog..her in an informal commune, others living in flatlets, hostels, etc. They have no social contacts outside the group. This pattern began ten years ago, when the founder members first came to the host country. They were not able to cope with the transition and sought comfort with each other. Their feelings of inadequacy were resolved by projection on to the various agencies which had unsuccessfully attempted to help them, and their cultural disorientation was resolved by tacitly agreeing that the new country was not worth adjusting to anyway. There was no place like the Old Country, no language like the old language, no food like the old food. ... The group was gradually enlarged by other refugees who failed to manage their first jobs and did not try again. The norms of the group were already established. They provided a ready-made defence against the demands of adaptation to a new culture, and the feelings of inadequacy and conflict which failure to meet these demands involved. Members speak only their mother language, constantly reminisce and idealize their country of origin, and invest much time in expressing dissatisfaction with the new country and its customs. There is an intense group bond. Minor attempts to approach the surrounding culture—such as buying a traditional local sweater, showing interest in a work-training scheme, finding a new friend or going with a local girl—are reacted to with scorn and are hastily discontinued for fear of group rejection. Dependence upon the group has become so total that no imaginable disadvantage can outweigh that of rejection by the group. Thus, dependence, socially inhibiting norms and rigid group control interact in a vicious circle to limit members' possibilities of ever solving their common problem.

To digress briefly, again, into the world of secondary groups, this question of dependence and conformity reminds us of an important early study on the membership of mass movements. Hoffer (1951) wrote penetratingly and very provocatively about mass movements—from early Christianity and other faiths, to modern nationalism and nazism—and was particularly interested in the "fanatical" member, the True Believer. He contended that it is not necessarily a profound conviction of the rightness of the Cause, but the need of frustrated and disaffected individuals to be consumed by global holy causes which produces the True Believer—who will convert you or kill you, and whose "identification with the collective whole" is so great that he will die almost as readily as he will kill. To the extent that we accept Hoffer's analysis—here crudely introduced—we would in the present context comment that it is precisely the extreme dependence of the True Believer upon his mass movement which explains both his total conformity to its precepts and his self-sacrificial commitment to its programme.

Group Cohesion

The potency of the group as an influence system has been shown to be related to the degree of dependence of the members upon the group and to the extent of their identification with its purposes. In this context it is relevant to introduce the concept of *group cohesion*.

The terms "group bond" or "we-feeling" have been used to refer to the experience of mutual indentification between members. The varying intensity of this experience is referred to as the degree of the group cohesion.

Group cohesion is a rather complex concept, since group bond to which it is so closely related is itself a compound phenomenon. It is therefore more satisfactory to regard group cohesion as the intensity of stated aspects of the bonds between members. The reader will have had life experiences which support such an approach. One might, for example, feel strongly identified with the aims of a given group and contribute a great deal towards their achievement. But while one is prepared for that reason also to accept such rules as the group may have, one might well have reservations about developing strong relationships with certain of the members. Conversely, many will have belonged to groups in which there have been quite intense, warm relationships, but where one has "drawn the line" at certain of the group's proposed objectives or activities.

There are, then, at least three separate elements involved in group cohesion. These are the relationships between members, the shared investment in group aims, and the acceptance of group norms. It is clear that these variables will usually be closely associated, as was already indicated at a general level in Chapter 2. However, closer observation suggests that the association is by no means always one of high direct correlation. In some groups one aspect of cohesion may be quite recessive, although the group is highly cohesive in the other respects.

This may be seen both in common life situations and in groups met in social work practice. A number of examples will now be given.

Example 10. Many students and other young people are currently living in various kinds of experimental communal groups, which often seem to be characterised by a considerable involvement in relationships. There is also a common investment in the aim of demonstrating the viability of alternative social and familial patterns. At the same time, they appear to be free of pressures to conformity, apart from the minimum essential rules enabling the group to survive. Otherwise they seem to permit an unusually wide range of behaviour and activities.

Example 11. The neurological department of a large hospital accepts patients for pre-operative diagnosis and post-operative control and treatment. Typical duration of stay is 3-4 weeks, although a few patients remain much longer. Medical and nursing care is of very high standard despite staff shortage but includes only minimal help with the emotional aspects of the patients' crises. While many patients make excellent recoveries, a few die, and some are diagnosed as having progressive degenerative diseases, such as multiple sclerosis or muscular dystrophy. Many have traumatic illnesses, such as cerebro-vascular conditions or head or spinal injury. These sometimes occasion severe handicap, both physical and intellectual. Many patients, less seriously ill, commonly fear at admission that they too are threatened with a bleak and limited future. Further, much neurological examination and intervention is unavoidably somewhat painful, and involves a period of discomfort afterwards.

The situation is one of protracted multiple anxiety. The fear of pain and death, of progessive deterioration, of extreme dependency and loss of ability to work pervades the atmosphere. The patients, using their own resources, must deal with this in some way which enables them both to perform their role as patients and to survive the crisis with minimum damage to their self-esteem.

During a period of observation, a number of patients were seen to "solve" this optimally by means of an informal open group, which had clear behavioural expectations and equally clear, though less conscious, aims. During each day's contact, members both gave to and received from the fund of defence against anxiety, which was the group aim. Fears were denied or minimised, and there was intense investment in mutual distraction—jokes, games, ward scandal, "social conversation" and TV. Where problems and pain inescapably obtruded these were often made the subject of black humour, a curious but effective control device. Similarly, where patients expressed fears or complaints or dramatised their situation, they were met with embarrassed sympathy, followed by change of subject or some other form of withdrawal.

The amount of interaction seemed, at first, to imply involvement in relationships. But these were in fact transient and superficial, members colluding in "discovering" patterns of compatibility, some of which were at the level of conscious pretence. Plans were made for later meetings—fishing trips, joint holidays, etc—in which no one really believed, but which contributed nevertheless to sustaining relationships at the level necessary for the achievement of group aims, and acceptance of its norms.

(This reminds of another group situation characterised by extreme external pressures, by fear and compelled intimacy, namely military units in time of war. Here too there is a high degree of shared agreement about aims, rules and behaviour, and "if we get out of this lot" there will be undying friendship. . . But the reunions seldom take place. If they do, they tend to be hearty meetings between embarrassed strangers. . . . . There seems to be a component of utility and mutual exploitation in the apparently strong but transient relationships developed under stress. This could profitably be examined more closely, not least in therapeutic settings.)

Example 12. The social worker in a psychiatric out-patients' clinic leads a group of five young men. Not all have been previously hospitalised, but all have suffered depressive illnesses and received treatment. While now functioning well enough to remain out of hospital they are still withdrawn, anxious and isolated from social contacts. Their self-esteem is low. This relates not least to distress and confusion about sexual identity in several cases. They are intelligent, sensitive but inarticulate. The group meets once a week over two years.

The members are extremely burdened by their situation. They all wish to decrease their social isolation, which is described as "crippling". It is hoped to achieve this by increasing self-esteem on the basis of successful participation in the group, as well as by behavioural and perceptual .modification arising from increased insight. The social worker therefore invests in helping the members to identify and develop relationships with each other. She also—not least by demonstrating her own accepting attitudes and ability to experience feelings—gradually enables members freely to express feelings, impulses and preoccupations. A climate develops in which there is little fear of criticism, ridicule or pressure. Members learn to permit both themselves and others a wide variety of behaviour and preferences, and in this accepting atmosphere are able to work on their problems and to increase their self-esteem.

These observations and case extracts accord well with certain research and theoretical formulation on group cohesion. Particularly relevant is the work of Feldman (1967, 1969) and Gross (1956). These investigators have also identified three constituents of cohesion, which are referred to as the group's "modes of integration", and which are differentiated from each other in the following manner:

Functional integration refers to the extent to which the group-as-a whole is mobilized towards the performance of its function, and to which the individual members are identified with and contribute towards the performance of that function.

Normative integration refers to the degree of group-member consensus about the behaviour and attitudes accepted or rejected by and in the group.

Interpersonal integration refers to the frequency and intensity of reciprocal liking between members.

In these terms we may say that Examples 10 and 12 both demonstrate high levels of functional and interpersonal integration, but that normative integration was a relatively unimportant aspect of their cohesion. The group in Example 11, although its aims were somewhat unclearly perceived by members, demonstrated high levels of functional and normative integration, while interpersonal integration was less clearly evidenced.

Many investigators have confirmed what must be a commonplace impression from everyday life, namely that the more cohesive a group, the greater the conformity. But we have already indicated that cohesion is a compound phenomenon, and both of Feldman's studies have shown that functional integration and interpersonal integration are more closely correlated than normative and interpersonal integration (as in Examples 10 and 12). This relationship must, however, be subject to the influence of numerous variables. Feldman's studies have mainly been conducted with camp groups of school-age children, but it seems likely that his findings have wider general applicability.[5] The tendency noted accords with our greater preparedness to support people whom we like, and with the correspondingly greater need for pressure, such as group control, to establish successful co-operation with people with whom we have more tenuous reltionships.

However, these are normally complementary and not alternative factors in cohesion. There are always relationships in a group, and there is always some normative pressure, or group control. It is in their quality and intensity that these factors vary as regards ability to further functional integration.

Reference Groups

This model of "modes of integration" is also useful in helping us to place such concepts as "cohesion" and "conformity" in their proper perspective and to relate less emotionally to them. Like "dependence", both "cohesion" and "conformity" are descriptive terms to which we readily and inappropriately ascribe value. Interestingly, although conformity (normative integration) is as we have seen one constituent of cohesion, there seems to be a tendency to ascribe opposite values to these two terms. Perhaps this paradox may be explained by their political connotations? "Cohesion" is very like "solidarity", and is therefore a good thing? "Conformity" is very close to "conservatism", and is therefore a bad thing?

But again, the question which should be asked is "what are the consequences of the high level of cohesion for these individuals in this group, and in particular of the high level of normative integration?" On this, Sherif and Sherif (*op. cit.*) say:

> Much of the unsavoury reputation of "conformity" in current popular literature reflects the tendency of the writers to condemn conformity itself, rather than examining what is conformed to, and *why* individuals conform to certain values rather than others. Conformity and non-conformity are, by definition, behaviours relative to some standards, which standards may be assessed as good or evil. Divorced from these referents, however, conformity or non-conformity cannot possibly be appraised in itself. The terms become meaningless.

Several of the case extracts already cited amply illustrate this, showing how high levels of normative and funtional integration may lead to social growth or stagnation, to life enrichment or impoverishment, according to the norms and aims on which there is consensus.

It is clear that we are all more highly normatively integrated in some groups than in others. Our fisherman, earlier mentioned, would be more so in his family or his trawler-crew than in the Child Care Committee, for example. Some of our memberships involve, or have involved, a very high level of normative integration— "for good or evil", as Sherif and Sherif have it. Certain periods of life and certain situations find us more ready, at least temporarily, to suspend the assertion of our individual identity in return for the advantages of high conformity to a particular group or groups. We then appraise the appropriateness of our behaviour in relation to the standards of such so-called *reference groups*. Their norms are vitally important determinants of our behaviour and our attitudes. Sprott (1955) has cogently argued that also our "self-respect" is in fact a reflection of the degree of approval which we are afforded by our reference groups:

> It is from the groups with which we identify ourselves that our standards come. We respect in ourselves those qualities and the behaviour that goes with them, which find approval in the eyes of the other members of the groups in which we are involved, or to which we feel we owe allegiance. We are to a large measure the artefacts of our affiliations.[6]

The family of our early childhood is such a reference-group. As we have earlier seen, the very roots of personality are formed by the processes of identification, imitation and conformity, conflict-resolution and conflict-suspension inherent in this primary reference group.

Adults in situations of isolation and stress, such as war, imprisonment, hospitalisation, organisational or political struggle, may become so cohesive that current referents make possible behaviour far removed from that of which they would be capable alone. Not only may such membership facilitate more efficient effort towards the common goals—whether these be well or badly chosen—but it may also have a profound influence on the self-evaluation of members. Individual impotence may become collective power, humiliation become pride, or private shame a collective bond of meaningful relationships.

Certain reference groups may have so decisive and lasting an effect that they enable members to withstand even the greatest external pressures towards normative change. This remains true even though other members of the reference group are not present. Its norms have been internalised and the group remains as what has been called an "invisible committee", lending support, strength and evaluative referents for behaviour even in its absence. This mechanism enables the lone trade unionist to remain loyal to his views and consistent in his demands when in confrontation with powerful, autocratic and persuasive employers. Despite pressure and perhaps threat, he is able to pursue aims and values consistent with his organisational and political affiliations, since these provide moral reinforcement even in their physical absence. The suffragettes suffered in solitary imprisonment extreme privation and humiliation. Despite all of this, they were able to adhere to their politically necessary programme of hunger-striking and to endure the agonies of forced feeding because of the intensity of their commitment to their reference group and their certainty of its spiritual solidarity. These situations are analogous to that of a professionally identified social worker, struggling to achieve change, flexibility and humane attitudes from a position within a rigid bureaucracy, who may be enabled to survive the isolation, manipulation or enmity which he may meet by experiencing support from the invisible committee of his professional reference group. We may profitably also here return to Bettelheim's (1960, *op.cit.*) descriptions of the remarkable dignity and high personal morality retained by many concentration camp prisoners who were members of such highly cohesive religious groups as the Jehovah's Witnesses, or who had been dedicated to an ascetic yet passionate political ideology such as the communism of Central Europe in the 1930s. This despite the fact that according to Bettelheim's analysis the purpose of the camp regime at the time was precisely that of conscious and systematic obliteration of all sense of both individual and group identity, rather than of life. This thread is taken up in Hoffer's (*op.cit.*) comments on Zionism in his study of mass movements. While confirming Bettelheim's observation that those who best resisted coercion were those with strong reference group affiliations, he also noted the corollary—that "individualists, whatever their nationality, caved in...the Western European Jew proved to be the most defenceless. Spurned by the Gentiles...and without vital ties with a Jewish community, he faced his tormentors alone, forsaken. ...." Yet when the survivors of the same vulnerable and resigned victims came to Palestine they fought British and Arabs alike as "formidable enemies: reckless, stubborn, resourceful. ... In Palestine the Jew felt himself a *member* of an eternal race, with an immemorable past behind it and a breathtaking future ahead. ..."

Concentration camps, women's suffrage, fishing trawlers and industrial dispute seem well removed from the concerns of social work treatment. Yet they provide useful analogies, for this concept of reference groups holds an important place in social work with groups. A major aim of this method is to enable members to relate to each other somewhat in this matter—not necessarily with the drama and fervour of some of these examples, but at least with a comparable sense of sharing aims, suffering and strength through a commonality of needs.

Heightened self-acceptance has been mentioned as one consequence of reference group membership. This is a common reason for choosing the group as the context and means of help. Certain clients are in situations of isolation and rejection. Both their self-evaluation and prevailing social attitudes burden them further with feelings of guilt, dependency and inferiority. Cases in point are young unmarried mothers, discharged psychiatric patients or prisoners, vagrants and alcoholics in hostel accommodation, lonely aged people, many homosexuals. Their possibilities for change are low. The right of others to attempt to inflict change is in most cases highly debatable. But it is consistent with social-work aims and principles to attempt to help such people to live as rich and satisfying a life as possible, and to enhance their self-respect, even within the confines of their life-situation and in the face of discriminatory social attitudes. Where groups of such people are formed they tend to become highly cohesive, and develop the characteristics of a reference group for their members. The heightened self-acceptance which results from this seems frequently to increase the members' ability to use their ego-resources, to defend their interests, and better to withstand the humiliating and judgemental social pressures to which they are daily exposed. Their "invisible committee" assures them that they *are* valuable. They may then demand the attention of the National Assistance clerk who intentionally keeps them waiting. (That the social worker should simultaneously be involved in influencing the attitudes of the clerk, his service, and the society which it represents is another and yet wider issue.)

In addition to forming such groups as these, the social worker may become involved in groups which are already the major referents of the members' behaviour and attitudes. This is especially true of work with youth.

During adolescence, the peer group becomes the major normative referent for its members. Identity and strength are in a sense "borrowed" from the group and used as a means of liberation from the expectations of continued conformity to the primary reference group of the family. This enables the adolescent to experiment with new behaviour, values, clothes and language. Above all, he may establish for himself his separateness from the family. Life revolves around the activities and maintenance of the peer group. The new reference group may often in fact be more controlling and demand more conformity than the family. (Josselyn (1952) refers to the "iron control" of the adolescent peer group). But he accepts this in return for the gains of membership. The intense cohesion of the group, based on high normative and interpersonal integration, helps him both to change and to distance himself from the guilt and discomfort which accompanies this change because of its seeming rejection of his family.

The intensity of such existing reference group influence may be the factor which determines the social worker's use of group service as the method of choice.

The author's own fumbling introduction to group-work came about for this reason. As a Probation Officer one sat in the office vainly striving to "reach" the teenage gang member, who—usually very politely—manoeuvered himself out of all attempts at meaningful communication and contact. All responses were submitted to the "invisible committee" of his reference group, the young men with whom he had grown up, attended school, started work and committed joint offences and who were also currently enjoying the benefits of one's supervision. His conformity to their expectations (in this case of a circumspect non-involvement in "treatment") hindeed the development of a relationship to the social worker. One gradually experienced the illogic of attempting to influence an individual client, leaving in the waiting room a reference group of three joint offenders whose possibilities for influence were infinitely greater than one's own could ever be. Whereupon the group were invited to attend jointly. Meetings thereafter were marked by an astonishing increase in spontaniety and directness. (Excitedly recounting this discovery to an older and untrained colleague, one was met with a deflating, "Oh! I've been doing it for years. It is the only way that makes sense, isn't it?") Eminent group dynamicists also agree that it "makes sense". Cartwright (1951) says: "Efforts to change individuals or sub-parts of a group which, if successful, would have the result of making them deviate from the group, will encounter strong resistance."

The social worker contacts many groups which have already become reference groups for their members. Street-corner groups, pre-puberty glue-sniffers, inmates of an old people's home, groups of derelict meths-drinkers, are cases in point. Possibilities for change and effective help, however slight they may sometimes be, are at least greater at the group level than at the individual level. The behaviour regarded as problematical has become incorporated into the group's norm system. Only by group consensus or by withdrawal from the group may change occur. The highly restrictive group of refugees in Example 9 (p. 63) was such a group. The members' presumed needs led to the planning of a long-term detached group work project led jointly by a woman and a man social worker. After the first winter the group began to show some willingness to question common assumptions and standards, and there was a certain weakening in the group control system. (Very regrettably this project had to be abandoned after one year owing to personnel changes, so no more conclusive change may be reported.)

Some groups seem to be aware at some level of the therapeutic advantage of bringing treatment into the reference group, rather than making individual sorties from it in order—ambivalently and defensively—to enter treatment. The feeling of security experienced in the group is no doubt an equally important factor in such situations.

Example 13. A school-psychology office became increasingly orientated towards family group treatment, following certain inspiring learning experiences. Family group treatment was offered to a number of families where a son or daughter was referred because of behavioural or learning problems. Most of these families accepted. In several cases, however, the "identified patient",[7] a teenage pupil, although motivated for treatment, refused to co-operate in this venture. These pupils said, however, that they "didn't mind coming with some of my friends who are in the same boat". This client-initiative led to the formation of a weekly counselling group of teenage pupils with behavioural problems related both to their family and school situations. A colleague concurrently helped the parents by supportive casework. (Problems at the school level were approached by staff group consultation led jointly by a psychologist and the social worker who worked with the group.)

With increasing maturity and personal security this close identification with the reference group or groups seems to decrease. Members consequently become less dependent upon them, though never entirely so. The process of differentiation becomes more strongly emphasised, and the tendency is to withdraw from the groups which demand most normative integration, or to dilute the impact of continued membership in such groups with other affiliations. This is seen clearly in social group work, where many groups which have been intensely cohesive at a time of acute and coincident need have become decreasingly cohesive with the approach of optimal problem solution, and have been well orientated towards termination when this has been suggested.

This is a familiar process in social work with many formed groups. Common purposes of such groups are clarification and solution (or partial solution) of a shared problem, which is frequently circumscribed and fairly clearly defined. It is hoped that members will identify with the group and receive its support. They may thus develop and integrate socially rewarding ways of behaviour, or may identify themselves with constructive solutions achieved or appropriate attitudes to common problems. These may then aid members in actively dealing with the problems and decisions of their life-situation outside the group in which they are discussed. Working towards these attitudes and solutions through shared activities or discussion intensifies the extent to which they are meaningfully integrated. This is further reinforced when the group becomes a reference group for the members within the relevant context. For most clients, however, the client-group will be only one of several referents. This implies that dependence upon the group will usually not be so high that they will need to submit to extreme normative pressure. This factor enables each client to temper the influence of this particular reference group and adapt it to his own individual needs.

Example 14. A social worker leads a group of wives of middle-aged and elderly men who have suffered cerebral haemorrhages. A group culture develops which enables members to express fairly freely their feelings about their changed role and about their husbands' sudden and extensive dependence. Some of these feelings would not commonly meet with social approval. While group norms encourage frank expression of feelings, members' dependence upon the group is not so great that group control may impel them into one common "solution". Rather, shared attitudes and feelings may and should lead to quite different consequences for each member, according to their individual resources and life-situations outside the group (including perhaps some other reference group—church, family, etc.). Thus, some members decide simply to "carry on as before". One decides to let off rooms to supplement her income and to gain time for the care of her husband. Most of them decide to apply for maximum home-nursing help. Some find it most appropriate and realistic to try to make arrangements for institutional care.

This reflects a central trend in the processes of integration and differentiation which have been discussed in this chapter. The individual is motivated towards integration up to the point where the group may better serve his perceived needs than isolated activity. But his need for self-assertion and independence remains active. This will lead him to invest more in differentiating himself from the group when his needs have been optimally met, or when group demands for conformity threaten his freedom to find solutions best suited to his unique life-situation, personality and resources. On this point we wish finally to quote from Storr's (1968) lucid book on human aggression:

Heretics are persecuted because they threaten the security of the believer; and the savage punishments which the orthodox have meted out to those who disagree with them bear witness not to the strength of their faith, but to its vulnerability ... One of the most difficult problems which human beings have to face is that of maintaining sufficiently close contact with others whilst at the same time preserving autonomy. The heretic is driven to rebellion because he finds his individuality stifled by the orthodoxy of the group. Conformity, based on close identification, at first promises reassurance, but easily becomes a restriction upon freedom to those who need to assert an individual point of view....

Just as the child must need rebel against even the least authoritarian of parents, so the adult who feels restricted by too close an identification with others will rebel against the confinement which this imposes upon him...

Whenever identity is threatened by too close an identification with others there will be an increase of aggression leading to differentiation. This process is closely analogous to the part aggression plays in territoriality. A certain distance must be maintained between myself and my neighbour or my identity is threatened. But I need my neighbour, for I cannot be fully human in isolation.

Notes to Chapter 4

1. There seems currently to be a renewal of interest in such notions of collective mental and emotional processes, perhaps because many social problems today manifest themselves at the group level or as inter-group conflict. Professional involvement in the problems of certain minority groups and inter-racial tensions involving the 3rd World necessarily stimulate thinking about collective processes. For example, Morales (1971) in a social-work symposium on the social, emotional and political problems of the "Chicanos"—Mexican Americans— postulates a "collective preconscious" as one important determinant of racist attitudes. His paper is a thoughtful and timely reintroduction of this kind of concept into contemporary social debate.

   In the context of analytical group psychotherapy, Foulkes (1964) and Foulkes and Anthony (1965) have developed the concepts of the "group matrix". This term refers to all the shared experiences of the group since its formation. The group matrix continually grows, both in its complexity and in its importance for the members. It is the source of shared associations, preoccupations and responses, and provides both the framework and the focus of the authors' model of treatment. They also use such terms as "group mind" and "group association". They propose that ideas and comments expressed by members have the value of unconscious interpretations, which are made possible by the shared history of communication and interaction which composes the group matrix. ...These are subtle and complex concepts, which will repay further study.

   The recent literature also contains a highly interesting analogy between the individual and the team, which reverses the more familiar pattern of applying individual behavioural and emotional concepts to groups. Pentony (1970) applies a number of propositions about the behaviour, identities and adaptive techniques of teams to the individual person. On this basis he tentatively suggests a model which may follow fresh reflection about such important concepts as self, insight, crisis and therapeutic change.

2. Concerning group names. The name chosen by a group will sometimes very succinctly characterise the self-perceptions and behavioural expectations of the members. A treatment group in a psychiatric hospital was initially led by a therapist whose treatment philosophy emphasised strongly the value of maximum openness and directness about members' experience of the institution, the group and each other. The unmodified expression of anger and frustration was encouraged. The anxiety-arousing aggression experienced from others, as well as fear of that perceived in oneself, was reflected in the group's self-chosen sobriquet—"the Wolves".

    This crystallizing of group culture in a name presents therapeutic material, of course. (It may also give the therapist occasion to re-evaluate his techniques.) It is sometimes of particular interest during a stage when a group culture is changing. One group in a large youth club—delinquent, violent and unpredictable—called themselves "the Sledgehammers". During their second year, in which some members had matured considerably, they debated a change of name. Those members who had markedly matured and who now partially rejected previous standards, suggested "the Pioneers". Those who wished to remain "Sledge-hammers" retained earlier behaviour standards. Until they too accepted the new name, they were referred to by the others as "the Sandtray-kids", an unexpectedly clear perception by "the Pioneers" of the immaturity of their earlier norms.

3. There is a wealth of literature on this subject. Students may particularly enjoy two companion studies of the varieties of attitudes and practices in child-rearing in an English coal-mining district. These share clarity of observation with a good-humoured warmth surprisingly lacking in our professional literature (Newson and Newson, 1963, 1970).

4. The term "culture" is commonly used to denote the norms and values of a group. It does not in this context have any evaluative connotations.

5. Feldman concludes his studies with a number of tentative but appealing suggestions about the implications of his findings for social work with groups. It is suggested that different modes of integration may become the focus of the worker's inter-vention according to the nature of the group goals, since his intervention may conduce to an increase or decrease in the levels of these various modes of integration. This contribution to establishing a more validated basis for social work with groups will repay further study and consideration. It is recommended for discussion in connection with social work method.

6. Reese (1961), Newcomb (1952) and other investigators have amply supported Sprott's contention, demonstrating experimentally various aspects of the close relationship between self-acceptance and group-approval.

7. Satir (1967) refers to the family member who is presented as "the sick one", "the different one" or "the one who is to blame", as the "Identified Patient", since his symptoms may often be seen as serving a family function as well as being a manifestation of his personal conflict. Elements of chance, constitution and manipulation determine who becomes "identified" as the patient in a dysfunctioning family, but it is the family as a whole which requires help.

CHAPTER 5

Communication in Groups

The processes of group formation, group cohesion and individual differentiation so far discussed necessitate communication and inter-action between group members. All group life does so. Aspects of these two concepts will be discussed in this and the following chapter.

First, to distinguish between them. The term "communication" refers to the process of conveying meaning by giving, receiving and exchanging signals of various kinds. "Interaction" is a wider term, which may be said to subsume communication. It refers to the process of mutual stimulation, response and influence between persons in contact with each other.

These concepts, then, deal with the most central features of all social life, including that of small groups. All other small-group processes—role formation, leadership, decision-making, development—are in a sense products of the exchanges of meaning and the mutual influence involved in communication and interaction. Sensitivity to these phenomena is thus indispensable for those working with groups.

Communication and interaction are, clearly, closely related. We shall, however, for the sake of clarity, discuss them separately. In this chapter, we shall look at some aspects of communication, and interaction will be discussed in Chapter 6.

Aims and Means of Communication

We communicate in order to give and seek information and instruc-tion, to impart experience and reactions, to elicit responses and clarify messages to and from each other, to demonstrate attitudes and opinions, and to influence others. In doing all this we use several media.

We tend to think of communication as consisting first and foremost of spoken and written words. Certainly no more extensive means of communication exists than that of language, through which an infinity of ideas and associated messages may be expressed. In learning, teaching, business, politics, organisation, entertainment and indeed in all of life we depend mainly upon words to convey meaning—either our entire meaning, or refinement and clarification of meaning already implied by action. The more complex our technology, our relationships and our social organisation, the more differentiated are the notions which must be expressed and clarified. Contemporary education therefore places enormous emphasis on skill with words and concepts, compared with the emphasis on practical skills of some generations past or that on survival skills in more primitive societies. Words are vitally important! The eloquent are admired and rewarded. The inarticulate are at a profound disadvantage. This is true in the highest political, administrative and cultural circles: it is equally true over the counter of the National Assistance office or in the dock of the Magistrate's Court.

But communication is by no means restricted to the use of words. Parallel to our learning of a verbal language or languages, and beginning in fact earlier, we also acquire and refine during our whole life an extensive repertoire of non-verbal means of communication. The beckoning finger, the resigned shrug, the disgusted grimace, the puzzled frown, the shaken fist, are examples. These are rich, expressive and often very subtle means of communication, with which we are all familiar. In some special situations, non-verbal communication has been formalized and refined into means of communication which excludes the needs for words. One thinks here of deaf-and-dumb language, of the rapid and intricate choreography of the tic-tac men and of certain dance forms. Currently there seems also, in some circles, to be a return of interest in mime, perhaps partly in reaction to the inescapable barrage of words with which we are continually bombarbed.[1] Similarly, some forms of therapy and sensitivity training are currently being introduced which encourage greater liberation from bodily tensions and inhibitions as well as paying much more attention to understanding bodily expressions of feeling and attitude.

Somewhere between the verbal and non-verbal means of communication we have the use of expressive sounds. Laughter—of hilarity, ridicule or sarcasm; weeping—with grief or relief; sighs—of resignation, sadness or demonstrative irritation, are among many examples. Grunting, according to earlier papers (McCullough, 1954, and Foren, 1954), has been elevated among social workers to the heights of a therapeutic technique!

Most communication uses, of course, a combination of these media. The way in which they are combined may substantially influence the content of the message which is transmitted and received. The gestures and facial expressions which accompany words greatly influence their meaning. "Come here", to take a very simple example, may convey and inspire feelings as divergent as eager anticipation, anxiety, guilt, tenderness or sexual awareness, depending upon the gestures and facial expressions used. The tone in which words are spoken is equally important for the meaning conveyed. One word, something as brief and familiar as "yes", can be given numerous different meanings by change of tone and inflection.

Cultural factors also play an important part in communication. Skill in communication is first learned, and preferred means of communication first established, in the family-group. These are then extended at school and in play, and further refined during all contact with both the immediate environment and with the mass media. Thus, cultural and subcultural usages profoundly influence our use and style of communication. Even where the same words are used, their flavour and sometimes their whole meaning may vary from one environment to another. "Topping" means "splendid" to debs, or used to do, but it still means "execution by hanging" among prison inmates. "Up Britain" means one thing to the campaigning politician, and quite another to the singularly disrespectful young people who are raising difficulties at his meeting. "Graft" to the Nottinghamshire coal-miner means "hard work" whilst to most people it conveys the opposite idea of "profit by corrupt means". Examples are legion. Tone, inflection, gestures, also vary both culturally and individually, although some facial expressions and certain bodily gestures seem to be used universally. Passivity and restraint in communication may have quite different implications in different cultures and subcultures, as may abruptness or volubility. Goldberg (1968) has an important point about this.

> There is a notion abroad that the more family members are able to communicate with each other, the better for the cohesion and functioning of the family. Yet the labourer's family in which the father raps out the occasional command to his children and has a short monosyllabic conversation with his wife on coming home from work is not necessarily functioning less well than the middle-class family in which long discussions and explanations take place on every issue that arrives. ... It is likely that many different styles of communication are perfectly compatible with normal growth and development.

There is an interesting reciprocity in this. Cultural factors influence our style and means of communication. But we tend for various reasons also to adapt our manner of communicating to the culture or subculture in which we find ourselves. We strive, for example, to "improve" our accent and in certain cultures to restrain our gestures as we ascend the socio-economic ladder. It is a culturally determined adaptation of communication, often quite conscious. Similarly, a social worker, engaged in a stimulating conference with colleagues, will use a different vocabulary than when he is spending nights by the railway sidings with homeless alcoholics or leading a group of mountain small-holders in discussing their problems as foster-parents.[2]

Levels and Distortions of Communication

Much of this is very familiar. Less familiar, at least less conscious, are some of the more subtle aspects of communication to which the social worker must be particularly sensitive. We may illustrate this by first considering a basic 2-person, 1-message communication situation:

A gives a signal or message, S, to B

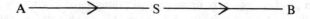

$$A \longrightarrow S \longrightarrow B$$

S might, for example, be a simple comment upon the weather ... "It is raining" ... This may seem an unambiguous and complete message. Perhaps it is.

But let A be a 3-year-old, the only child of his unmarried mother, B.

Let the situation be 06.45 on a dark winter morning, with the child in rain-clothes standing in the door. The mother is hastily packing his satchel with dry clothes and sandwiches, prior to his being picked up by an elderly neighbour who "minds children". She is also anxiously watching the time because she must clock in at the nearby factory at 7 o'clock. She will work all day.

The communication situation is now more involved.

A's "It is raining" carries a number of subterranean messages and probably means also:

> "I wish I didn't have to go, Mummy," or
> "I wish I could stay here where it is dry and warm," or
> "I wish I could stay with you," or
> "How can you, of all people, do this to me day after day?" or
> "I am wretchedly unhappy and it's your fault. And you get so cross these days I daren't even say what I'm thinking."

B registers his sadness, his confusion and his feelings of being deserted by her. She feels both accused and guilty. Instantly repressing her guilt feelings, without solving them, she becomes tense and defends herself by anger. She snaps at the boy, "Don't be such a baby. A drop of rain won't hurt you". He bursts into tears. She feels even more guilty and therefore more angry. She desperately shakes him to make him quiet. The hooter goes in 5 minutes and that damned woman hasn't come yet. He cries even more.

Two people, dependent upon one another, have hurt each other through their failure to communicate clearly, and thus to interact appropriately. It happens all the time, and many common sources of such failure are involved in the above example.

A is frequently unable to articulate his message, S, clearly, and completely. Even if he does, B is not always able to perceive its content accurately.

The obstacles may arise from A's poor verbal ability, his own lack of clarity about S, including his feelings about it, or from language problems. They may also arise from his uncertainty and anxiety about how S will be received by B, his relationship to B, and other emotional obstacles in A himself preventing clear and complete presentation of his message. Obstacles may also arise from B's inattention, his preoccupation, and his attitudes to S. B's attitude to S may be coloured by preconceptions, prejudice, rejection, guilt and defences against guilt or anxiety. These will cause distortion, blocking or selective perception of S. His attitudes to A, whether of dislike, mature love, idealisation, status anxiety or superiority, etc., will similarly influence his ability accurately to perceive A's message.

Such factors may enter any communication situation, including that of a small group. Communication in a group is, of course, more complex than in our 2-person, 1-signal example above. This is both because of the greater number of participants, with their manifold combinations of attitudes and needs, and because the senders and receivers are the same persons, at different times, these being in practice interchangeable roles.

If we extend our example from an A to B situation, to one including a number of clients, as well as the social worker, we may see how differently a single signal may be received and distorted. Further, in the following case extract, we may see how the differences in the recipients' perceptions of the original signal lead in their turn to different responses. Thus there is a tendency towards a progressive diffusion of communication into areas of steadily decreasing relevance, unless the social worker or a perceptive and sensitive member intervenes.

Example 15. The Child Guidance Clinic in a large dormitory high-rise estate had in individual psychotherapy a number of patients in early-puberty with acute behavioural problems. Some of these were also on probation or under supervision of the Child Care Officer. The social worker worked with a group of parents of these patients. A major aim was clarification of the parent-child conflict and of the mutual manipulations within the families represented. Without inviting to excessive projection, the worker hoped also to gain some material on environmental contributions to the problems presented. This would be included in representations to the appropriate local authorities. The group worked seriously with these issues, encountering both resistance and culpability also in themselves. At a stage where the group were beginning to perceive the behaviour as something wider than "the child's problem", the following episode occurred, illustrating our present point.

X said with an unsuccessful laugh, "I begin to see that the best thing to do must be to buy the biggest book on child psychology I can find ... and then give him a good old-fashioned thump on the head with it."

Y,Z,V and W's response to this seemed to indicate that they had received widely varying messages. Y, enthusiastically but not yet securely adopting new insight into child behaviour, heard this as a sarcastic rejection of psychology and was irritated. Z, a rather humourless and moralistic member, heard it as advocating hitting children and murmured a half-hearted reproof. V, a gregarious, but geographically isolated woodsman, the only member living outside the district, found important social satisfactions in the group, and related only to the humour. He therefore laughed uproariously.

W alone appears to have heard the real message behind the joke, namely, "I am getting confused and anxious. Maybe a bit angry with the social worker too. This group has made me see that the simple and satisfactory approaches I earlier had were really over-simplified and unsatisfactory. I am now in conflict as to whether I can use these new insights I have got from the group or whether I shall go back to where I started. It is all very difficult and I feel a bit of a failure."

W's response to what he "heard" was first to laugh mildly at the joke and then to say, "I think I know what you mean. I've been feeling like that. I call my 12-year-old a dirty sod and stop his pocket money because he still messes himself. It's his fault. All right? Or of these batteries we live in! Until coming here I honestly hadn't thought it might help if I tried to see a bit more of him, let him be a kid now and then with an Old Man he can talk to. He's no happier up here than we are, but we don't expect him to trouble us with it. ... Know what he said last time he filled his pants?—"I'm in a mess, Dad". . . . Know what Dad did? Locked him in for the weekend. Good old Dad! Talk about understanding. . . . Psychology! . . . If I could work less overtime, be less tired, less edgy, calm down a bit. ... But here's the crunch. Who's going to pay these rents? And we're so far from town I spend £10 a month just on travel. Can anybody here conjure me up a job in my trade 5 minutes from home, or find me a place to live at with a rent a man with one job can pay? . . . No? . . . So I'm back where I started, only now I know I'm to blame too."

We see here how V, Y and Z perceived selectively and insensitively because of their own needs and problems, their wishes and presuppositions. Their responses were in consequence irrelevant to what X was really trying to communicate. W, however, was able to see the complexity of his own situation and to experience its frustrating and guilt-provoking conflicts. He could thus allow himself, without threat to defences, to register and respond to the hidden elements in X's bitter "joke".

We shall now introduce some relevant concepts. Where a signal, whether verbal, semi-verbal or non-verbal, conveys a message in its *expressed* content, this message is referred to as *overt or manifest communication,* or the overt or manifest *part* or *level* of the communication. Where a signal sent by whatever means contains other *concealed* or *implied* messages which supplement or modify the overt or manifest message, then such a concealed or implied message is referred to as *covert* or *latent communication*, or the covert or latent *part* or *level* of the communication.

Thus, in our example of the little boy on the wet morning, A's *overt* or *manifest* communication was "it is raining". His *covert* or *latent* communication was "I wish I didn't have to go" . . . to . . . "daren't say what I'm thinking". In Example 15 above X's *overt* or *manifest* communication was "I begin to see" . . . to . . . "thump on the head with it". His *covert* or *latent* communication was "I am getting confused" . . . to . . . "bit of a failure".

Yet other terms for these phenomena have become current in the field of conjoint family therapy. These are of particular interest since they draw especial attention to the part played by relationships and feelings between communicators in determining the level of communication at which various messages may be placed. Satir (*op.cit.,* pp. 75-90) speaks of the *denotative* and the *meta-communative* levels. She defines these respectively as "the literal content" and "a comment on the literal content as well as on the nature of the relationship between the persons involved".

It may well be that the sender himself is not fully—perhaps not at all—aware of the latent content of his communication. It is therefore common also to use the terms "conscious" and "unconscious" communication. Manifest and conscious communication will usually coincide, as will latent and unconscious. This is an over-simplification, however, since latent communication will also often be conscious, the sender being for various reasons unable or unwilling to articulate his real message and consciously sending out indirect signals instead. While there is in most cases a clear distinction between the latent and manifest communication, the differences in conscious and unconscious communication will often be differences only in degree or level of consciousness. In the example above of the small child in the rain the latent communication was probably quite conscious. In Example 15 it was much less so.

Communication may also be either clearly manifest, or have rich and apparent latent content, yet be *accidentally* or unintentionally expressed. This could occur where "forbidden" impulses or feelings were being suppressed or were preconscious. The familiar Freudian "slips of the tongue" come readily to mind.

Example 16. To return to example 7 (p. 47). One of the social workers leading the group of delinquent teenagers in the climbing and survival project ruefully recorded the following episode.

One rather disturbed member, David, had taken a path above the cliff-face which was being climbed by others in the group. These were roped together with the social workers on a part of the climb which was somewhat exposed and looked relatively hazardous. David began rolling rocks down upon the group and narrowly missed dislodging them.

Later back in the camp, the members threw him into the lake and threw large stones all around him. The social worker anxiously ran out of his tent to *stop* this persecution. He called, "Stop it! you might *miss* him!" . . . This was not quite what he had intended to say!

Double Communication

Because of situational, emotional and cultural obstacles to satisfactory communication or simply because of the participants' lack of facility in communication, some signals may be not only unclear and incomplete, but also ambiguous. Where signals are sent which are open to more than one interpretation, this is called *double communication*. This places the receiver in a position of uncertainty and perhaps anxiety.

A common example of this is where an affirmative or negative reply is given to a question which poses alternatives. Consider the classic parent/child exchange:

Parent: "Well, are you staying in or going out?"

Child: "I decided not to."

This ambiguous reply may be caused simply by the child's lack of communicative skill, or is perhaps intended to provoke the parent into a state of irritated uncertainty. In either case, it may be readily clarified by a reformulation of the original question. Double communication is, however, not always so readily clarified, since both its expression and its sources may be more complex than this. It seems often to be the case that double communication is less conscious than this, and that it reflects an unresolved conflict in the sender. This conflict may concern either the message to be sent, or the sender's relationship to the receiver(s). This in its turn arouses anxiety about the receiver's reception and response to the message. Conflict breeds confusion. Ambivalence breeds ambiguity.

Example 17. A Child Care Committee was discussing the case of a 14-year-old girl, who had recently been aborted, following a rape in which she had apparently been an unusually co-operative victim. The issue under discussion was whether this should be dealt with by offering the girl and her family informal supportive help, by seeking a formal supervision order, or by planning institutional care.

The Chairman, a doctor, had expressed the view that the girl was undoubtedly promiscuous, suggesting her physical maturity as a possible explanation of this. "In another time or place this girl would by now be a mother, and—for all we know—a good one.'' He felt that the wisest course would be to dramatise the situation as little as possible, and to offer informal help, directed not least to teaching her effective contraceptive techniques and helping her family to accept this practice.

Another member, Mr. Brown, a teacher and lay-preacher, reacted to this. It was ''incomprehensible'' that the Chairman should ''make a bagatelle of so grave a case''. Further, the suggestion that the Committee should request some public servant to teach the girl to use contraceptives was ''tantamount to encouraging her to go onto the streets.'' The Committee would be ''neglecting their duty to the girl'' if they did not try to ''arrange for her proper care and protection in a suitable institution.''

The Chairman and Mr. Brown had clearly, completely and unambiguously communicated their views. The issue, now polarised, was offered for further discussion. No takers. The Chairman addressed himself to a new member, a Health Visitor, ''You meet this kind of girl daily, I should think, Mrs. Jones? . . . Mr. Brown suggests she is in need of placement: I suggest a quite different course. What, in the light of your wide experience, do you think?'' . . . After some hesitation, Mrs. Jones said, ''There's no doubt about it. One does meet a great deal of this sort of thing. It is a fact that young girls today do go to bed with their boys, and they should know more about it than they do. It's a fact of life. But I don't think either that we should treat the matter lightly, and some sort of standards and example have to be set somewhere. Some limits. Or where will it all end?''

Mrs. Jones' contribution was such double communication as is now under discussion. Both the Chairman and Mr. Brown could interpret it as support for their view, and Mrs. Jones could still move less ambiguously in either direction if and when she chose to do so. Her double communication was a product of ambivalence and uncertainty which may have had several causes. Perhaps she simply had not yet clarified her standpoint. Perhaps she was anxiously half-aware of the Chairman's attempt to manipulate her to support him. Perhaps, as a relatively new member, she might wish to hear more from other members to avoid taking what might be an unpopular minority view. She was certainly in conflict between her habit of accepting medical authority in other settings and her identification, on both religious and political grounds, with Mr. Brown.

In the above examples the double communication is already evident at the manifest level. This is often called simply ''contradictory communication''. A closely related but more complex phenomenon is that where the ambiguity lies not in alternative possible interpretations of the manifest signal, but in disharmony between the manifest and the latent signals. As we saw earlier, latent messages usually refine and supplement the manifest message. But where they contradict each other there is a highly confusing ambiguity, usually referred to as ''incongruent communication''.[3]

A special case of double communication, involving both contradictory and incongruent elements, has in recent years occupied researchers and clinicians engaged in work with dysfunctioning families. This is the concept of *double-bind* communication (Bateson *et al.,* 1965, 1963). Central to this is the observation that many such families distort their communication, not merely by ambiguity, but by including mutually exclusive signals in messages which call for response from the receiver. Thus, the receiver's positive response to one part of the signal can only be interpreted as a rejection of the other part. He cannot choose correctly.[4]

Consider the fastidious and secretly rejecting mother, demonstrating her lovingness to visiting members of the bridge club. She calls her little boy to come and give her a kiss. As he dutifully approaches her, reaching out with his sticky hands and offering his sand-and-toffee-stained mouth, she wrinkles her face and withdraws a little. He must now choose whether to approach and disgust, or withdraw and disobey. . . .

No doubt most families and groups occasionally "communicate" with such mutually exclusive signals. It is an unavoidable product of ambivalence, which we all experience from time to time. But where contradictory and incongruent communication is a persisting character-istic of the family's interaction, this leads to an ever-increasing confusion and frustration and to a pervading fear of disapproval and rejection. The insolubility of the conflict and the impossibility of rational solution leads to withdrawal as a defence. Laing and Esterson (1964) and subsequently others have proposed that such withdrawal may well be an important aetiological factor in childhood schizophrenia.[5] The child seeks refuge in manifest madness from the impossible demands of the family which is ostensibly healthy. (A central question in much of Laing's work is that of "who is really ill and who healthy?" This question is equally relevantly addressed to society as a whole as to single families.)

Aids to Understanding Covert Communication

Several levels and types of communication have been mentioned. The social worker needs to be keenly attuned to these, for only through observing what is communicated in some way or other may he gain understanding.[6] He may never, however, permit himself certainty about his interpretation of the content of the group's communication.

Like all other aspects of social diagnosis this is tentative, and must continually be open to confirmation or rejection in the light of new signals and evidence. Our understanding is more at the level of tentative hypothesis providing a defensible provisional basis for helping action. It is no more than a guide to appropriate intervention and is to be used with care and humility.

The social worker has few tangible and no infallible tools to use in his attempt to untangle the multiplicity of messages exchanged in the group at various levels. Certain aids do exist, however, which increase his ability to identify the latent and unconscious communication with at least some degree of confidence. They include certain qualities in the worker himself, his awareness of the group's aims and problems, his knowledge of defence mechanisms, his perception of non-verbal and semi-verbal signals, and his interest in behaviour as communication. These will be discussed and exemplified separately.

1. It is hoped that *selection, training, self-awareness and a critically evaluative attitude* to his own professional functioning will enable the worker to minimize distortion and selective perception caused by his own problems and biases in his reception of group members' messages.

For example, the social worker often—and realistically— feels inadequate when faced with the magnitude of some clients' problems. If he lacks the self-awareness necessary for contact with these feelings he may collude in clients' denial in order to protect his own feelings of worth and potency.

Example 18. One member of a newly formed open group at an alcoholics' treatment institution is already approaching discharge. He says rather assertively, "What I want to talk about is getting a job. That's the important thing for us—and the most difficult. We needn't sit here endlessly talking about drink. ... If I can't take care of that problem after all the treatment I've had here —and I'm lucky, I've been seeing Dr. X— then I never will!" Members nod their agreement and discuss work problems. Relevant and appropriate discussion. But whether the group will later be able to help this member with his major anxiety about "never being able to take care" of his drink problem will be largely determined by whether the social worker has registered the latent message conveying this anxiety, or whether his own feeling of hopelessness will cause him to collude in avoiding the problem.

Among other traits of the social worker, which could lead to such blocking in his perception of latent communication, is that of over-protectiveness and its attendant satisfactions.

Example 19. An old people's club met at an old people's home. Some members were resident and others lived alone in the neighbourhood. A social work student had taken the admirable initiative of forming this group, and was pleased with its initial success. The activities she had suggested and the materials provided had met with members' approval and interest. Her suggestion for a bus excursion to a local beauty spot was well accepted. She had booked a bus and was collecting money from members, when one remarked to the others, "We *are* lucky to have Miss J. to give us such a nice time . . . It's for all the world like having a daughter to look after us."

Miss J. was brought up abruptly by this. She recalled that this member, a widow, had earlier described her own daughter as being " . . . like a fussy hen . . . she clucked around and smothered and protected me all the time . . . and never let me do a thing . . . I spent the first day here (in the Home) just sitting and enjoying the quiet." Recall of this earlier conversation helped the student to register the latent message—"You are over-protecting and infantilising us", and to see the need to return to members the responsibility for themselves of which she was depriving them. In supervision, the student was well able to see how her over-active leadership related to the satisfactions which the roles of protector and provider gave her, and she worked very constructively on this.

Examples 18 and 19 illustrate fear of inadequacy and protective needs respectively as potential blocks to contact with covert communication. Other common obstacles are fear of strong feelings, over-identification, stereotypy, moralism, manipulative (power) needs, denied anger towards the client or, simply, lack of empathy. (Such attributes, of course, hinder all aspects of social work, not only that under discussion. This provides the rationale for the attitudinal probing in the more satisfactory intake procedures and for the practice of stimulating students to intensive subjective involvement in the social work learning-process both during and after the initial training.)

2. *Awareness of the aims and problems* which have motivated the group's formation is perhaps the most important aid in understanding latent communication. These aims and problems are a continuing preoccupation of the members, and are the focus of their activity. While the focus at times seem very unclear indeed, it is seldom that communication in the group does not in some way relate to these common preoccupations. Sometimes the group-as-a-whole and sometimes an individual member will signal the common concerns. Sometimes they will be manifested directly and sometimes by defensive avoidance of some area of the common preoccupations, members engaging themselves with surprising intensity in apparently irrelevant or peripheral matters. But the needs underlying the group's formation

are constantly present. Awareness of these as the reason for their being together presses upon the members and comes to expression as what McCullough and Ely (1968) have called "the recurring themes". Certain topics or activities, directly or indirectly related to the shared problems or some aspect of them continually recur. They do so until the group have optimally resolved the problem or that part of it. Then the group move on, and new "recurring themes" arise related to some new aspect of the problem. In the context of analytical group psychotherapy an important therapeutic model has been built on similar observation of this recurring phenomenon and the different approaches to its solution. In this context, these central and recurrent preoccupations of the group are called the "group focal-conflict" (Whitaker and Lieberman, 1965) or "common group tension" (Ezriel, 1950).

The "focal-conflict" postulated is between wishes and associated fears. Certain wishes, referred to as "disturbing motives", are present in each group session. These relate either to the current group situation, the problems motivating members to belong, or both. Fear of some kind is associated with or aroused by a disturbing motive. This is called a "reactive motive". The work of the group in each session is seen as finding a "solution" to this conflict, which optimally satisfies the wish, while maximally alleviating reactive fears. These writers present their material in a simple diagrammatic framework. The symbol "X" is used to denote "opposed by" or "in conflict with". Thus,

disturbing motive		*reactive motive*
wish to be unique and		fear of disapproval
singled out by the therapist	X	and retaliation by
for special gratification		the therapist or group

solution
all be alike

Where members disagree about an emerging solution, the group is said to be in a state of "solutional conflict". This will often arise where some members' want to satisfy the disturbing motive ("enabling solutions") and others' low anxiety tolerance causes them to favour solutions which mainly reduce reactive fears ("restrictive solutions").

The solutional conflict must then be resolved. Whitaker and Lieberman's model then looks like this,

disturbing motive   X   reactive motive

group
solutional
conflict

group solution   X   alternative solution

modified
group
solution

These notes are an almost barbarically simplified presentation of a highly refined model. We believe it important, however, for social workers to be introduced to these concepts and to pursue them further. While the therapeutic contracts and the techniques of analytic psychotherapy and of social work differ in many important ways, there is no basic difference in the group processes which occur. The concepts which we have introduced enrich understanding of communication and interaction also in social work groups.

While much manifest communication may not be directly addressed to the group focal-conflict, most latent communication may be so directed. In this context, the *observation of members' associations* is the main diagnostic tool. This includes associations which follow a comment thereby shown to have latent content, the preceding events or comments to which the manifest message in question is an association, and the possible associative relationship between overt comment or behaviour and the total situation of the group.

Example 20. A group of parents of mentally defective and physically handicapped infants located early in their first meeting a topic of apparently intense common concern. This seemed not to be their own problem at all, however. They took up a recent newspaper article about the "problem" of gypsy families who gathered in the city during winter months. The group united in strong moral condemnation of the gypsies' way of life. In particular, members expressed contempt for people who "brought unwanted children into the world" and who then, having done so, "did not even care properly for them". It was a "well-known fact" that "half of the poor mites had to go into Homes" where they were "yet another burden on the ratepayer".

This topic was apparently irrelevant to the common life-situation of the members and to the chronically painful preoccupations motivating them to membership. This suggested to the social worker that the discussion (manifest communication) was associative material arising from a group focal-conflict. She perceived the discussion as being pregnant with latent communication indicating a possible focal conflict between members' wishes to express some of their resentful and rejecting feelings about their own children and their fears of meeting condemnation from other members or from the worker if they did so. The worker perceived their behaviour as representing the "restrictive solution" of projective defence.

She therefore provisionally understood the latent communication as meaning ... "We understand and believe it morally right that irresponsible and rejecting parents are condemned. But our lives have been so changed with the birth of our defective children and our disappointment is so great that we wish, partly, that we did not have them. Are we therefore "bad"? Perhaps some kind of Home exists? ... But then we would feel even worse. Not only guilty about "having brought unwanted children into the world", but also making "the poor mites" a "burden on the ratepayer", and thus being as "irresponsible" as the gypsies. This is how we see ourselves, and no doubt others would regard us similarly if we exposed our feelings." . . . Further work with the group confirmed that these were in fact central preoccupations of the parents, and much of the treatment was directed to clarification and support in these areas.

In Example 20 the group focal-conflict related mainly to the precipitating problems of the group members. Such conflict may also frequently relate to tensions precipitated by the group situation itself. This may arise from internal struggle between group members, or from the relationship between the group-as-a-whole and the worker or agency he represents. Here too, if this does not come to some kind of direct expression, the latent messages about the tension may be located through observation of associations, as in the following case extract.

Example 21. An adoption agency initiated a programme of group work services for future adoptive parents. This included several groups for applicants who had waited 6 years of more without having yet received a child. The agency had little or no contact with them since accepting their applications. These applicants could now expect to be offered a child within a year. It was believed that they could profitably come together to discuss general questions about child and family development, role and activity changes following adoption and their feelings about these, and in some cases perhaps to re-evaluate the decision to adopt made several years before, and not since reconfirmed.

One social worker in the programme was aware of a certain cautious formality, a propriety, in the deportment of her group. This, reasonably, was attributed to members' anxieties, both about the group situation and the imminent offer of a child. At the third' meeting, however, the worker was delayed some few minutes and arrived to find the group already in heated discussion. The topic was the new Shop Closures Act, an issue apparently far removed from their joint aims and problems. The discussion continued in her presence. It became clear that the main issue was their common anger at legislation which extended greater freedoms to shopowners in deciding when they should open and close. Members' experience was that many grocers, bakers, butchers, etc., were already choosing to close at precisely the time when the public found it most convenient to shop.

The worker noted that the central element in this curious exchange was anger and resentment at the whims of possessors, who had the power of both dispensing and withholding valued commodities. She also registered that this was shared by all members, although it was manifestly related to a matter entirely outside the area of the group's common aims and problems. In reflecting about aspects of the common group preoccupations to which this could be associated material, she thought it probable that she was witnessing latent communication of group anger and resentment at the powerful and manipulative adoption agency which withheld children from them. Direct expression of this was not possible, owing to members' phantasies about the possible consequences of criticising the agency. Indeed it seemed that some of this anger was so intense that it was repressed or over-compensated into an understanding of "how difficult it must be for the agency". Communication was not only latent, therefore, but in some cases also preconscious. This tentative diagnosis of the latent communication was confirmed by the response of the worker's subsequent interpretation.

Like the previous case, Example 21 may also be described in Whitaker and Lieberman's terms. They would probably represent it thus:

disturbing motive		*reactive motive*
wish to express angry		fear of retributive
and resentful feelings	X	rejection by agency
against agency and worker		or worker

solution
displace feelings
onto external
objects

Note that this solution is also "restrictive", i.e. is more aimed at the alleviation of reactive fears than at the gratification of wishes. This observation brings into relief the worker's function of helping the group to locate more "enabling" solutions. In this case, this was achieved first by tentative interpretation and then by supportive demonstration of acceptance of the feelings latently communicated.

3. Both training and experience will have made the social worker aware of the enormous range of feelings and behaviour which different human beings may experience and demonstrate in problem situations. Nevertheless, certain signals may so deviate from what we might call the *range of appropriate responses* that the worker will register the gap between the signal and the sender's probable meaning. He will therefore reflect about the existence and possible content of latent communication. Laughter in a grief-stricken situation may be an incongruent communication of the fear of possible dissolution if sorrow is allowed

expression. Apparent indifference by parents to some family disaster—
the discovery of a child's drug addiction, for example—may in fact
latently communicate the massive extent of their pain, fear and
perhaps guilt, all so intense that it must be avoided by denial.

In this, as in so much diagnosis of communication, knowledge of
and sensitivity to *defence mechanisms* is essential. Understanding of
Example 20 above may be approached through the understanding of
projective defences. Example 21 similarly shows the defence of affect-
displacement, concealing the more meaningful level of communication
in the group. The relevance of defence mechanisms to interpreting
various levels of communication becomes very clear when we reflect
that the use of covert levels of communication has partly, often
mainly, defensive purposes.

4. A point already illustrated, but which might profitably be made
more explicit, is that observation of *non-verbal* and *semi-verbal signals*
is a source of increased contact with the less manifest aspects of
communication. The social work student is often made acutely aware
of this when he first writes process records and finds how difficult it is
to convey the clients' signals by means of words only. Much readily
apparent latent content is conveyed by such supplementary methods
of communication as gestures, facial .expressions, inflections and semi-
verbal sounds.

As well as these familiar media, certain other forms of non-verbal
communication are worth mentioning. Particularly relevant in group
work are the possible implications of silence or passivity, position in
the group, and eye-contact.

Silence or *passivity* is also communication. It is easily misinterpreted,
perhaps because it arouses anxiety in many workers. The mute group
arouses feelings of helplessness and ineffectuality in the worker and
these may seriously disturb his professional judgement and functioning.
He may project upon the group, experiencing them as "hopeless" and
"inadequate". Or he may believe them to be apathetic and disengaged.
In all of these cases he must first deal with his own feelings of hostility
towards the group. Only then is he free to address himself to the
problem of understanding their passivity. This poses a diagnositc
question with innumerable possible answers. While it is usually
somewhat easier to sit in a silent group than it is to break a long silence,

it is nevertheless a tense and uncomfortable experience. The student must accustom himself to the idea that the group which sustains silence may at a certain level be working hard. *Something* is being intensely experienced and potentially signalled. To take but one example, such vital issues as incongruence between the group's perception of their needs and the worker's apparent assumptions may emerge from this diagnostic approach to such apparent "non-communication". The silent group may also be communicating fear of manipulation, suspicion or repressed aggressive feelings (Example 3, p. 29), is a case in point). They may be conveying the intensity of their social discomfort or their anxiety about being able to cope with the demands of the group. Pessimism or depression in the group also finds expression in this way in some cases. ... While the newly trained group worker may not be expected to agree that "silence is golden", it is valuable if he can, in the middle of the tension, remind himself that it is pregnant with important though unspoken meaning.[7]

Lake (1970), in an engaging essay on the varieties of communicative experience, has some remarks we wish to quote here:

> (However) the persons in the room may constitute a group in their various refusals and resistances. ... These persons may be aware implicitly of their temporarily combining to resist what they think the group leader wants them to do. They are communicating defiance, hostility, nonconformity, social isolation, rejection of invitation, and possibly other things. If their resistance endures, they may be said to be demonstrating cohesion. They accomplish work. They manifest organisational ability in the pursuit of recognisable goals. Who is to say that their goals are unacceptable, their methods negative and therefore valueless, their techniques unlearnable, their achievement despicable?

Physical position in the group may also be unconscious non-verbal communication.

Approach to and avoidance of others communicates feelings of alliance, disengagement or antipathy, and may thereby tell us something about the interests, identifications and feelings between members.

In a mobile and flexible group setting some members may be seen to place themselves focally, "where the action is". They move into the most active sub-group, or it may gather around them. They thus communicate anticipation of being accorded an active role, of being acceptable, and of having a contribution to make. Such assumptions may be the realistic evaluations or valid impulses of motivated and mature members, who may be of great value to the group; or they may be the uncritical or over-compensated responses of immature or anxious people. These may need help lest they commit the group to unfruitful paths or expose themselves to painful rejection. Yet other members place themselves peripherally—either rejected or withdrawn into a geographical isolation which mirrors their social image. Low self-evaluation, lack of identification with the group, fear of rejection, or fantasied superiority are common traits of such marginally placed members.

When the group spends its time, or part of it, sitting in a comparatively structured discussion situation, observation of seating arrangements may sometimes stimulate the worker to reflect about the reasons for choice of place. We suggest that information about both motivation and the way in which the group is experienced may be latently communicated in this manner.

Practice suggests that certain positions and movements may tentatively be described as regularities. There is a tendency for highly motivated members to place themselves initially near the worker, as if nearness intensified the potency of his help. Perhaps some experience this nearness as protective. But usually it seems to derive from a wish to gain more of the worker's attention, since it is believed to facilitate communication. However, immediate closeness is in fact an obstacle to communication in groups sitting in circular or similar patterns! Those immediately to either hand of the worker may easily be overlooked. Physical effort is required to keep them in the field of vision, and they may be "forgotten" if they do not make their presence felt. The seat farthest away is perhaps at first attractive to the least motivated or the most insecure. But this seat is usually directly opposite the worker, and therefore most exposed to observation. It has been referred to for this reason as the "hot seat". If members change their places, this may say something about the way in which they experienced their original positions and therefore about their motivation and feelings.

Not infrequently, highly motivated clients have placed themselves as near as possible to the group worker and have been observed thereafter to move further round the circle — further from the worker — in order to achieve better contact with him. We have also observed such members change places with more threatened and insecure clients who had initially placed themselves in the more exposed positions *vis-a-vis* the worker. The "hot seat" seems very often to be occupied, after the group's first re-adjustments and shufflings, by an active member. The use he makes of his active participation can, however, vary greatly. Sometimes the worker has most direct eye-contact with a highly-motivated member who is eager both to contribute to and to get something out of the group. But it seems also quite frequently to be the case that the occupier of the hot seat is either aggressive or in active defence, or both.

These quite unscientific impressions from social work practice are, comfortingly, supported by a number of research studies, notably by Steinzor (1950).[8]

In a circular group with ten members, the positions on both sides of any member may be numbered from 1-5. Steinzor found an average distance of 3.6 positions where interaction was significantly greater than could be explained by chance. In that context, interaction was defined as giving direct response to a speaker's contribution. Subsequent findings also confirmed that seating position, irrespective of both content and duration of the preceding contribution, had significant influence on the amount of new communication which occurred. Steinzor illustrated his findings by this simple diagram:

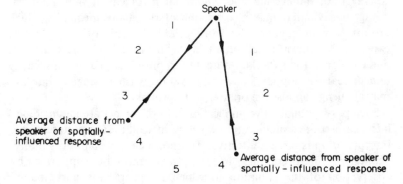

Steinzor tentatively suggests some practical implications of these findings. Assuming that a high level of interaction and participation is desirable, it could be arranged that a rather expressive individual sat opposite a quiet one; or two members who normally monopolized discussion might be placed next to each other in order to decrease their mutual stimulation. Such manipulation would rarely be either possible or appropriate in social work with groups. But awareness of these regularities has nevertheless some practical value to the social worker. It reminds him that he may at least partly counteract their potentially distorting influence on the communication pattern by his own activity in both stimulating and limiting certain members. Similarly, Steinzor's study serves to remind the social worker consciously to include all group members in equal, face-to-face contact with himself. Experience confirms that this in fact requires both practice and the exercise of some discipline.

Eye-contact. A related subject is that of *looking* and *eye-contact.* This is an important feature of interaction in small groups, and may also serve as communication. The worker soon becomes aware of a continual and shifting exchange of glances and looks both among the members and between them and himself. In different situations, and accompanying different verbal comments, these may convey many messages. Listeners' looking and attempts to gain eye-contact may express interest and support. Particularly if prolonged, they may convey critical or sceptical evaluation of the speaker's contribution. Looking at the worker and seeking eye-contact with him may convey both intellectual and emotional involvement in what he is doing or saying. It may also be one of the many means by which groups may manoeuvre the worker into the role of focal leader, expert and authority. Accompanying senders' verbal signals, looking and eye-contact may seek and invite response, may convey insecurity and appeal for support, or may show the wish to engage interest, may challenge opposition or attempt to provoke.

Such possible qualitative implications of eye contact are innumerable. It is an aspect of communication which is difficult to subject to research. Interpretation is largely intuitive. To approach any claim to validity, qualitative interpretation of eye-contact must be supported by observation of the situation in which it occurs, the participants' relationships, and the accompanying or preceding verbal signals.

The quantitative aspects of eye-contact are, however, more amenable to research. Some findings on this merit our attention. Kendon (1965), whose unpublished work is quoted in Argyle (1967), found, perhaps surprisingly, that eye-contact between two people in discussion usually occurs for not more than 10-30% of the total interaction time. The average duration of eye-contact is not more than one second. Some other regularities, usefully summarised in Argyle (*op. cit.*), include looking as a signal of wish to initiate interaction, although we typically look away immediately we begin to speak! We look back while listening about 60% of the time, precisely twice as much as we look while speaking. Not surprisingly, therefore, looking away is easily interpreted as disinterest and disturbs the speaker, often causing him either to terminate hurriedly or to accelerate his delivery, often at the expense of clarity. We customarily look at the listener immediately before we close our contribution, and at critical points. The more we look while talking, the more likely we are to be believed and to be accorded influence. (Every used-car salesman knows this, but it is perhaps comforting to have scientific validation.) Most interaction is accompanied by a series of short glances. There is much to suggest that prolonged looking implies greater interest in the person speaking than in the content of what is said. Avoidance of eye-contact, on the other hand, signals such problems as fear of rejection, fear of manipulation and authority, wish to conceal prevailing emotional state, and of course guilt (Laing, 1960; Exline *et al., 1961*).

5. Point 4 above introduces and already exemplifies the notion of *behaviour as communication*. Behaviour is not only an invaluable aid to understanding messages which are latent in a manifest signal. It is sometimes the only signal given. Everything we do, whether as a product of conscious thought or not, communicates intent and attitude. It may therefore reinforce, supplement or contradict the signals of intent and attitude which we give verbally. This remains true even if communication is not intended. Fetching a glass of water communicates to the observer that one is thirsty, although one's behaviour has no other purpose than to quench one's own thirst.

Similarly, the member of a street-corner group of glue-sniffers conveys a message to the social worker by his verbal signal, "At last I have given it up". He then conveys the message that he has not done so by stealing a bottle of paint-thinner from a local shop, although he did not intend this communication. His behavioural communication is indeed the opposite of his manifest verbal communication. It is "incongruent". His latent communication might also, since he allowed himself to be caught, include the message that he is frightened and that he feels a need for help which the norms of his reference group may prevent him from seeking. (This would remain speculative until further evidence were found.) Behaviour as such a "cry for help" is, however, a communication phenomenon with which all practising social workers are familiar.

Since behavioural communication is often unintended, it may be a more reliable guide to meaning than the verbal messages of unhappy, conflicted and disadvantaged persons. Arnulf Øverland, the late Norwegian poet and philosopher, has said that Norwegian consists of three languages—"Old Norwegian, Modern Norwegian and a good punch-up". (It puns in Norwegian, which improves the formulation somewhat.) That the punch-up will normally be a more reliable guide to feeling than guarded, inarticulate or diplomatic wordage is self-evident. The discrepancy between feelings and needs as expressed in behaviour and in words is often wide. Family-group therapy today builds extensively on communication theory. One of its major techniques is the supportive confrontation of family members with this discrepancy. Similarly, in social work with other groups, members' behaviour may communicate their needs, conflicts and feelings to each other and to the worker much more clearly than their words do. This applies both to behaviour in the group itself and to their reports in the group of events which have occurred elsewhere. These behavioural impressions will always supplement and will frequently modify the impression of intent and attitudes given by speech. Where the behavioural and the verbal communication are incongruent, this may bring into sharp focus precisely the areas of ambivalence and conflict which are most problematical for the clients concerned at that moment.

Example 22. Mrs. Y, a member of a foster-parents' group (see e.g.s 5 and 8, pp. 37 and 56) continued to disparage the parents of "all" foster-children. As the rest of the group came increasingly to accept the misery and problems of the natural parents, Mrs. Y seemed to intensify her moralistic and punitive comments. This had earlier given her a central position in the group, which she was now gradually losing. At one important meeting, about half-way through the series, she mentioned with a kind of angry defensiveness that she had written to her foster-son's mother, inviting her for Sunday, and gave some kind of "excuse" for this. Her behaviour communicated an incipient conflict around her prejudices and fears. It was in sharp contrast with what she said. This conflict had perhaps been both delayed and repressed either because of the satisfactions derived from her earlier high status, or because she had failed earlier to register the change in group attitudes. For the first time she gave some hope for a more purposeful and understanding attitude to the natural parents. At that time, however, she was not at all able to express this verbally.

In the above example we see latent communication of conflict and change reflected in incongruence between reported behaviour and verbally expressed attitude.

Behaviour in the group situation itself will also convey messages about conscious but "inadmissable" feelings. This behavioural communication, though unintended, may at times be remarkable specific.

Example 23. An informal group of neurological patients was earlier discussed in relation to modes of integration (e.g. 11, p. 65). The norms described were formed by defences of denial and over-compensation. The tone achieved was occasionally hilarious. Behavioural communication was particularly informative not least on such occasions.

The Joke of the Day on one occasion was a pantomime description by a patient of the conclusion of an examination by the professor in the latter's office. The patient vividly mimed his shuttling in Tati-like confusion between the three alternative exits, hoping desperately to choose the right one. "As everyone knew", one door led straight to the pathological laboratory, one to the psychiatric ward, and one came back to the "home" ward. It was only when he realised that the last-mentioned must, of course, be the smallest that he managed with great relief to make his choice and get back to his friends! With retelling and improvement, a fourth door was introduced into the story. This one led to the street, but was so well concealed that no patient had yet found it. ... (There was in fact only one door, as all knew.)

The Joke of another Day occurred during a visit by the ambulant members of the group to the hospital cafeteria. It became a tradition of the group to spend an hour thus each evening. They used lifts and walked the underground corridors to reach their goal. One patient, unable to walk at that time, was taken on an ancient stretcher-trolley which the group had characteristically "acquired" and kept hidden in the basement. One evening a nimble fellow-member ran all the way there and back with the trolley at great speed, at some hazard to them both. A near-collision with a member of the maintenance staff was dealt with by prompt explanation that the supine patient had recently "left us", and had to be delivered to the pathological laboratory while still warm! ... This macabre joke was recounted with great apparent enjoyment many times during the following days.

In the terms of our discussion, all this was behavioural communication of conscious but inadmissable fears. Such themes as death, mental illness, and dependent immobility recurred in the joking and play of the group and indicated very specifically indeed the areas of anxiety against which the members had to defend themselves.

Some behaviour will communicate messages of which the sender is quite unconscious. This is frequently true of the "cry for help" for instance. Much apparently self-destructive behaviour has this quality. Attempted suicide is a case in point.

Even more familiar is the early recidivism of the highly institution-alized discharged prisoner, whose behaviour seems often to convey the message that he feels frightened in freedom and that he in fact prefers to be in prison. We have not thereby said that he *likes* it: he merely tells us that he is less intimidated by it. It is familiar and he knows that he is accepted. He can function and survive there. So it is "back again!", despite his earnest assurance to the Governor that he would go straight and has learned his lesson. Such assurances were expected of him, and both he and the Governor know how meaningless they were. Both know well the rules of the empty game they were playing. Despite this, his almost immediate reconviction arouses strong retributive reactions. He has "fooled" the authorities with his verbal expression of attitudes which he immediately contradicts by his behaviour. Instead of this being regarded as further evidence of a chronic social problem, both of that individual and of the society which resists his re-integration, it is taken as evidence of his incorrigibility, instability and untrustworthiness. This view is usually reflected in the severity of the sentence for the new offence.

The tendency to disorientate and disarm other participants is perhaps what makes this form of incongruent communication both frustrating and infuriating. It seems to be a common source of confusion, tension and frustration in many life-situations and in groups of many kinds. It is, for instance, commonly met at the centre of unrest in dysfunctioning institutions and organisations. Here the incongruence may be at a more conscious level. People in authority—policy-formers or purse-holders—may verbally articulate one set of views and behaviourally express another. The frustration of expec-tations which they have themselves stimulated then causes confusion, anger and a bitter helplessness among people lower in the hierarchy. Today, for example, the leader of a psychiatric hospital, social agency or university may often feel compelled by the forces of history, politics and expendiency to acclaim enthusiasm for the notion of institutional or student-democracy. But clearer signals of his real attitudes are given by the private arrangements he may make with senior civil servants or his committee, and by the regretful *fait-accompli* presentation of policy decisions for which "The Ministry" or "They" may then be held responsible. The familiar results of this are the alternatives of withdrawal (high staff turnover), internal conflict, revolution or institutional inertia.

In brief, the practising group worker must regard behavioural communication as a feature of all groups in which he works. He will meet it in treatment groups, in action groups, and in rehabilitative or leisure-time clubs. He will meet it in the team of which he is a member and in other groups to which he is an adviser or consultant. Central and continuing questions in his attempt to understand the group's problems and needs are: "What are the possible implications of what these people are *doing?* ... Is it consonant with what they are saying? ... Does their behaviour refine and modify my own impressions hitherto and the impressions given by their current verbal communication? . . . Does it in fact contradict those impressions? . . ." In the latter cases, the worker will probably find that the latent and incongruent communication which emerges illuminate important areas of the group focal-conflict.

Patterns of Communication

In addition to means and levels of communication, patterns of communication are also of interest and will be briefly touched upon.

It is clear that listening to a lecture in an auditorium where seats all face one way reduces the possibility of communication between members of the audience. The reader's own school and university experience will readily confirm this. It is partly a question of the implied authority of the speaker and the expectations of passivity inherent in the arrangement of the seating, but also of the sheer physical difficulty of cross-communication. Conversely, in other everyday situations which presuppose communication there is a tendency to place participants in face-to-face positions—the priest and the communicant, a school of poker players, committee meetings, discussion circles, etc. These common-place observations are of some relevance to social-group work, since its aims usually require a high level of communication and interchange.

We will draw attention to one well-known study which observed the consequences of different patterns of communication. Leavitt (1951) devised an experiment which compelled five people, who were jointly solving certain problems, to adopt various communication patterns. The number and sequence of both mutual and one-way communications were predetermined both by the instructions given and by the limitations imposed by special seating arrangements.

The patterns which were studied may be diagrammatically represented (Fig. 1):

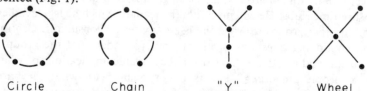

Circle   Chain   "Y"   Wheel

Certain of Leavitt's findings deserve emphasis in the present context. The circular pattern, in which communication might occur in either direction, gave most satisfaction to members. It also maximized participants' activity, despite having no formal leadership. It did, however, generate some errors during problem-solving, but the group was able through communication to correct these.

The "wheel' was the communication system with the most clearly defined leadership. It was much less fallible than all others, since one person received all the others' signals, obtained an overview and made appropriate decisions and judgements. However, members obtained markedly less satisfaction and participated less than in the circle.

"Y" members, with the exception of the most central person, felt little satisfaction, although the pattern functioned fairly well. Satisfaction among members of the "chain" was not high, and the pattern functioned slowly.

This summary hardly does justice to an imaginative and important experiment, but it does enable us to make the point with which we are concerned. The "Y" and the chain pattern are unlikely to have counterparts in social work treatment or action situations. Perhaps the internal organisation of institutions with a particularly rigid hierarchy might be compared with the chain. The wheel and the circle, on the other hand, are communication patterns which invite association to alternative ways of organising client groups in social work. The wheel pattern, with its clearly defined leadership and high degree of imposed structure, contrasts sharply with the unstructured and egalitarian circle. While both are efficient, there are substantial differences in the extent of members' participation, and in their subjective experience of both their achievement and the group situation. Leavitt's findings suggest that a free and egalitarian communication pattern will normally be more appropriate where, as in social group work, results are to be measured in terms of success in relationships, improved self-esteem, and experience of achievement in optimal solution of own problem. The alternative of a pattern which gives the worker, or a member, an authoritarian, directive and expert role, while equally efficient, is inconsistent with these important aims. We suggest therefore that Leavitt's findings may be interpreted as experimental support for aspects of established social-work practice and principles.

We have elsewhere discussed the development of certain features of the social-work role (Heap, 1968). The concept of "giving up the role of central person" was introduced. We proposed that the social worker, in harmony with the group's increasing capacity for independent activity, clarifying attitudes and solving problems, consciously abrogates the central position and the structuring functions which he has initially in most groups. Among other changes, this involves change in the pattern of communication. In Leavitt's terms, the most appropriate and customary change is from his "wheel" pattern to something like his "circle", though communication in social work groups should also occur freely accross the circle as well as round it. The immediate and intended consequences of this are increased member-to-member communication and diffusion of leadership.

Notes on Chapter 5

1. Dittmann *et. al* (1965) and Ekman (1964) have conducted studies which compare the ability of psychotherapists and professional dancers to register and interpret bodily signals about the subjects' feelings. These studies suggest that even very experienced psychotherapists are inadequately alert to cues about emotional states which are conveyed by body movement and posture, compared with their sensitivity to facial expression. The implications of such studies for training are, however, largely ignored.

2. On this theme, Leonard (1966) proposes a brief but important basis for discussion and further study. He refers to the work of the sociologist Bernstein (1960, 1964) and the social worker Nursten (1965). It is suggested that different "speech-systems" prevail in lower working-class and middle-class families. These are referred to as

"restrictive" and "elaborated" systems respectively. The former is not only less abundant. It is also especially ill-suited to communicating experiences which are unique and personal. It is more orientated towards the sub-cultural "us". "You" often means "I" or "we". (for example "I did so-and-so ... Well, you do, don't you?") Differentiated and separate experience, particularly feeling, is very inaccessible to this restrictive speech system. It tends rather to be expressed by behaviour, by demonstration. The "elaborated speech system" attributed to the middle-class is, however, well suited to expressing this kind of experience.

To the extent that social workers are middle-class (are they?), or have acquired the middle-class speech system (perhaps they must?), this—according to Leonard—raises problems (does it?) in the application with lower working-class clients of casework, "which relies largely ... upon verbal communication".

The provisional findings of one current study—the Child-rearing Study of Low-income Families in the District of Columbia (Lewis, N.I.M.H.)—suggest that the "communication gap" is a myth. So do the daily experiences of many practising social workers. ... The issue remains one of dispute, and further research and discussion is required.

3. Satir (*op. cit.*) discusses congruent and incongruent communication with unusual clarity and rich exemplification and refers also to further literature. The reader who is quite new to communication theory will also find rewarding a book on communication with children (Ginott, 1965) written for parents. Without using these concepts, Ginott readily and charmingly conveys a great deal about them. (In Norway, his book has been criticised because he incidentally ascribes in his illustrations somewhat stereotypic, perhaps archaic, sex roles to Mother and Father. Agreed. He does. But he is still good on communication.)

4. Current with Bateson's early formulations, a blackly humorous illustrative story went the rounds. This told of the guilt-provoking widowed mother who bought her unmarried son two ties for Christmas. He came down to Christmas dinner wearing one with a proud, grateful but anxious expression. His mother looked sadly at him, wiped away the tear, sighed with long-suffering resignation and said ..."so you did not like the other one then?"

5. The journal *Family Process,* in print biannually since 1962, has devoted numerous articles to these phenomena.

6. Lambrick (1962) writes clearly and very sensitively about the understanding of covert communication in the treatment of very sick and dying patients, and shows the implications of this understanding for the social worker's role. While her examples are drawn from a casework setting, her comments are equally applicable to communication and social work in groups.

7. Slavson (1966) both proposes categorisation and offers some interpretations of silence in therapeutic groups from within a psycho-analytic frame of reference. This is recommended.

8. Since Steinzer's early research, a number of other studies have been conducted in this area, notably by DeLong and Sommer. In DeLong (1971), a study of these so-called dominance-territorial relationships is introduced by a brief review of the recent literature.

The ethological concepts of dominance and territoriality have yet more recently been applied to analysis of the behaviour of institutionalised boys suffering from behavioural disorders or borderline psychosis. These concepts were shown to illuminate such important features of institutional life as fighting, isolation, status, sub-grouping and conflict with staff (Esser, 1973).

CHAPTER 6

Interaction

"Interaction", as we have seen, refers to the mutual influence of people who are in contact with each other. By "influence" we do not only mean modification of behaviour. The term is used here to include both modification and reinforcement, and not only of behaviour, but also of attitudes and self-concept. This is an important point, since changes may occur in the latter two areas without immediate manifest change in behaviour.

Indeed, where social work is concerned, changes in self-evaluation and attitude may often be goals in themselves. These less tangible products of group interaction are just as important as manifest behavioural change. Social workers are often involved with clients whose possibilities for behavioural or situational change are very limited. Their problems are often increased by society's attitudes and by social pressures towards a normative adjustment of which they are not capable. The resulting isolation, and their introjection of society's low evaluation of them, may in such cases be the main foci of social work treatment. Far from contributing to these pressures for conformity—of which he is often accused—the social worker's function is to help such citizens to the maximum self-realisation possible within the confines of their handicaps. Further, his function is to encourage resistance to social pressure and criticism, and thus to increase self-evaluation. In both casework and groupwork, the relationship to the worker and the worker's own attitudes are important resources in such support. In group work, however, the increased self-evaluation resulting from involvement in the group bond is an equally potent resource.

Where the more tangible objectives of problem-solving, maturation, and—by implication—behavioural change are involved, these same processes are main means of treatment.

All of these group processes are dependent upon the occurrence of interaction. It is the very nucleus of the social group work process. There is no reason for bringing together a group of clients unless we genuinely believe that they have something to give each other, that they can in some way help each other. And to do this, they must interact. At another level we could say that the dynamic processes of group identification and cohesion, group support, group control, recognition and generalization, which are fundamental to social group work treatment (see Heap, 1974, *op. cit.*), depend on interaction between the members. No interaction, no identification. No identification, no group support ... , etc.

We need therefore to consider the nature and consequences of the interaction process and the conditions under which it occurs. Some of these matters will now be discussed.

Forms of Interaction

Like communication, interaction is a manifold process. It may involve different degrees of intent and chance, consiousness and unconsciousness, importance and superficiality.

A number of classificatory systems have been proposed for distinguishing between various forms and levels of interaction. Some of these extend the use of the concept to include situations where no communication takes place. One participant in the interaction is perhaps not even aware of the other's presence, although he is influencing him. Macarov (*op.cit*) illustrates this with two people meeting in a deserted and fear-inspiring place. One or both may think "I am glad someone else is here too", without knowing whether the other is glad to see him, indifferent or afraid of him. Much social control occurs in this way. When we are alone waiting for a bus we may well pick our nose, or we may do a little jig for the joy of the morning. These are socially forbidden impulses, however. They will be restrained in the presence of a queue, although the others present will not be at all aware of their inhibiting influence upon us. Many social situations are pregnant with this kind of mutual awareness and control, although communication does not occur and no relationships are present. A student once described the silent daily journey in the lift with strangers as the most emotionally exhausting experience of the day!

These unconscious and often unilateral processes are both important and interesting, but the usefulness of including them in the concept of interaction is rather doubtful. Macarov himself opens his chapter on interaction with a definition by Zadrozny (1959) which includes the phrases ". . . *mutual* stimulation and response among persons in contact with each other . . . (and where) the behaviour of *each* participant . . . is modified by that of the others". This clearly is a meaningful approach to the interaction process in the context of social work with groups.

One formulation of considerable interest to the social worker proposes a distinction between the more diffuse aspects of interaction and the kind of social exchange and engagement which are more commonly associated with the term.

Goffman (1961) distinguishes between what he calls "focused interaction" and "non-focused interaction".

Focused interaction occurs where people communicate with each other in *relation to some common purpose* and where there exists an explicit or implicit agreement that they are meeting in order to serve that common purpose. Thus, the visible and audible stimuli and responses of football-players, of the officers on the bridge of a ship, of clients attempting to clarify feelings about a common problem, of a childcare committee working towards a decision, would all exemplify this, provided that their exchanges related to the agreed common purpose.

Non-focused interaction occurs spontaneously whenever people come together. The concept refers to the modifications of self-evaluation, confidence, tension, demeanour, attitudes and behaviour which result simply from our awareness of the presence of others and the influence of that awareness upon. This is a more inclusive concept than that of unconscious interaction mentioned earlier, since it raises the questions of how do we modify our self-evaluation, behaviour, etc., and in relation to whom? These changes will occur in different directions and degrees, depending upon how the participants in the encounter experience each other.

Non-focused interaction, as described by Goffman, is by no means a trivial aspect of interpersonal encounters. This more emotional and often less rational level of interaction often quite over-shadows the more purposive and reasoned "focused interaction". It may influence substantially both the content and outcome of an anticipated—perhaps planned—encounter. It may change it entirely.

Example 24. A young priest has recounted to the author his first contact with a group of spirit-drinkers living under a bridge in a major city. He met a foreign, desperate, and, for him, alarmingly primitive culture. The very appearance of its members caused him a sense of guilt, failure and total alienation. This affected his self-presentation profoundly. Usually a relaxed, calm and modest man, he found that he was talking with a volubility and a false joviality which he experienced himself as pompous and insincere, but which he was entirely unable to get under control. The spirit-drinkers, a defensive and cohesive in-group, sensed his vulnerability, but also resented the apparent implication (his dog-collar) that they were a moral problem. Therefore they were both scornful and rejecting. At the same time, they exploited him and the material things he had to give them.

Interactional experiences of this nature are surely common? Many readers will have experienced a fluttering in the belly, a stiffening of posture, a flowering of the wish to please, in the presence of people of whom they have been in awe. Others will have sensed something unpleasant about themselves, something manipulative and cruel, in contact with people who are excessively self-effacing and apologetic— the "victim" type, to whom one may react with one's less admirable characteristics. John Le Carré, a keen observer of this kind of process, has an illustrative episode in *The Spy who Came in from the Cold*.

"...Having himself no particular opinions or tastes, (Ashe) relied upon whatever conformed with those of his companion. He was as ready to drink tea at Fortnums as beer at the Prospect of Whitby...; his voice would tremble with sympathy when he spoke of Sharpeville, or with indignation at the growth of Britain's coloured population. To Leamas this observably passive role was repellent; it brought out the bully in him, so that he would lead the other gently into a position where he was committed, and then himself withdraw, so that Ashe was constantly scampering back from some cul-de-sac into which Leamas had enticed him...."

The stimuli and response in this kind of interaction do not necessarily relate to the participants' aims, but rather to what they seem to be, and how they experience each other. The above examples perhaps tend towards the dramatic, but in all interaction we adapt and modify our behaviour to some extent in relation to our experience of the people with whom we are in contact. They in their turn adapt their responses to both our presence and our self-presentation. The reader may reflect on his own experiences of various professional and social groups and his different adaptations to them. He will see that his behaviour and his self-feeling are substantially influenced by who the others are and what they are like, not least in respect of how much he experiences commonality with them.

Goffman's concept of focused and non-focused interaction is of considerable relevance to social work groups. Members usually meet for relatively clear common purposes. However, the pressures of the life situation which brings them to the group and their consequent vulnerability will also cause them to be particularly prone to the tensions, defences, comparisons and evaluations which underlie the non-focused interaction process. The social worker will therefore observe that these two processes occur simultaneously. Further, they have the important effect of reinforcing or opposing each other at various times. This point may be illustrated by reference to the confering of prestige in the group.

Evaluative comparison is inherent in non-focused interaction. It must therefore influence the distribution of status. This may have fortunate results where it contributes to conferring high status on a member who is orientated toward the common group goal and is well equipped to lead the group towards it. In such a situation we may say that the non-focused interaction reinforces the focused interaction. But the opposite also occurs. Feelings of antipathy or sympathy, and superiority or inferiority, which are generated at the level of non-focused interaction may be reflected in a status distribution which seriously inhibits the group in its work.

Example 25. Annual school-readiness tests were held at the School Psychology Office in a small market town. A number of parents were advised to wait a further year before allowing their children to commence school. The social worker had observed that this often led to undue pressure on the child during the intervening year and to the development of defensive/negative attitudes to the school. As an experimental preventive measure he offered all of these parents the opportunity of meeting together for a brief series of discussions of this situation. Several groups were formed.

One such group included Mr. and Mrs. Brown, who were prominent in local political and business life. From the outset the group regarded this couple with something approaching awe. They were accepted quite uncritically as the natural initiators of opinion and as centres of attention. However, these highly successful people felt ashamed of the "failure" of their child to achieve school-readiness. This contrasted sharply with their accustomed success and eminence and also threatened their ambitions for the child's future. Mr. and Mrs. Brown dealt with this situation defensively by a furious projection of what they experienced as inadequacy upon the testing psychologist and the social worker. They stimulated the group to join them in attacking the absurdity and irrelevance of testing methods. This influenced strongly the group's initial approach to the common problem.

Present also was a divorced mother, Mrs. Green, who had a number of children from her two marriages. She was commonly known in the district to receive social and welfare help of various kinds. Mrs. Green was initially accorded in the group the low prestige with which she was commonly regarded in the district, quite irrespective of whatever contribution she may have had to make in the work of the group. Her attitude to the common problem and openness about her feelings and concern made her, ironically, a potential resource in the group, but they were not able to take advantage of this until they slowly became aware of the respect with which the social worker manifestly regarded Mrs. Green's comments and were encouraged by him to explore her contributions further. The worker's concurrent help to Mr. and Mrs. Brown was aimed at supporting them in their very evident concern. At the same time he tried to help them to experience and articulate their underlying feelings. He intended this also to help the group, since the Brown's experience of inadequacy in themselves and their child was only different in degree from that of most other members. While the group-as-a-whole were able to accept this, the Browns unfortunately were not. They became less active, which was desirable, but withdrew somewhat demonstratively before the group terminated.

In this case extract we may see how the non-focused interaction in the group influenced status and attitudes in such a way as to detract from the effectiveness of the focused interaction. This was illustrated in contrasting ways by interaction involving both the Browns and Mrs. Green. One function of the social worker was also exemplified, namely that of attempting to influence the non-focused interaction in such a way that it reinforces rather than opposes the focused interaction.

Interaction Process Analysis

A more refined system of differentiating and classifying interaction in small groups is that first developed by Robert Bales (1950, 1970) and his colleagues at the Harvard University Social Relations Laboratory. This is known as Interaction Process Analysis.

In developing a research instrument for scoring interaction in small problem-solving groups Bales needed first to develop categories for types of observable interaction. He devised a set of categories based

Social-Emotional Area: Positive

A

1 *Shows solidarity,* raises other's status, gives help, reward:

2 *Shows tension release,* jokes, laughs, shows satisfaction:

3 *Agrees,* shows passive acceptance, understands, concurs, complies:

Task Area: Neutral

B

4 *Gives suggestion,* direction, implying autonomy for other:

5 *Gives opinion,* evaluation, analysis, expresses feeling, wish:

6 *Gives orientation,* information, repeats, clarifies, confirms:

C

7 *asks for orientation, information,* repetition, confirmation:

8 *Asks for opinion,* evaluation, analysis, expression of feeling:

9 *Asks for suggestion,* direction, possible ways of action:

Social-Emotional Area: Negative

D

10 *Disagrees,* shows passive rejection, formality, withholds help:

11 *Shows tension,* asks for help, withdraws out of field:

12 *Shows antagonism,* deflates other's status, defends or asserts self:

a b c d e f

Key:

a	Problems of communication	A	Positive reactions
b	Problems of evaluation	B	Attempted answers
c	Problems of control	C	Questions
d	Problems of decision	D	Negative reactions
e	Problems of tension reduction		
f	Problems of reintegration		

on the behaviour actually demonstrated by group members. Some speculation as to the intent of members' comments and behaviour seems also, perhaps unavoidably, to be implicit in this means of observation.

In developing his categories, Bales begins with the postulate that interaction relates to two main areas of concern; the *task* of the group, and the *relationships* between the members—(without reference to the task). This latter is called the social-emotional area. (It will be noted that this starting-point is not unlike Goffman's formulation referred to above.) These two kinds of interaction are again subdivided. Task-orientated contributions are subdivided into two main groups, concerned respectively with *giving* information, opinion and suggestions and with *asking for* them. Activities in the social-emotional area are in turn subdivided into *positive* and *negative* contributions, according to whether they further the emotional cohesion of the group or inhibit it.

Thus, there are twelve categories which are arranged in Fig.2.

In addition to the twelve subdivisions it will be seen, on the right-hand side of the model, that Bales indicates yet another dimension, namely a subdividing into sets of pairs. The key to these is given below the model.

Thus, categories 1 and 12 are concerned with contributions relating to the social-emotional activities of integrating/disintegrating relationships in the groups. Categories 3 and 10, though classified as problems of decision, concern contributions relating to the important social-emotional activities of accepting/rejecting, and so on.

It is not chance that these groups of balancing pairs are found. This reflects an observation which is fundamental in Bales' approach: that if the group is to remain in being, there must be available classes of contribution to the interaction which complement and counteract those which cause disharmony, fragmentation and insecurity. Negative social-emotional contributions (group D) must be balanced (though not necessarily immediately) by contributions from group A. Asking (group C) is met by answering or giving (group B). This notion of *equilibrium* in the group interaction (see also Bales, 1955) reminds one of the homeostatic principle familiar from the psychoanalytic model of individual personality structure. It is one of the features of group life which invite us to make comparisons between the individual and the group as social organisms. But it is probably more helpful to view this kind of complementary interaction in groups in the light of the concept of the group as a "social system". Systems Theory proposes just such a mutual dependence of participants in interaction processes. It regards the continuity of the group as dependent upon a reciprocity of interactive contributions—any actions or comments calling forth complementary reactions and re-adjustments from others. Equilibrium is achieved and the group preserved by such reciprocal interaction for the life-span necessary for its purposes.

It is, of course, most useful that Bales' model provides concepts which enrich and inform the social worker's thinking about the interaction in his groups. It is, however, an elaborate research method, and does not have immediate utility as a diagnostic tool for the practising social worker. The application of interaction process analysis requires practice and training, but also a situation facilitating systematic observation of the group. The social worker is clearly unable to walk around or sit with his group busily filling in large and complicated score-sheets.

However, some of the findings which have emanated from the application of interaction process analysis are very relevant to various questions on the functioning of small groups. It is well, at the same time, to bear in mind Talland's (1955) caution about the application of laboratory findings to treatment groups.

> They (treatment groups) meet in order to discover problems rather than to solve one neatly formulated for their attention; they neither have to reach a solution nor must they finally close a case and resolve at the end of a meeting. In so far as the psychotherapeutic technique stresses spontaneity, the discussion is allowed a free course, whereas in the laboratory its trend is implicitly determined by the task even in the absence of directive chairmanship. Finally, discussing a hypothetical or didactic case and a transient acquaintance do not lead to the deep emotional involvements that occur when patients grapple with their own and each other's personal problems, baring their inmost thoughts and experiences week after week in intimate fellowship. Consequently the process of interaction would be expected to differ in the two situations, and more particularly in such dynamic aspects of the model as the phase sequence of acts indicated by and the equilibrium properties of the interaction system inferred from observations made in laboratory debates.

Talland applied interaction process analysis to a series of therapy groups at the Maudsley Hospital. He did not find there the tidy pattern of problem-solving found in Bales' laboratory groups. Nor did he find the tendency to establish equilibrium in successive cycles, beginning with the introduction and ending with the resolution of a disturbance. (These are two of the group processes described by Bales to which considerable attention has been paid.) Social work with groups, however, in terms of specificity of problem and degree of imposed structure, may fall somewhere between Bales' laboratory groups and the group psychotherapy model represented by Talland's groups. The applicability of these two findings to social-group work remains therefore untested.

Other findings, however, seem to confirm impressions from social-group work practice and to suggest useful lines along which to gain some increased system in one's observation and diagnosis during such practice.

The essence of the model, as indicated, is that the group is seen as a field of tension wherein two main forces operate. One of these is directed towards performance of a task, and one towards the maintenance of some kind of social-emotional equilibrium. The interdependence of these two sets of forces is repeatedly demonstrated in Bales' research, and is similarly seen in social-work groups.

Example 26. A group of elderly clients met to find a new meeting place, having been evicted from their customary clubroom. There were clearly seen spurts of task-orientated interaction—suggestions about advertisements, vacant rooms seen, content and formulation of letters, etc. These would develop a little way, then differences of opinion—sometimes rational, sometimes based on expressions of personal hostility—would introduce tension at the social-emotional level. The group would then be occupied with these before they could proceed with their task.

These two tendencies may sometimes conflict with each other. This threatens both the efficiency and the emotional cohesion of the group. Thus, if dominant individual members are over-eager to "get the job done", or, alternatively, "to keep a good atmosphere" they may hinder the activation of one of these necessary sets of forces. This perhaps partly explains the finding that high popularity and leadership are by no means synonymous (Bales, 1955 *op.cit*). Bales found that such aspects of leadership as initiation of ideas, quality of ideas as judged by the group, and acceptability as discussion-leader, all correlated highly with popularity at early stages of group life. Such individuals, judged in Bales' terms as the "most productive", became less liked as the group became increasingly able to function. Highest popularity seemed at that later stage to be accorded those placed second and third in terms of productivity. This is familiar to the social worker. The concerned, rational, goal-orientated member with more psychic energy, perhaps more able to acknowledge problems is a step before the others all the time. He therefore arouses and contends with the others' defences and resistance. He brings them along, they need him, but they do not necessarily like him for it. Another member, slightly less productive but more highly attuned to the social-emotional climate, is more popular. We return to this point in our later discussion of styles of leadership.

Another regularity, seen in social work practice and revealed experimentally by Bales, is the tendency for the most productive member to be a focal point for the group. Without intervention of some kind, this crystallizes into a pattern wherein the indigenous leader, the most "productive" member, receives a disproportionately high degree of attention. Most communication is addressed to him. He, in turn, communicates most with the members nearest to him in rank and vice versa. The least productive members barely communicate with each other at all. Their few contributions tend strongly to be addressed to the leader. These interaction patterns tend to be increasingly rigid with time. Members "get stuck with their roles", to use a phrase of Macarov's. If the group objectives presuppose a high degree of participation and mutual exchange, the worker will often find it appropriate, quite early, to try to temper this hierarchic pattern.[1]

Interaction process analysis has also shown a certain pattern in the development of problem-solving by small groups. (Bales and Strodtbeck, 1951; Heineke and Bales, 1953.) As members feel safer with each other, they seem to spend less time in expressing feelings, both positive and negative. They seem to tolerate more disagreement, and are less conciliatory towards each other without increase in anxiety. The Heineke and Bales study also showed an increase in contributions from group D (hostility, rejection disagreement) around the second meeting. In groups which quickly agreed upon a leader this dissipated quickly: in groups which did not, it continued. This suggests that, after initial exploration of the group situation, some kind of leadership struggle takes place. This accords well both with what we commonly observe in practice and with other research studies.

The general developmental pattern described by Bales is one of three phases—with emphasis successively on orientation, evaluation, and control. But, as Talland points out (*op.cit.*), this is both logical and possible where a group of uncommitted people over few meetings are faced with one specified and limited problem to solve. Its relevance to psychotherapy groups is disputed by Talland, as we have seen. Practice suggests that such regularities as seem to exist in the development of social work groups also involve a more complicated pattern. (This question is more extensively discussed in Chapter 8.)

In the wake of Bales' work have followed other models and techniques of interaction process analysis. One such approach merits special attention here since, unlike Bales', it is designed specifically for the study of interaction in treatment groups of various kinds. Hill (1966) has constructed the Hill Interaction Matrix, a conceptual scheme often referred to simply as HIM. The very design of the HIM scheme draws attention to important differences in interaction processes and emphasises the varying levels of relevance, openness and defence in treatment groups. The incorporation of these factors in a readily applicable research instrument represents a considerable step forward in facilitating scientific studies focused on process, validation and method in treatment groups. The basic design, however, is not complicated in conception. It is built on the observation that the interaction in a group may be characterised by different levels and styles of content, and by different levels and styles of work.

The content/style dimension consists of categories referring to "topic, group, personal and relationship" items. Statements described as "topic" items relate to general matters external to the group and to its members' common immediate concerns. "Group" items are statements concerning the treatment group-as-a-whole. "Personal" statements are about a group member independently of his relationships with other group members. "Relationship" items are statements concerning relationships between members or between a member and the group-as-a-whole.

The work/style dimension consists of categories referring to "conventional, assertive, speculative and confrontive" ways of approaching the "content" with which the group is currently concerned. The statements scored as "conventional" are social pleasantries and neutral comments, appropriate to any group situation, which evade the issues and consequences of the patient or client role. Those scored as "assertive" are argumentative and hostile, often including projective defences against involvement in treatment. "Speculative" statements, while focused on the issues of treatment, do so in an intellectualised and speculative manner. Those contributions categorised as "confrontive" serve to confront individual members or the group-as-a-whole with therapeutically relevant aspects of their behaviour and attitudes, including material which is usually avoided.

The analysis of verbal interaction using this scheme consists of scoring all statements by placing them on the 4 × 4 matrix formed by combining these two sets of categories, thus:

		1 Topic	2 Group	3 Personal	4 Relationship
W	Conventional	1W	2W	3W	4W
X	Assertive	1X	2X	3X	4X
Y	Speculative	1Y	2Y	3Y	4Y
Z	Confrontive	1Z	2Z	3Z	4Z

We shall selectively and briefly exemplify this. While a research study would require rater-reliability tests, we would expect the following comments to be placed in the cells indicated:

"How pleasant the weather has been since we last met." . . . 1W

"It is time we faced the fact that the staff in this clinic are as sick, if not sicker, than we are. There is no help to be found here.". 2X

"A funny thing happened to me on the way to the group." . . 3W

"I have often thought of beginning in analysis. Kleinian, probably. But binding exclusive and expensive resources in individual treatment has political implications which bother me." . . . 3Y

"I'm fed up with the way we bicker and attack each other. Or if we're not doing that, we're agreeing that there is something wrong with somebody else outside the group. If you ask me, we use time, energy and each other in order to evade the problems that really bring us here." . . . 4Z

The 16 cells of the matrix represent a continuum which progressively rates the therapeutic intensity of the verbal interaction in the group, ranging from topical/conventional, 1W, in cell 1, to relationship/confrontive, 4Z, in cell 16. We hesitate to use the terms "least" and "most" therapeutic to describe these contrasting styles of interaction, and prefer to use the term "intensity". The qualitative terms "least" and "most" which are customarily used in this context imply assumptions about aims, needs and methods which are not necessarily always applicable. Topic/conventional and relationship/confrontive interaction would normally be regarded as, respectively, least and most therapeutic in such contexts as analytical group psychotherapy, marathon group therapy,[2] and most forms of sensitivity training and encounter groups. This would also be the case in some areas of social work with groups. But many social work groups also come to mind which have such central themes as mutual support, life-enrichment in an impoverished situation, or planning social action. In such groups, a relationship/confrontive style might not be the "most therapeutic", but might in fact inhibit the work of the group. It would, however, still merit description as the "most intensive" style of interaction.

The HIM scheme is important to the social worker for two main reasons. For the first, the simple structure of the scheme brings clearly into focus the central questions of group diagnosis with which the worker is concerned throughout his entire contact with the group. "What is the group currently occupied with? Is this relevant? In what manner are they working with this content? Is this purposive?" The second reason for our interest in this scheme is that it is a flexible research instrument which may readily be applied to many questions concerning social work groups. It will be clear to the reader that it makes it possible to test hypotheses regarding treatment-group experience where amounts, levels, foci and intensity of therapeutic or evasive interaction are relevant variables.

The Hill Interaction Matrix, in both its original or subsequently modified forms, has as yet been little utilised in social work research. Group therapists and group-training leaders, on the other hand, have been less tardy in subjecting their work to the rigours of scientific and critical study using the HIM scheme. The following examples of such studies may interest the reader. Parks and Antenen (1970) conducted a study of marathon group therapy with institutionalised alcoholics, focusing on the development of the interaction process. This was part of a study of the potential value of this type of therapy as a supplement to more traditional group counselling. The investigators were stimulated by their clinical impressions that counselling groups who also experience a marathon session have better survival chances and subsequently work more intensely, having apparently a greater commitment to the total rehabilitation programme. Sklar, *et al.* (1970) report a study of the effects of a "time-extended" session,[3] on the subsequent course of therapy groups with psychiatric out-patients. It was shown that significant increase in both inter-member involvement and member-group involvement occurred following a single time-extended session, and that the stage of group development at which such an innovation is used may be a determinant of its productivity. Robinson (1970) reports a study of the effects of focused videotape feedback in group counselling of hospitalised psychiatric patients. This provides some further confirmation of the value of such feedback to treatment groups in increasing the adaptive quality of patients' behaviour. The results also raise important questions about the discrepancy or time-lag between adaptive behavioural change and attitudinal change, or willingness to accept responsibility for the possible implications of such change.

Factors Influencing Interaction

The circumstances under which interaction occurs are also of interest to the social worker. He wishes to offer his clients a situation which assists them in communicating with each other and in helping each other, both in solving problems and developing relationships. Much of this is a matter of common sense and everyday observation. It is, however, always useful to have common impressions confirmed and quantified by research and other systematic observation. They are often all too fallible. In the following, both common impressions and some relevant studies will be discussed.

Let us begin by imagining a familiar, everyday social situation. A cinema contains a thousand people, all engaged for several hours in the same activity. Despite this, interaction is virtually non-existent. We can learn quite a lot from this banal anti-example. Why does so little interaction take place? For the following reasons. The cinema is dark;

the seats all face the same way; the number of members is very high; the participants do not need to relate to each other to gain the satisfaction on which they are intent, and the pursuit itself requires no contribution from the participants other than their presence. (In fact since the common aim is to absorb stimulation from the screen only, interaction would be very disturbing and is strongly discouraged, such as by the "shushing" of couples talking, etc.) We shall now look a little more closely at these factors of *mutual exposure, group size, relationships* and *activity* and briefly indicate some of their implications for interaction.

INTERACTION AND MUTUAL EXPOSURE

Interaction is most likely to occur where participants are able to see each other, to have a face-to-face contact. Thus they need, among other conditions, a room which is light enough to enable them to see each other and to pick up non-verbal responses to what they say from the others' facial expressions and gestures. In general they have the advantage of a visual contact with the environment and people which are the sources of most of their impulses to communication.

There is probably a law of diminishing returns here, however. If lighting and attention are too intense, many participants seem troubled, as it they feel exposed and vulnerable. One experiment, concerned with one-way communication (Argyle and Dean, 1965), shows that the speaker's comfort and clarity of formulation are in fact greatest when he is standing behind the group, having no eye-contact at all, and next greatest where he is wearing dark glasses! Whilst this finding may not be applied to a situation presupposing mutual interaction, it does reflect the degree of anxiety commonly experienced in speaking to or as a member of a group. Approach-avoidance ambivalence (the conflict between forces motivating towards engagement in the group and those motivating towards restraint and self-protection), is probably present to some extent whenever a group member makes a contribution. The group worker needs to recognise this and to provide conditions in which the conflict is most likely to be resolved in the direction of "approach".

Where members are face-to-face, unlike in our cinema example, there is feedback and stimulation, whose potency was indicated by

Steinzor's findings, noted earlier. Both expectations and evidence of mutual interest are also present in face-to-face situations and these make interaction more probable. This, however, assumes that the worker and the members are able to co-operate in reducing the social anxiety which may also result from such arrangements by developing a safe and accepting atmosphere. Where motivation is relatively high and unambivalent, it is usually possible, if otherwise appropriate, to arrange the group in some kind of circular seating pattern so that all members can see each other. The worker would make sure that room was sufficiently well lit for members to see each other clearly, but without feeling that they are spotlighted.

Where motivation is more ambivalent or feelings of insecurity are high for other reasons, it is often appropriate to avoid the circle altogether. Many flexible and more mobile arrangements are possible, but these will also be determined by such factors as the group's form for activity and its size. More flexible arrangements are generally appropriate in groups whose purpose is to reduce isolation or to promote social growth, fulfilment and learning, rather than more specific problem-solving, or where the group consists of immature or unstable members or of people under great tension.

INTERACTION AND ACTIVITIES

This is one reason why planned activities play so important a role in social work with groups. These are often referred to as "programme". Activity, as distinct from discussion, may have many purposes. These include attaining improvement in members' own environmental conditions, promoting a sense of achievement, sublimating and canalising certain impulses, actualising problems in an on-going social situation, and working through or articulating symbolically problems and feelings which members are unable to express verbally. But activities also always have the purpose of stimulating interaction.

Sometimes the activity is a secondary focus of interaction—a permissible distraction, as it were, helping insecure or inarticulate people to approach each other. The expectation of talking about common problems is often overwhelmingly threatening. Activity may then legitimise some degree of necessary, though transitory, avoidance.

Such activity may gradually become a more recessive aspect of the group culture owing to the increase in inter-personal familiarity and security which it has promoted.

This could be illustrated by something as simple as sharing the preparation and distribution of tea and biscuits at the first meeting of a psychiatric out-patients' club. This activity provides a familiar and unthreatening focus of interest and comment. It does not necessitate any discussion of anxiety-arousing material, and it can be performed without failure. Thus it is a shared positive experience, which also requires these anxious strangers to interact. On the basis of such experiences they may tentatively enter relationships with each other and develop feelings of security which eventually make possible the articulation and working through of painful common problems.

In other situations, appropriately chosen activities may be the primary focus of the group. Verbalisation of problems and feelings may either not ocur at all, or may have only secondary importance as an element in treatment. "Sitting around a table to talk" may simply not arise.

In most areas of learning, "doing" rather than "talking" has pedagogic value, which many social workers have been slow both to recognise and to act upon. This is perhaps partly because the role of learning and the possible relevance of learning theory have, until recently, been given scant attention in the literature.[4] This reluctance to integrate learning theory into social-work practice may be caused partly by anxiety about apparent intrusion into the terrain of yet another profession, namely teaching. But resistance has also been aroused by the highly manipulative nature of some techniques of behavioural modification proposed on the basis of learning theory. However that may be, group work practice has for many years fostered experiential learning as a major means of treatment, although its theoretical frame of reference has usually been either unclear or non-existent. Much work of this nature has been candidly intuitive. It is only now *post-factum* being belatedly clothed in the more seemly attire of theories and models of treatment. (Schulman (1971), Middleman (1968) and Heap (1977)—for the reader of Norwegian—are alternative introductions to the subject of "programme".

Much social work with groups consists of achieving attitudinal or behavioural change primarily, or exclusively, by just such "doing things together". This may be illustrated by the group of young probationers mentioned in Examples 7 and 15. There can be little doubt that the experience of each being dependent for their safety, success and satisfaction upon the movements, decisions and responsible behaviour of the others provided possibilities for social learning of an intensity which might never be achieved by verbalisation alone. This would be particularly true of such immature, inarticulate and aggressive young people. Similarly, the milieu of treatment homes, "mini-societies" for young drug addicts, or such progressive penal establishments as Grendon Underwood (Parker, 1969) provide rich opportunities for social learning through purposive and relevant activities and through control by corrective group response to the individual's behaviour. These activities should maximally be orientated towards engagement in planning and executing the myriad functions of the institution's daily life. This is the major therapeutic and maturational resource of such institutions. To regard the "therapy" as a scant 40 minutes with a visiting psychiatrist every few weeks is a manifest absurdity. It is a valuable, but only supplementary, activity.

Whether activity is the primary feature of treatment or only secondary, one of its aims will be to promote interaction since relationships cannot develop and mutual influence cannot occur without interaction. Thus, the activities encouraged will be those which favour or necessitate interaction and which are most relevant to the perceived needs and interests of the group members. Different activities provide more or less opportunity for interaction. Where the group activity does not require co-operation, as with our cinema audience, interaction will be limited. Obvious though this may seem, observation suggests that some social workers are remarkably ready to adopt quite irrelevant practices from occupational therapy, and eagerly encourage members of activity-centred groups to engage in pottery, weaving, basketry, copperwork and the like. Such programme may certainly be creative and satisfying, and for that reason appropriate for certain clients. But it seems that clients who by definition have problems in social, not manual, functioning may best be helped by supported involvement in activites requiring the exercise of social and co-operative skills. An infinity of possibilities exist. Choice is determined by the needs, problems, motivation and resources of the group. While detailed exposition must await a discussion of group-work practice, we can already indicate such activities as committee and planning work, campaigning for organisations and disseminating information, camping and climbing, team games, producing news-sheets, dramatics and dancing, making film and videotape, preparing food and drink, decorating group premises, arranging events, providing home services for the aged and handicapped, and so on. While each of these may be chosen or rejected in relation to different group's needs, they all have in common that they encourage interacting in the group.

If, however, we wish to be taken seriously in our claim to a scientifically based treatment method, we must go yet further. We should be able to suggest with some degree of clarity and validation that activity X is more likely than activity Y to stimulate meaningful and relevant interaction between given clients in given situations. So far only a few studies have approached this question.

Gump and Sutton-Smith, American social workers, conducted a series of experiments during the early 1950s. One method-orientated study on the relationship of interaction and type of activity was reported by these investigators in 1955. This was addressed to the question of "how activities limit, provoke or coerce the expression of children's needs and problems". These questions were made operational by formulating categories of interaction which were then applied during observation of a group of pre-puberty maladjusted boys in a summer camp. The number of interactions in each category was scored and compared during equal periods of time spent in two different forms of activity. The activities chosen were those of a joint swimming trip and handicrafts (boat-building).

While the average number of interactions during swimming was significantly greater than during handicraft, their classification into the categories of "sharing, helping, asserting, blocking, demanding and attacking" made possible a more differentiated and informative comparison. It was, for example, shown that while all other interaction categories were more numerous during swimming (including the negative ones of "blocking" and "attack"), the category of "helping" was substantially greater during the craft activity. It was also shown that the proportion of the total craft interaction which involved the social worker was 46%, while that during swimming was only 26%. This too was differentiated, showing that the worker-involved inter-action in craft activity was predominantly "helping"—41% as compared with 17% in swimming. This contrasts with the predominance of "demanding, blocking and attack" in swimming (34%) as compared with 17% during handicraft.

This study, though modest in scope, raised questions and developed research instruments whose potential contribution to a more selective and purposive use of activities may be considerable. It is encouraging to note that their scheme has recently been revised and extended by the very productive University of Michigan group workers (Vinter, 1967) and that Vinter's work in its turn has been incorporated in a study of the selection and use of activity in a therapeutic milieu (Whittaker, 1974). These studies facilitate a continuation of this productive avenue of inquiry into the relationship between activity and interaction.

INTERACTION AND RELATIONSHIPS

Our cinema audience were not required to relate to each other in order to achieve their comon objective. We saw this as one factor militating against their interacting. It is a matter of common observa-tion that people who have relationships with each other interact more than people who have not, whether these relationships are negative or positive.

This interdependence of relationships and interaction has a number of consequences. Whether these consequences are seen as desirable or not, depends upon the demands and philosophies which prevail in different life situations.

In some situations the development of friendly relationships is regarded as undesirable. We may therefore find both customs and regulations whose conscious purpose is to restrict interaction. Military services provide a good example of this. Napoleon proposed that the "brave" soldier is one who fears his sergeant slightly more than he fears the enemy. The acceptability of this dictum has been reflected throughout the history of most countries by rigid regulations or traditions which prevent officers and "men" from interacting with each other and thereby developing positive relationships, which might inhibit the immediate and unquestioning obedience of command as well as the ready issue of commands which exposed the recipient to risk.

The cultural trappings of medicine include similar devices and make comparable assumptions. The medical hierarchy, with the doctor at the apex and the patient at the base, provides a series of layers of insulation against all but essential sympton-focused interaction between the participants. In this way, affective relationships are minimised and personal-emotional factors may be prevented from disturbing the clinical processes of diagnosis, decision, treatment and disposition.

Is the converse of this true? If non-interaction hinders relationships, may we say that interaction fosters their formation? This belief is certainly commonly held. "If we could just get these people together, I am sure they would learn to get on. . . ." Variants on this theme are heard from many sources. There is the "radical-chic" hostess,[5] dizzily mixing the militant New Left with shipping magnates and the cultural eminences. There is the Borstal governor who invites public schoolboys to spend their holidays at Borstal, on the debatable assumptions (a) that interaction will occur, (b) that positive relationships will develop and (c) that the visitors will thus imbue the inmates with their supposedly superior attitudes and standards of behaviour.

It is certainly true that relationships cannot be formed without interaction. It is tempting to infer from this common observation that relationships will develop proportionately with the amount of inter-action which occurs. Bovard (1952) showed experimentally that greater mutual liking was generated in "group-centred" groups, where inter-action was stimulated, than in "leader-centred" groups, in which interaction between members was discouraged. In this context Homans' (1951) proposition that mutual liking will increase with increase in interaction frequency is also often quoted. But it is important to add his rider that where participants do not gain satisfac-tion from their interaction, yet are unable to withdraw from it, they may on the contrary become hostile to each other "like two rats in a trap". Sartre in *Huis Clos* presents an unorthodox but strangely chilling vision of Hell as an eternity spent in a small closed group of people whom one dislikes. The implication is certainly not that the resulting interaction fosters more liking.

One can accept that when dislike, tension and defensive awareness of differences exist, compulsory contact and propinquity are as likely to stimulate negative as positive relationships. There is empirical evidence for this.

Star *et al* (1958) report observations of attitudes in racially mixed groups of American military personnel during the Second World War. It had been hypothesised that their interaction in a sustained situation of stress and mutual dependency would lead to the dissolution of negative stereotypes and thus to more positive relationships. But in so far as such development occurred at all, it was found to be individual, situational and—most importantly—temporary. The prejudiced were easily able to find evidence supporting their prejudices when interacting with large numbers of the disliked group. This would probably have remained true irrespective of the number of contacts. In the dynamics of prejudice a much greater part is played by the emotional needs of the prejudiced person than by the objective qualities of the person(s) for whom it is held.

From the area of macro-social planning comes a further observation relevant to this question. We read in Macarov (*op.cit.,* p.20) that

> . . the planners of new villages during the days of mass immigration into Israel sought to ensure rapid integration of immigrants from over a hundred countries by sending to each village people from different origins and backgrounds, feeling that the interaction which would necessarily ensue would lead to good relationships. Instead, many villages were the scenes of tension and strife, with entire groups leaving, blood feuds developing, and mutual discrimination between groups. The revised plan, in effect for several years now, recognises that certain conditions determine the success of interaction in leading to good relations. Now, outlying villages are planned around central towns, and populated by people from the same country of origin, and sometimes even from the same city. Essential services, such as tractor stations, medical services, schools, and stores, are located in the central town. This allows people from the various villages to interact in a limited manner in the central town, with the opportunity of withdrawing when the pressure becomes intolerable, or of participating further, in parents' committees and the like, as they become able to accept each other.

In summary we may say that while there is a general tendency for interaction to promote positive relationships, it does not always do so. The extent to which it does so is dependent, among other variables, upon volition in group formation, the degree of freedom to withdraw or express dissatisfaction, the existence of some degree of commonality, consensus on objectives and activities, and the emotional health of members.

In social work some of these factors may be under the control of the worker at the inception of the group and he may make decisions about them. Others are to some extent amenable (if appropriate) to his and the group's influence during their contact with each other. Since both the stimulation of interaction and the development of satisfying relationships are central aspects of social work with groups these brief comments should be regarded as a minimal introduction to a theme of central importance to practice.

INTERACTION AND GROUP SIZE

Where the social worker leads voluntarily or compulsorily formed groups, he frequently decides the number of people who compose the group or at least to whom membership is offered. This is not so in agencies where he works with natural groups, but there too he must be aware that the size of the group influences the group situation and therefore his own function and intervention.

A comprehensive discussion of the determination and consequences of group size in social work would include its relation to the aims of various kinds of groups, to the activities and treatment methods most appropriate to those aims, and to both the initial and potential levels of group functioning of members. We shall limit outselves here to introducing some observations on the influence of group size upon the intensity and quality of members' interaction. We shall refer to a small number of selected but important studies. For a critical and more extensive review of the literature on this subject we recommend Thomas and Fink (1963) who discuss the findings and methodology of thirty-one empirical studies on the influence of group size. Some of the studies mentioned in this chapter are, however, not included in Thomas and Fink's review.

We shall first look at the extremes of group size—"very small" and "very large"—and then at what we might term "the middle range".

Is there a "group of one"? We have already drawn attention to analogies which have been proposed between the individual and the group. These have involved both the application of individual personality theory to group dynamics and the reverse. It does not seem incongruous, within a psychoanalytical frame of reference, to speak of the components of the personality—the id, ego, and super-ego—as "interacting" with each other. In another approach, Mead (1934) has written on the nature of "self". The self—the "I" which is the primitive and uninhibited proposer of self-serving behaviour, and the "me" which is an organised set of attitudes—is seen as "essentially a social structure, which arises in social experience". What we are, and how we experience our "selves", is seen as a product of the response of the surrounding culture to our presentations of ourselves. It is important to note that this culture is itself dynamic. At different times and in different places it gives dramatically different responses to the same kinds of self-presentation. Through this circular process of "self"-assertion and environmental response, each person "internalises a generalised impression of others". To proffer a simplified version of Mead's refined conceptualisation, we may say that each "self" converses and interacts continually with this "generalised other". This is how cultural and sub-cultural *mores* are enabled to play their vital role in personality development. Mead's work, here superficially reported, is demanding and rewarding reading.

A recent and succinct statement of this notion of the individual interacting with himself was made by Lake (1970):

> Interaction may take place when the interacting individual is in a state of physical isolation. A person habitually and constantly interacts with memories and with learned and acquired values, symbols and referential systems. He also interacts with constant or predictable behaviour and response patterns which he recognises in himself or attributes to others.
>
> The point is that all behaviour is interactive behaviour even though it be solitary . . . (he) assumes the existence of other persons and functions as a social entity within the existence of probable or implied relationships between himself and others.

Yet despite all this, something stubbornly pragmatic tugs at the sleeve of our reason and insists that the individual is *not* a group, and may only profitably be regarded as such in the service of analogy. The smallest groups, insists our reason, consists of *two* or *three* people . . . Do we know anything about these?

Two-person groups, often referred to as "dyads", are subjectively experienced as "most intimate". This was shown by Fischer (1953), in a study where subjects were invited to rank the primary groups to which they belonged in terms of their relative intimacy. The groups included varied in size from two to twelve members. This is perhaps not a surprising finding. However, it helps to illuminate an interesting and less obvious finding by Bales and Borgatta (1955). In a study of discussion groups ranging in size from two to seven members, they showed that dyads generated most tension, were relatively unstable, and yet overtly demonstrated least conflict (i.e. categories D10, showing disagreement, and D12, showing antagonism, in Bales' scheme). This is consonant with a later finding by Slater (1958) who also studied groups ranging in size from two to seven. He concluded that forces which inhibit the expression of disagreement and dissatisfaction exist in the smallest groups. The explanation proposed for this is that the smaller the group the more severe are the consequences of alienating a single member.

It is interesting here to speculate on the possibility of a causal relationship between the dyad's instability and high tension and its low rate of overtly expressed disagreement and antagonism. We know that in general the repression of negative feelings leads to their progressive intensification. One way of dealing with this is by withdrawal from the situation. In a dyad, this means dissolving the group, i.e. instability.

The presence of a third member, forming a so-called "triad", substantially changes this picture, whether or not the third person is another indigenous member or is an "outsider" such as some kind of clinical worker. Each participant now has to consider how his behaviour will be seen by the new member. Thus the presentation and protection of "market images", the consciously desired impressions of one's self, becomes more marked. Triads are also characterised by more overt competition and manoeuvering for status and influence. A common interactional pattern is the formation of a dyad-alliance of the weaker members against the dominant member. If the latter is very intimidating, however, it frequently occurs that one of the weaker members strongly identifies with him and joins in showing superior attitudes to the third, now isolated, member. (Readers need go no further than observing the behaviour of their own or neighbours' children when in groups of two or three to confirm these observations.)

Robson (1966) contends that the pattern last described is much more typical of male than of female triads, the latter being less competitive and more cohesive. He also contends that where a triad consists of two males and one female, the males will compete for the attention of the female. We are back with Morris and with Freud; the naked ape rears his sexy head. . . . However, the intervening decade has seen changes in sex-determined role behaviour, and Robson's findings might well be modified in a replicated study.

At the opposite extreme of group size, very different interactional patterns emerge. One basic observation, with a simple arithmetical explanation, is that the larger the group becomes, the less can any one member participate. After a certain point members become less involved with each other and the group-as-a-whole. Their feeling of responsibility for the group and its performance therefore also decreases. We have earlier cited Bales' observation that in larger groups contributions tend to be confined to a high-status élite. Similarly Psathas (1960) has observed: "Instead of interacting with each other, members (in large groups) tends to direct communication to the highest-ranking initiator, who in turn responds to them as a group rather than as individuals."

There is a corollary of this, mentioned by Loeser (1957). He suggests that as group size increases, transference reactions become weaker, until the members experience no meaningful relationships with each other.

We must conclude from all this that the initiating and active roles in large groups become focal and are imbued with very considerable potential power. This being so, we would add a rider to Loeser's observation. Although inter-member relationships are weaker and transference between members less, the concentration of attention in large groups upon the few and the consequent tendency to formalise leadership, must cause such "leaders" to be particularly available to members' transference feelings. We would suggest that this explains why many people leading large groups, whether with formal or informal authority, seem often to be "loved" or "hated" or "feared" to an extent quite disproportionate to their behaviour and personal qualities. Members occupying such roles arouse feelings and reactions in others which are connected with early unsolved problems of dependence and authority, submission and control. This, like all interaction phenomena, is reciprocal and there is a tendency for individuals with such unsolved problems to place themselves in that kind of subordinate group relationship.

This tendency reaches, of course, its most extreme expression in mass movements, which are characterised by the "complete assimilation of the individual into a collective body", and where the True Believer perceives himself as "having no purpose, worth or destiny apart from his collective body. ... His joys and sorrows, his pride and confidence spring from the fortunes and capacities of the group rather from his individual prospects and abilities" (Hoffer, *op.cit.*).

The characteristics of the "very small" and the "very large" groups to which we have drawn attention do not encourage us to regard them as ideal for social work practice. Circumstances may sometimes compel us to work at these levels, and thus to find ways of minimising their disadvantages. The high tension, instability, competitiveness and repressed aggressivity of the very small group is in fact itself the focus of much counselling and family treatment. But in general, social group-work takes place in groups of medium size. Do we know anything about this middle range?

Interaction process analysis has something to tell us. Bales and Borgatta (1955) found with increase in group size from two to seven members that associated increase occured in the giving of orientation (B6), the giving of suggestions (B4), the showing of tension release (A2) and the expression of solidarity (A1). Simultaneously, decrease occurred in categories D11, A3, B5 and C8, i.e. showing tension, showing agreement, giving opinion and requesting opinion. Moreover, the groups with four members showed most negative activity in the social-emotional area, and those with three members were next highest. This seems to suggest that groups whose membership increasingly approaches seven are increasingly well adapted to task-centred discussion and are less disturbed in their work by social-emotional needs precipitated by the group situation. Such observations, however, emphasise the difficulties inherent in applying interaction research findings to social work and other therapeutic groups. Some social-work groups have a clearly defined and circumscribed task. But in many groups the task itself consists of working through psycho-social problems in members' life situations. Group treatment may have been selected as the method of choice precisely because social-emotional problems which echo those members' life situations may be precipitated and dealt with in the group. Thus, this "negative social-emotional interaction", far from being a troublesome and peripheral aspect of interaction, may provide material of central relevance to treatment.

Here we can see the suitability of Hill's scheme to such studies. Much of the "negative social-emotional interaction" of Bales' model would be included in Hill's categories of "confrontive/relationship" and "confrontive/group" interaction. Far from being peripheral, these might be the very foci of treatment. Replication of some of these studies, using Hill's Interaction Matrix with groups in social work treatment, could usefully illuminate some of these questions.

To return to amounts rather than quality of interaction. Stephen and Mishler (1952) studies groups of similar size-range to the Bales and Borgatta studies, namely three to seven members. They showed that with increasing size there was an increase in activity from the already active members, and a corresponding decrease in contributions from the relatively passive. Fewer and fewer members said more and more, while more and more said less and less. A number of other studies, as well as our own daily life experiences, suggest that this trend becomes yet more marked as numbers increase, until we attain the centralisation and formalisation of leadership characteristic of very large groups.

The feelings of comfort and satisfaction with which these different interaction rates are connected have been studies by both Hare (1952) and Carter *et al.* (1951). Comparing groups of five and twelve members and four and eight members, respectively, both investigators found that members felt freer to express themselves and to participate in the smaller groups. In the larger groups it was more common to feel inhibited and unimportant. The more active members in the larger groups were experienced as both more formal and more domineering. (It is not entirely frivolous to remind here of the little group of renegade rabbits in "Watership Down", fugitives from both man's encroachments and from the self-defeating, inflexible hierarchy of the over-populated home burrow. Early in their flight, they developed democratic, effective and informal ways of utilising their various skills. This had much to do with group size. Hazel, who was elected Chief Rabbit when the group later increased in size, said during the early days, "there are too few of us for giving orders and biting each other" (Adams, 1974).

We will include one final observation, involving variables of size, structure and group control. Asch (1951, *op. cit.*) studied groups of up to fifteen members. He was particularly interested in the possibility of group size influencing the amount of pressure upon members towards conformity. He made the interesting finding that the intensity of group pressure increased steadily in groups up to the size of eight members. With additional members, however, pressures to conformity again slowly declined. Of potential practical importance was the observation that, concomitant with the decrease in group control in groups from eight to fifteen members, an increasing tendency to the formation of sub-groups was exhibited.

In summary we may say that these findings help the social worker to determine group size. These findings, and others not discussed here, will influence his choice and decisions. According to the type and objectives of the group with which he is working, the members' ends will best be served by different intensities of individual participation, different degrees of formalisation of indigenous leadership, the avoidance or stimulation of sub-group formation, and greater or lesser confrontation with social-emotional material. As we have seen, these variables are influenced by the size of the group, among other factors.

Notes on Chapter 6

1. This notion accords well with certain formulations on social group-work practice. Sarri and Galinsky's model of small-group development (see Chap. 8) also includes the emergence of a potentially dominant leader or leader-clique at an early stage of group development. Sarri and Galinsky suggest that the worker's functions during this so-called Formative Phase include attempting to prevent such dominance becoming a permanent feature of the group. "... the worker is careful not to give positive sanctions to leaders who hinder the treatment process ... (he) attempts to forestall premature formalisation or stabilisation of the leadership structure in order to preserve opportunities for more members to assume leadership functions subsequently."

2. Marathon group therapy was introduced during the 1960s as a technique for intensifying the group experience. At first it seemed to be yet another of the "way out" Californian "human potential" innovations. But it has shown itself rapidly to be widely acceptable and capable of both refinement and some validation. Bach (1966) is credited with introducing it. Stoller (1968), another pioneer of this technique, defines it as " ... a use of groups for the purpose of personal change which utilises continuous group interaction over several days as its major source of impetus. Other important ingredients of this new approach are time-limited contact, negation of the illness model, and the promotion of plans for the future." Marathon therapy focuses intensively on cause and effect in present behaviour rather than on past history or current situational difficulties. A brief but informative review of the literature is included in Parks and Antenen's paper (*op.cit*). A more extensive review study is to be found in Dinges and Weigel (1971). Sohl (1967) has written a successful novel, *The Lemon Eaters,* which gives a clear impression of the conduct of marathon group therapy.

3. Time-extended group therapy, like the marathon, is intended to enhance investment, involvement and intimacy in the group. It is also intended to encourage members to disclose themselves more quickly, and to accept an "honest" and confrontive mode of communication. It is not conducted for such long periods as the marathon, however. For example, the time-extended sessions in Sklar's study (*op.cit.*) continued for 6 hours. The conventional sessions in the therapy series were of 1½ hours' duration.

4. A useful addition to the literature is Jehu's book (1967) in which the principles of learning are first concisely expounded, then applied to problems of personality adjustment and maladjustment, and finally examined for their relevance to social work practice. This exposition is continued in Jehu *et al.* (1972).

5. The tongue-in-cheek term "radical chic" has been coined by Wolfe (1970). It refers to a wealthy social clique, cultured and comfortable. While not finding reason to shed their own affluence, they proclaim a liberal political position and publicly espouse fashionable radical causes.

CHAPTER 7

Group Structure

Any small group, shortly after formation, will begin to show an increasingly clear pattern of relationships, mutual expectations and differentiation between individual members or sub-groups with regard to their function, influence and contribution to group life. This pattern of roles, ranks and relationships is customarily referred to as the group structure.

Group structure is often unspecified and informal, developing in some spontaneous and unclear manner out of the group process. In other groups, important components of structure are defined and formalized, as a result of some kind of decision or elective procedure, or by appointment or by tradition. In either case, whether formally or informally determined, structure is a decisive factor in determining any group's efficiency, its ability to use its resources, and the degree of satisfaction which members derive from the group.

Many aspects of group structure continually affect us, for better or for worse, in our daily lives. Typical of these are, for example, leadership and role distribution. We may see a group of poor children, envious of a more fortunate child's possessions, reject or isolate him, thus increasing their own frustration and thereby damaging the group climate. Or if they are better able to deal with their envy, they may be able to draw him into the group and accord him some appropriate status and role, thus increasing both his and their own satisfactions. Or only too often one sees how a manipulative or more openly authoritarian leader of a staff or team causes members to lose interest in the common task, and inhibits their creative fantasy. Fragmentation also occurs because of the different responses of individual members to anxiety and aggression. Rival cliques are therefore formed. Or we may observe a committee whose members recognise and respect each others' skills and specialised knowledge. They will probably appoint chairman, secretary, treasurer, sub-committees, etc., on the basis of this recognition and so be able to maximise both their efficiency and their harmony.

These random examples of common structural phenomena illustrate some of the consequences of structure to groups of all kinds.

Structure is always important in social-work groups, because of its implications for the value derived from membership, because it provides a key to further understanding of the group, and because much social-group work method attempts to influence structure in such a way that it serves the interests and needs of the members.

Roles, ranks and relationships are closely interrelated components of group structure, each profoundly influencing the other. However, we attempt, for the sake of clarity, to discuss separately some selected aspects of these three concepts.

Roles

DEFINITION

Role is mainly a behavioural concept. The various functions, tasks and ways of behaving which are associated with given social positions (statuses) are the "roles" ascribed to those positions. This common interpretation of "role" is reflected in Merton's well-known definition (1957). "(Role is) the behavioural enacting of the patterned expectations attributed to a stated position in a social system."

The term is however used somewhat differently in the various social sciences. Deasy (1964), in a discussion on the relevance of the role theory to social work, points out both differences and similarities in the use of the concept by sociologists, social psychologists and anthropologists. These differences in usage unavoidably lead to difficulty in formulating consistent definitions. Sarbin (1954) achieves some clarification of the definitions of role appearing in the literature and his review is recommended.

As social workers we are concerned with attitudes and emotions, as well as with behaviour itself. We therefore seek a formulation of role which also refers to these important aspects of our functioning. If, in any small group, we become leader or follower, newcomer or isolate, scapegoat or clown, we have feelings about the position we occupy and about the role-behaviour associated with it. The other group members also have feelings both about our behaviour and their own role. This important dimension of the role concept is included in two useful formulations. Perlman (1961) states: "Role implies that certain emotional values or sentiments tend to be injected in any human activities that involve relationships with others, either into the activities themselves, or into the reciprocal relationships, or both."

Park and Burgess (1924), quoted in Sarbin's review, offer a definition of role which includes the phrase, "a pattern of attitudes and actions".

This inclusion of emotional and affective components brings us a little further. It provides a useful starting-point for considering how role differentiation occurs in groups and with what purpose? It is often assumed that the individual's wishes and capacities are the determinants of his role in the group. "He is a born leader" ... or ... "a natural scapegoat". Alternatively, the group's pressures on the individual member are often thought to be decisive. "They led him astray" ... or ... "He had no real wish to be Chairman, but ... ". Both of these views are simplifications. Role is, in fact, a product of a complex interplay between individual, group and environmental forces.

FACTORS INFLUENCING ROLE

Each member brings into a group situation his particular attitudes and forms of behaviour. As we have seen, these are in large measure a product of earlier life experiences in other social groups. These experiences have formed the individual's self-image and self-evaluation, which in their turn influence his expectations of acceptance, indifference or rejection in new group situations. His expectations influence his approach to new groups and therefore to a considerable extent the response which he receives. His earlier experiences also influence how much he is able to invest in new groups, whom he associates with, his attitude towards the group's norms and values, and his ability to accept or adjust to them.

This point may be illustrated by reference to the family as a primary group.

A wanted child is born to relatively mature parents. In his first years he experiences love, respect and security. He will develop a generalised feeling of being valuable and is able to approach groups outside the family (for example in the neighbourhood, kindergarten, or school) optimistically and with little anxiety. He has no strong need for self-assertion or for reassurance about his own worth. His behaviour as a new member is therefore on the whole acceptable to the group and unthreatening to them. This eases his integration into the group and will later make it easier for him to find a role and a status which optimally meet both his own and the group's interests. The success of his membership in this new group will in turn reinforce yet again his ability to function well in later groups.

This briefly sketched history may be contrasted with that of an unwanted child, whose parents are immature and rejecting. This child experiences little consistency, security or warmth. Very early indeed he senses his parents' rejection, and this strongly influences his self-respect and self-confidence. He develops a need to defend himself against his experience of insecurity and worthlessness. He may do this by withdrawal, by denial, by attention-seeking, by destructive behaviour or by other means. His behaviour becomes progressively irrational, and is increasingly marked by self-defeating patterns of defence. This behaviour is demonstrated when he approaches each new group because the situation arouses more expectations of rejection, more anxiety and therefore more aggression, whether inwardly or outwarding directed. His inappropriate behaviour will therefore influence in turn the group's response to him. This will probably be at least indifferent, and perhaps yet again directly rejecting. Thus he becomes trapped in a circular and self-defeating pattern of repeated social failure.

However, this same person, precisely because of his defensive behaviour, may enter harmoniously into the culture of a particular group. If his defence against rejection has been, for example, an over-compensated and aggressive demonstration of his own independence, he may be accorded high status in a group which needs the stimulation of such a person, and where aggressive behaviour is accorded high status, perhaps even earning the role of leader. The attraction of the delinquent gang to the rejected child can be clearly seen in this perspective.

These very brief and schematic examples show the importance of the individual's attitudes, resources and behaviour in determining his place in the group structure. The last example, however, also shows how the norms and needs of the group itself are an equally powerful determinant of the individual's status and role. This is an important point.

We may perhaps say that most groups accept and absorb those individual members who fit the group's aims and needs. The group needs individuals in order to exist as a group, and in order to realise its objectives. As we have seen, the individual on his part has to join groups in order to satisfy his needs. These factors are indivisibly woven into each other. We therefore see that the individual member's ability to contribute to the group's aims is often a vital determinant of the role which he can play in the group and of the status which he is accorded. A member may well be disliked because of his behaviour and attitudes, but may have possessions or abilities which the group needs. This may cause the group to accept him as a member and even give him high status. For example, he may be verbally gifted in an inarticulate group which needs a spokesman. He may have a bottle or money in a group of destitute alcoholics. He may have experience or knowledge which the group needs in order to solve a problem which is important to them. He may be the child with relatively prosperous parents, possessing toys and sweets in an impoverished street.

Thus an individual may be accepted as a group member without arousing warm feelings or friendship; he may merely be *acceptable* to the group at that point of time. And we usually see that the more he is able to contribute to the group's goal-striving, the more acceptable he becomes. Thus, one of the most decisive determinants of the individual's position in the group and of his opportunities for self-realisation, is the group's need.

But the group's needs change! They change in harmony with the group's development, with maturation on the part of individual members and with the group's changing relationship to its environment. In consequence, the relationships between individuals in groups are also steadily subject to change.[1] Thus, sub-groups dissolve and new sub-groups are formed. A leader may withdraw, be deposed or lose his influence in some other way. After a series of successful experiences, a group may no longer need a scapegoat who has earlier been subjected to much contempt. In a guilt-determined reparation they may give him a new role with relatively high status, which he may enjoy for a period. Almost any member may experience different degrees of approval and acceptance at different stages in group life. Role, rank and relationships in the group change in accordance with change in the group's perceived needs. Thus, group structure is a highly dynamic process whose understanding may give valuable insight into the needs which the group and its individual members experience at any point of time.

To summarise our discussion so far, role may be seen as a product of interplay between:

1. individual members' needs and resources,
2. the situation in the group, and
3. the forces acting on the group from the environment.

All three of these factors are subject to change during the life of any group.

Clearly, the group's need to assign given status and roles and the individual's need to accept them do not always coincide. This common disparity is another cause of the shifting patterns of rejection and acceptance within groups, the manoeuvering between the group and the individual as they attempt to meet, to compromise with, or to avoid each others' demands and expectations.

It is relevant to introduce at this point the concepts of the "external and internal systems". Homans (1951) sees group behaviour as directed towards solving two sets of problems and needs, namely those arising from outside and those from inside the group. The repertoire of adaptive behaviour which enables the group to survive in its environment and to cope with other environmental pressures is referred to as the "external system" of the group. But given survival, the group has to deal with the myriad problems of co-operation, competing interests, relationships, and organisation inherent in group life. That part of the group's behaviour which is directed towards these problems is referred to as the "internal system". Neither system is more important than the other. The group must survive in its environment in order to achieve its internally derived purposes, yet unless its purposes are attainable its survival is not important. Thus the external and internal systems are interdependent processes. Different groups, or the same group at different times, will necessarily be more concerned with problems of one or the other system, according to the prevailing sources of pressure and tension. However, some work goes on continually in both systems in all groups.

The approach to understanding role distribution which we are proposing here uses these concepts.

The group's environment impinges in various ways upon it. The external system of social work groups may have to deal with discrimination or repression, with threat or moral rejection, with support, encouragement, or offers of help—all depending upon the nature of the group's problem and the environment's reaction to its members. These influences from the environment stimulate needs on the part of the group, and may add to the burden of the basic problem which brings them together. In order to meet as many of these needs as possible, the group must mobilize its members' resources, which at once engages the internal system. Since needs are multiple, and since the members' personalities and capacities are necessarily various, this must lead to differentiated role-behaviour on the part of individual group members.

Example 27. An approved school, its regime and the society on whose behalf it functions, compose the environment and activate the external system of the group of young persons committed there. The staff of one such school were experienced by the boys as punitive, authoritarian and moralistic. This increased their problems, arousing new needs to counteract the feelings of worthlessness, injustice and powerlessness which the environment imposed and a need to express the resultant aggressive feelings. The headmaster's house and garage were therefore ignited in his absence. This group action, though an expression of its external system, required differentiated role-behaviour from the members. One or several members had to inspire and organise this demonstration. Others had more passively to support them. One or more steal and conceal the necessary paraffin. Others check the movements of the staff, and others again simply to follow orders. One member, by no means centrally involved, was afterwards cast for the role of scapegoat and for a time accepted it. Different characteristics, skills and needs on the part of the individual members determined the distribution of these roles. Any attempt fully to understand a single member's role would therefore be incomplete which did not embrace the factors of environmental pressures on the group, the internal processes of the group, and the personality dynamics of the individuals concerned.

Example 28. Eight young unmarried mothers in a working-class district accepted an offer of group work help at a family counselling agency. All had previously submitted abortion applications which had been refused. There were many practical problems concerning work, income, accommodation, baby-minding, etc. Members also experienced painful emotional problems arising from social isolation, from rejection and consequent feelings of worthlessness, from anger and self-abasement arising from others' moral condemnation, and from the ambivalence with which some of them related to their children. Again, we see the environment impinging upon a group and giving rise to needs. The group had to mobilize to meet these. This, again, gave rise to differentiated role-behaviour by the individual members.

Some members expressed angry rejection of the society which discriminated against them, thereby protecting their self-evaluation. Others expressed moral conflict and a partial identification with society's rejecting attitudes. These members thus located and articulated another part of the group problem. Others became impatient with this and tried to keep the focus on their more concrete problems. Others again seemed more occupied with the internal concerns of the group. These members fulfilled a kind of mediating and negotiating role, as if afraid the group could not tolerate the tensions arising from these different kinds of role behaviour.

The group situation was further both enriched and complicated by the social worker's presence. She was initially associated with the judgemental and condescending attitudes which were common in their environment. But in fact she introduced new external forces of support, understanding, respect and material help. The group had to learn to use these and to relate to her in a more appropriate way.

Further refinement and differentiation of role-behaviour was therefore required before the group could work towards clarification of attitudes and at least partial solution of some common problems. As with the other roles mentioned, the final determinants of who filled which role were the needs and the personality resources of the individuals concerned, while the determinants of which roles where necessary were to be found in the impact upon the group members of their environment.

The movement towards problem solution, which results from the differentiated role behaviour described above, usually involves some degree of conflict, as well as mutual support and supplementation of each other's resources. In this sense the development of group process may be regarded as a resolution of many forces which sometimes reinforce and sometimes conflict with each other.[2] Growth and maturation in groups, as in other organisms, seems inseparable from some degree of conflict or abrasion.

Maintenance, Task, and Individual Roles

These observations and examples suggest that different kinds of roles must be performed, both to express and to deal with the forces generated in group situations. In our examples we saw that some roles met needs arising from the external system, while others were aimed at resolving problems within the group itself—the internal system. The examples also indicated a relationship between role assignment and individual needs and proclivities. These observations are in close accord with important formulations on role by Benne and Sheats (1948), which we shall now summarise. Jennings' (*op.cit.*) concepts of socio- and psyche-dimensions and Bales' (1951, *op.cit.*) task-centred and social-emotional interaction will be seen to harmonise with these formulations.

Benne and Sheats propose a classification of the roles which may be performed by members of small groups. While this is based on work in group-training laboratories, experience and observation suggest that it can be more widely applied. Their classification falls into three broad groupings, as follows.

1. *Group task roles*

The purpose of these roles is to "facilitate and co-ordinate group effort in the selection and definition of a common problem and in the solution of that problem". It is emphasised that each member may enact more than one role in any given interaction ("unit of participation") and a wide range of roles in successive participations. Any or all of these roles may be played at times by the formal leader as well as by members. However, the authors comment that participants usually confine themselves to playing a limited range of roles. In the context of group membership training, an increase in role flexibility and in skill and security in a wider range of roles is seen as desirable. In this respect it resembles many examples of social work with groups. Twelve group task roles are proposed, thus:

(a) The *initiator-contributor* suggests new ideas or ways of regarding the group problem or goal. These may take the form of suggestions for a new group goal, new definitions of the problem, or of suggested solutions to a difficulty that the group has encountered.

(b) The *information-seeker* asks for clarification of suggestions made in terms of their factual adequacy, for authoritative information and facts about the problem being discussed.

(c) The *opinion-seeker* does not ask primarily for the facts of the case, but for clarification of the values pertinent to what the group is undertaking, or of those involved in suggestions made.

(d) The *information-giver* offers facts or generalizations which are "authoritative", or relates his own experience pertinently to the group problem.

(e) The *opinion-giver* states his belief or opinion about suggestions made. The emphasis is on his proposal of what should become the group's view of pertinent values, not primarily upon relevant facts or information.

(f) The *elaborator* spells out suggestions in terms of examples or developed meanings, offers a rationale for suggestions previously made and tries to deduce how an idea or suggestion would work out if adopted by the group.

(g) The *co-ordinator* shows or clarifies the relationships among various ideas and suggestions, tries to pull ideas and suggestions together or tries to co-ordinate the activities of various members or sub-groups.

(h) The *orienter* defines the position of the group with respect to its goals by summarising what has occurred, points to departures from agreed upon directions or goals, or raises questions about the direction which the group discussion is taking.

(i) The *evaluator-critic* subjects the group's accomplishment to some standards of group-functioning in the context of the group task. Thus, he may evaluate or question the "practicality", the "logic", the "facts" or the "procedure" of some aspect of group discussion.

(j) The *energizer* prods the group to action or decision, attempts to stimulate or arouse the group to "greater' or "higher quality" activity.

(k) The *procedural technician* expedites group movement by doing things for the group—performing routine tasks, e.g. distributing materials, or manipulating objects for the group, such as rearranging the seating or running the recording machine, etc.

(l)   The *recorder* writes down suggestions, records group decisions, or the product of discussion. The recorder role is the "group memory".

2. *Group building and maintenance roles*

The purpose of these roles is to build group-centred attitudes and orientation among members, or to maintain such group-centred feelings and activity. There are seven such roles, thus:

(a)   The *encourager* praises, and indicates warmth and solidarity in his attitude toward other group members, and shows understanding of other points of view, ideas and suggestions.

(b)   The *harmonizer* mediates between other members, attempts to reconcile disagreements, relieves tension in conflict situations by joking, pouring oil on the troubled waters, etc.

(c)   The *compromiser* operates from within a conflict in which his idea or position is involved. He may offer compromise by yielding status, admitting error, or by meeting others "half-way".

(d)   The *gate-keeper* and *expediter* attempts to keep communication channels open by encouraging others to participate or by facilitating the flow of communciation.

(e)   The *standard-setter* or *ego-ideal* expresses standards for the group's functioning.

(f)   The *group-observer* and *commentator* records various aspects of the group process and feeds such data, with proposed interpretations, into the group's evaluation of its procedures.

(g)   The *follower* goes along with the movement of the group, more or less passively accepting the ideas of others, serving as an audience in group discussion and decision.

3. *"Individual" roles*

These roles reflect attempts by members to satisfy individual needs which are irrelevant to the group task, and which are irrelevant to group building and maintenance or antagonistic to it. According to these authors, a high incidence of such roles indicates a low level of skill-training (group functioning) among members and/or leader, authoritarian or *laissez-faire* attitudes to group functioning, and immaturity among members. It may also be that the group task is inappropriately chosen or inadequately defined. It is emphasised that this set of roles does not include self-expressive and self-realising behaviour which also serves group maintenance or the group task. Five "individual" roles are described, thus:

(a) The *aggressor* may work in many ways—deflating the status of others, expressing disapproval of the values, acts or feelings of others, attacking the group or the problem it is working on, joking aggressively, showing envy of another's contribution by trying to take credit for it, etc.

(b) The *blocker* tends to be negativistic and stubbornly resistant, disagreeing and opposing without "reason", and attempting to maintain or bring back an issue after the group has rejected or by-passed it.

(c) The *recognition-seeker* work in various ways to call attention to himself, whether through boasting about personal achievements, acting in unusual ways, or struggling to avoid an "inferior" position, etc.

(d) The *self-confessor* uses the audience opportunity which the group setting provides to express personal, non-group oriented, "feeling", "insight", "ideology", etc.

(e) The *playboy* displays his lack of involvement in the group's processes. This may take the form of cynicism, nonchalence, horse-play and other more or less studied forms of "out-of-field" behaviour.

THE DYNAMICS OF SOME COMMON ROLES

The role-types in the above classification are so numerous and differentiated that few of them are likely to be consciously registered and remarked except by people with some kind of professional interest in group phenomena. Certain roles, however, are so familiar in everyday life that they are embraced by more commonplace observation of behaviour. "There is no doubt who is the boss there" ... "Oh! him? He's always clowning" ... "Me? Why is it I always get the blame?" ... "He's a proper Johnny-come-lately". ... The familiar roles of leader, clown, scapegoat, newcomer and isolate, among others, occur with such frequency that some tentative generalisations about how they arise can be attempted. While this may involve the danger of stereotype, it can provide a useful framework for presenting some common dynamics of role assignment, which is, in general, an important component of diagnostic skill in social work with groups.

The following notes on some selected and familiar roles are therefore not intended to be categorical, exhaustive and proven statements. Rather, they illustrate our general approach to the understanding of role assignment. The roles of scapegoat, central person and clown (or jester) will be discussed. Once again, we shall emphasise the interplay of environmental forces, internal group processes and individual proclivities in determining role assignment. Discussion of the leader role will be postponed until the concept of status has been introduced.

Jester or clown

It is common to find in small groups one member whose role may be called that of jester or clown. He can be relied upon to "see the funny side of things", he is always ready with a joke, a quip or a piece of clowning. It costs him nothing, apparently, to raise a laugh also against himself. In a relatively problem-free group or friends or colleagues, this is accepted as both natural and amusing. In more loaded situations, however—for instance in social work groups or similar contexts—we should observe this role with more interest.

The clown role may reflect a symbiotic relationship between the individual and the group; it may be assigned and perpetuated on the basis of the mutually dependent needs of the individual concerned and of the group-as-a-whole. He needs to play it; they need him to play it.

In certain situations of stress, anxiety, or threat, the clown's behaviour may help the group to avoid a problem or to survive a crisis. For instance, anxiety is often generated in a new social situation where participants and their potentialities are unknown to each other, and where behavioural expectations are either unclear or threatening.

In this familiar situation, tension may rapidly be relieved by a partici-pant who makes a joke about the situation or about something else. He thereby enables the others to displace tension and discomfort by their first shared positive experience, namely laughter. Further, by attracting attention to himself he relieves others of the burden of responsibility for a social initiative which they lack the skill and confidence to carry through. The group are grateful to him for this, and give him attention and approval. But he has now defined his role, and the group may often continue to expect such amusing behaviour from him. He is "stuck with his role". Often, his clownish behaviour will be amusing, appropriately timed and serve positive social purposes. But the group may also later demand that he clown for them in order, as before, to help them to evade a painful issue which otherwise must be experienced, rather than primarily to amuse. Where he fulfils these expectations, we may perhaps describe this member and the group as colluding in a denial defence.

The clown's own investment in his role is of interest. Is his behaviour a chosen response to group expectations by one who in fact possesses a much richer repertoire of role behaviour? Or is it the only behaviour of which he is capable, since he has already become dependent upon this way of defending himself from problems in life and relationships? This question will become important as the group develops. The group will usually become more at ease, increasingly able to solve their group-building and maintenance problems, and to communciate freely with each other in order to do so. Where this is so, their need for the jester declines together with the need for manic or other defences against social anxiety. Such increase in maturity of group functioning then gives the jester an opportunity for more varied and appropriate behaviour. If he is capable of performing other roles, he and the group can grow together. If he is not, there is a problem, for he may well increasingly irritate the group members and so become isolated or even rejected by the very group which earlier so valued his amusing behaviour. In Benne and Sheats' terms, we may say that because of his individual-centred needs, he is then performing an inappropriate group maintenance role (their "harmonizer") at a time when group maintenance problems are minimal and when approval is given to those who perform group-task roles. We see again how group needs influence role formation and attitudes to role behaviour, and how the appropriateness and flexibility of the individual's role performance is determined and limited by his own personality characteristics.

Central person

In discussing group formation in an earlier chapter, it was observed that groups usually form because of some shared aim, ideal or need, and that strong common feelings about some other person or persons may also be a basis for group formation. In such cases, the individual concerned is called the "central person", a concept introduced by Redl (1942).

In a study of group formation and emotion, Redl reported certain observations of group behaviour in school settings. He found a variety of situations in which groups had formed around some person who had evoked common emotional responses in the members. On the basis of this shared feeling they "developed group emotions towards each other", mutually identifying and so developing group cohesion. Redl defined this "central person" as "the one through emotional relationship to whom the group formative processes are evoked in the potential group members". In summarising his findings he classified the bases on which the central person role may be assigned as follows:

As an object of *identification*

      On the basis of love

Incorporation into conscience	Type 1
Incorporation into the "ego ideal"	Type 2

      On the basis of fear

Identification with the aggressor	Type 3

As an object of *drives*

As an object of love drives	Type 4
As an object of aggressive drives	Type 5

As an *ego-support*

Providing means for drive satisfaction	Type 6

Dissolving conflict situations through
  guilt-anxiety assuagement
Through the technique of the initiatory
  act in the service of drive
  satisfaction   Type 7
and in the service of drive defence   Type 8
Through the "infectiousness of the
  unconflicted personality constellation
  over the conflicted one" in the service
  of drive satisfaction   Type 9
  and in the service of drive defence   Type 10

This summary conveys little of the flavour of Redl's perceptive observations, and the reader is warmly referred to source. Two very brief case extracts may at once illustrate the relevance of this role concept to social work.

Example 29. A number of tenants of neglected slum property are helped by the social worker to organize, formulate, present and publicise their claims to the property owners in the most effective manner. Initially, the property owner, as object of aggressive drives, would fulfil the role of central person for the group and facilitate their initial cohesion. On the basis of this cohesion they are enabled to work effectively. (This exemplifies the Type 5 central person role, in Redl's model.)

Example 30. A group of cardiac failure patients meet to discuss their condition and its impact on their life situation. Traumatized and afraid, some members defend themselves by denial, while others exaggerate their invalidity. The oldest member, who has had several attacks before, is calm, realistic, open about his feelings and practical about his plans. The members, previously tentative and inhibited, engage themselves in his views and proposed solutions. He functions as a focal point for the group and also as an ego-support. The members become less defended, and become better able to use their own ego-resources in solving their own problems. (This case material appears in Goldner and Kyle (*op. cit.*). This extract exemplifies both Types 2 and 7 in Redl's classificatory system.

The central person will often, as in Example 30, also fill the role of leader, either formally appointed or informally chosen. But as in Example 29, he may well also be the object of very strong negative feelings and neither acceptable nor interested in a leader role. The intensification of group cohesion by the indication of suitable "hate or fear objects" is a familiar and related device which has been employed throughout history by skilled political leaders faced with the threat of national fragmentation. Where social and economic dissatisfaction, or loss of national pride and prestige, have led to destructive internal strife, unification and cohesion have been regained by indicating some person, group or nation as objects to be feared, blamed or hated by the populace as a whole. The effect of this is to revitalise the sense of national identity and cohesion. It is also this same manipulative and exploitive process which Hoffer (*op. cit.*) has in mind when he says that, "mass movements can rise and spread without belief in a God, but never without belief in a devil", and when he goes on to describe hatred as "the most accessible and comprehensive of all unifying agents".

It is evident that the role of central person need not necessarily be filled by a member of the group. A fan-club is a commonplace example of such formation. However, whether the central person is or is not a member, we may learn a great deal about the needs, standards, problems and prestige criteria of a group by noting the characteristics of the individual to whom this role is assigned, just as we learn much about the individual concerned by noting his or her response to being assigned it.

It is particularly important for the social worker to familiarise himself with the dynamics of the central person role, not least since he frequently performs it himself. We have elsewhere argued that the notion of the social worker as "leader" of the group is both ambiguous and confining, and that a more useful light may be cast on his significance to the group members by reference to the central person concept, (Heap, 1968).

Both the emotional needs and responses of members and the professional situation itself are conducive to placing the social worker in this role. The worker's initiative in forming or contacting the group implies that he possesses facilities, knowledge or skills relevant to their needs. This factor inevitably brings him into a focal position. His presumed knowledge and his tentative notions about appropriate ways of using the group situation involve the members in a degree of dependence upon him. This is transient, but persists at least during the intial phase, where he is active in clarifying aims, contract, resources available and perhaps constraints on behaviour in the group. In some situations, as for instance in closed institutions, the worker is focal because he is a link in communication with an inaccessible external environment, and also because he is commonly assumed, rightly or wrongly, to represent the norms and values of the external environment. During the work of the group, the social worker gives support and he both experiences and demonstrates accepting and non-judgemental attitudes towards members' feelings and wishes. He shows his belief in their ability to use their own resources, but may also in certain situations impose some limits. He may infuse rationality and consistency into distorted, loaded and conflicted situations. These aspects of the group situation and of the worker's function inevitably cause him to be variously an object of identification, an object of drives (both love and/or aggression) and to be experienced as ego-supportive. The duration and intensity of this will vary in relation to the needs, setting, maturity and phase of development of the group concerned. In any event, it is consistent with social-work method and principles that the social worker consciously withdraws from this focal role in rhythm with the group's increasing capacity for independent, purposive and democratic activity.

Scapegoat

We shall now discuss the role of scapegoat at some length. This is not because the role is necessarily met more frequently than those already discussed, but because it shows particularly well the interdependence of individual and group behaviour and needs in determining role. In addition, understanding of scapegoating is an aspect of group diagnosis which clearly suggests appropriate intervention by the social worker, because of the immediacy of its relation to the common group problem. Thus, while we will both describe and illustrate some of the dynamics of scapegoating, we shall also briefly indicate some of their implications for the social worker's intervention. (The following observations are extracted from a previously published paper (Heap, 1966).)

The origin of the term "scapegoat" appears to be the Old Testament. We read in Leviticus, chap. 16:

> V.10 But the goat, on which the lot fell to be scapegoat, shall be presented alone before the Lord, to make an atonement with him, and to let him go for a

scapegoat into the wilderness.

V.16 And Aaron shall lay his hands upon the head of the live goat, and confess over him all the iniquities of the children of Israel, and all their transgressions in all their sins, putting them upon the head of the goat, and shall send him away . . . into the wilderness.

V.22 And the goat shall bear upon him all their iniquities into a land not inhabited. . . .

In the use of the term scapegoat suggested here we retain the main elements of this highly purposive biblical practice—namely, projection and expiation. In social work with groups we also see the assignment of the scapegoat role as a projective defence on the part of the group. The group possesses feelings and wishes which it cannot bear to acknowledge within itself, and deals with the resultant conflict by ascribing them to a selected individual, who is then isolated and scorned for possessing them. The members thus gain a measure of relief from their own super-ego strictures; but since ego-work has been avoided by projective denial, the guilt-provoking impulses remain unsatisfied. Projection and scapegoating thus have to be actively maintained until further maturation takes place, or guilt and anxiety are relieved in some way.

This will be illustrated by three case extracts. Examples 31, 32 and 33 will describe the scapegoating episode at the group level. After some comment, each of these cases will be re-introduced in order to focus on the individual member assigned the scapegoat role.

Example 31. Elizabeth. A group of fifteen girls, aged 14-15 years, were members of a large youth club in an industrial city. They had their own group room, their own evening in addition to the club's "open" evenings; and had had their own group worker since the beginning. The worker was a qualified single woman, aged 25.

The group was clearly divided into somewhat hostile sub-groups characterised by very contrasting behaviour. One of these was usually noisy, rough and highly excitable; the other was over-controlled, critical and rigidly "lady-like". There was some contact, and a very limited degree of mobility between these sub-groups, and there was also a small number of "uncommitted"—but not isolated—individuals. One of the few issues about which the group was able to express a common view was the behaviour of one of the members, Elizabeth, aged 15½. Elizabeth dressed provocatively, had slept with boys and openly boasted about it. She had the position of "rejected isolate" in the group, all of whose members expressed contempt of her and her "low standards". The group had moralistic and consistently condemnatory attitudes towards her, implicitly and explicitly contrasting her behaviour with their own "respectable" conduct. (They had in fact virtually no contact with boys outside the club or school.)

These girls were meeting the inescapable adolescent conflict between increasing sexual wishes and curiosity, and prohibiton—both internal and external—against fulfilment of these wishes. Difficult enough; but the members of this particular group had additional problems. One had earlier been the victim of a sexual assault. Two had brutal alcoholic fathers. Several had divorced parents, adultery by one or both parents having been a factor in the divorce. Their sexual fantasies would thus be exceptionally loaded with guilt and fear, since their experience and observation had been that surrender to sexual impulse is highly destructive, that sex is in every sense "bad". Thus the members had to suppress recognition of their own growing sexuality. Some of the members (the over-active group) attempted to deal with this by sublimation. This sub-group's tomboyish behaviour also implied a denial of their vulnerable feminity. The other sub-group dealt with their feelings by repression, over-compensation and rigidly ladylike behaviour. But these defences could not eliminate the discomfort and guilt, since the sexual impulse and fantasy remained and renewed itself. In the absence of more mature solutions, the group projected their sexuality on to Elizabeth—who, conveniently, was in fact somewhat promiscuous—and punished her for its own internal badness. She was the scapegoat, both acting out for the group and being punished for doing so.

Exaple 32. Michael. The boys in a mixed youth club, aged 15-17 years, acccidentally broke in upon one of their co-members, Michael, aged 15 years, who was masturbating in the club lavatory. Up to this point Michael had been a retiring, rather colourless member of the group—a "born-follower" was the phrase used in an earlier report. The boys were quite disproportionately disturbed by this; some expressed violent disgust, others ridicule, and yet others made unsuccessful rude jokes. Michael became for a short while the scapegoat of the group. He was scorned and teased, and it was hinted to the girls that he was homosexual.

This was a hobby-oriented group, engaged in a great deal of sport, and associated actively with the Church. The members tended to be conforming lower-middle-class boys, who placed a premium on the "done thing" and were not a little occupied with moral issues. Clearly then their own masturbation would be the source of much guilt and anguish. Further, in a milieu where such practices simply "were not done", fear and fantasy remained unresolved, and for some of the boys—possibly most—the confusion of masturbation with homosexuality was a source of anxiety and self-doubt.

What to do with the guilt and the self-doubt? The group sublimated in sport; distanced itself by moral debate; performed reparation in its active church work, and had "healthy relationships" with the girls.

But the members still masturbated, in secrecy and in guilt. Then Michael was found doing the terrible thing, and with great relief and excitement the group was able for a time to shed its burden by projecting its badness on to him and so making him their scapegoat. They supported each other in their denial and projection, and found a temporary relief from their own guilt in his chastisement.

Example 33. Anne. A mixed group of young patients in a psychiatric hospital had a leisure-time club, which they organised to a large extent themselves. A social worker was the formal leader of the club, however, and saw her functions as being supportive and enabling.

    The patients were producing a play. Readings and rehearsals went from bad to worse, and the atmosphere in the club became strained. Increasingly the group blamed and complained about one of their number, whom we may call Anne. She was responsible for things going so badly; she could not remember her part or be relied upon for anything; she was "stupid" and "practically crazy". In fact, Anne functioned at about the average level of the group.

    Again we see the scapegoat receiving the projections of the group. The members, meeting frustration in their task, unable to organise and function effectively, were in danger of feeling themselves to be "stupid" or "practically crazy". Unable to contemplate this possibility, they resolved their feelings by projecting precisely these qualities upon a scapegoat and scorning her for possessing them. Thus, the group was able at least temporarily to feel less anxious, having asserted their own strength and sanity. Further, had the play eventually failed, the group could have convinced itself that Anne was to blame, thus making her carry the burden of their inadequacy and denied anxiety.

    So far, we have commented on the implications of scapegoating for the group-as-a-whole. But what of its implications for the scapegoat himself?

    There seem to be a number of factors determining the choice of a given group member as scapegoat. Chance, of course, plays some part— he may be a newcomer, for example, so that pillorying him does not damage the group bond or individual relationships. No aspect of group cohesion is at risk if he responds by withdrawal. He may be in some ways "different" from the others, so that group members feel somewhat less identified with him. Such a difference may be in appearance, cultural background or speech. Equally important are differences in behaviour, and this factor in scapegoat choice has much less to do with chance.

The member who becomes scapegoat is often distinguished by forms of behaviour deviant from the group norms. If this deviance expresses the repressed problem of the group he is very likely to become the focus of the group's projected guilt and therefore also its aggression. For example, it was almost inevitable that Wilde, provocatively deviant in many other respects than the sexual, should eventually be subjected to a tragic and savage ostracism. The rigidly conformist norms of the time could only have been established at the cost of enormous repression, and the guilt and envy resulting from such repression must have been greatly stimulated by Wilde's apparent enjoyment of his own highly non-conforming life; so that immediately he became vulnerable he was cruelly punished both for his own deviations and the uncommitted deviations of others.[3]

However he is selected, the scapegoat is in the painful position of being ostracised, and his wish for acceptance by the group is frustrated. He may deal with the situation in various ways according to his social maturity. He may withdraw from the group, or react with open aggression, or with a seemingly servile acceptance, repressing his angry impulses. Or he may deny to himself that he has this role, and so go on seeking the positive attention and approval of the group in different ways—perhaps by becoming a clown for the group, or by trying in various ways to buy or curry favour with the strongest in the group.

However, it seems that scapegoating may sometimes perform a function not only for the group, but also for the scapegoat. That is, the group may well be playing into the scapegoat's own needs when it assigns him this particular role. One sees this, for example, where the scapegoat has a great need for attention, and experiences even this negative limelight as satisfying, as proof perhaps of his identity and existence for others. More truly symbiotic relationships between the group and the scapegoat are occasionally seen, where scapegoating seems to be a mutual exploitation of group and individual for the satisfaction of their respective repressed needs. A guilt-laden, masochistic member seems sometimes to be able to manipulate the group into making him the object of its projections; thus both his need for punishment and the group's wish to avoid their own super-ego strictures are met. This tends to be a stable and mutually satisfying situation, first threatened when either the group or the individual makes some more positive step towards maturity, and has thus less need either to project or to accept projections.

To return to Example 31. We have already described the group's symbiotic relationship with *Elizabeth*. This girl's home life and upbringing were an appalling confusion of parental instability, sexual pathology and poverty. Elizabeth herself had deep feelings of worthlessness and insecurity. Her promiscuity, however, gave her some feeling of importance, of having some value, however dubiously regarded. Her boasting in the group, which attracted projections of its own sexual guilt, gained her yet more of the attention and status which she so badly needed, and may well have also assuaged her own guilt about her behaviour. Her scapegoating met the needs both of the group and of Elizabeth, but in a way which protected them both from having to deal with their growth and identity conflicts, and prevented them from using their group experiences constructively.

Elizabeth was then temporarily taken into care because of family crises. This produced a number of problems for the group. The one they had rejected was in fact removed, stimulating further guilt both towards her (as scapegoat) and towards their own sexuality. The sexual fantasies hitherto projected on to Elizabeth could no longer be dealt with in this way, and new solutions had to be found. The group began to act in concert for the first time following Elizabeth's removal, and engaged in noisy, provocative and destructive behaviour clearly aimed at testing out the social worker. Her accepting and non-judgemental response to this display of their "badness" enabled them to feel less anxious about their internal sexual badness. This they then began to take up in the group and with the worker in a number of ways—talking about boys, some tentative dating, and seeking information about birth, V.D., menstruation, etc., both directly and by telling rather confused dirty stories. Some of the group began to talk privately with the worker about their particular personal problems.

One result of all this was that the barriers between the sub-groups to a large extent fell away during this period. The members seemed more able to identify themselves with the group, recognising their common needs and problems.

When Elizabeth returned three months later, the group was

able to accept her and accord her a role much more in harmony with both her maturational needs and their own. There was an apparently conscious reparative approach to her, the members making a point of showing that they had missed her. She was also voted to be in charge of the Cola-bar, a central and somewhat status-giving function within the club. Elizabeth highly prized her new position, and seemed in some way to be aware of the changed expectations of her. Whether her relationships outside the club were in anyway changed is unknown, but at least she no longer found it necessary to provoke the group as before, and derived a much more healthy satisfaction from her new role than from her earlier role as scapegoat.

In Example 32, the choice of *Michael* as scapegoat was chance-determined, and served no discernible purpose for the boy concerned. Indeed, for one so anxious to be accepted and to conform, it was a painful and negative experience. However, with the possible exception of the most influential group members, almost any member of that group would have been the target of its projected guilt and anger had he been found masturbating by the others. Here, the scapegoat's allegedly deviant behaviour directly stirred up the group's repressed problem, and brought to expression not only its guilt about masturbation, but also the fear about this being a perversion.

The worker saw this as indicating the group's need for reasurrance. This he gave in terms of his own friendly and accepting attitudes towards the scapegoat, specific expression in the group of the universality of masturbatory practices, and direct reassurance about its not being a sign of homosexuality. Thus, support and acceptance reduced guilt and anxiety, and information provided a more rational basis for modified attitudes. The group quickly ceased to use Michael as scapegoat, but needed a long time to work through this problem, coming back to these questions in different ways on many occasions.

In Example 33, concerning *Anne*, it was symptomatic of this rather sick young woman that she attracted the projections of the group. The assignment to her of the scapegoat role again exemplifies scapegoating as mutual exploitation. Anne seemed convinced of her own utter worthlessness, and was admitted to the hospital after an attempt at suicide. In the group, as in other contexts, she was constantly testing out her value to others, and manipulating situations and relationships so as to confirm this picture of herself as useless. The hate-filled aggressive wishes (mainly towards parents) whose repression led to her self-castigation were thus inwardly turned, and in the scapegoating episode described we see her using the group as her agent.

It was not within this group worker's mandate to take up and interpret this material. All of the members were in individual or group psychotherapy in the hospital, and the agreed function of her group was to provide a supportive experience, encouraging achievement, facility of expression, and the stimulation of social skills. Understanding that the need for a scapegoat at this point arose from the demands of the group project, the worker was, however able to reduce the pressure by increasing her support to the group and taking a greater part in its planning activity and decision-taking. (This is consistent with Wilson and Ryland's (1949) formulation on the inverse ratio between social health of group members and the appropriate degree of intervention from the worker.) Thus the group-as-a-whole was protected, and enjoyed the ego-building experience of achievement at a pace more consistent with its potential. The group's decreased anxiety reduced the need to project their inadequacy upon Anne, and thus reduced their responsiveness to her neurotic needs.

It is of interest, in summary, to point out that the cases of Elizabeth, Michael and Anne and their groups all show the worker intervening in a particular way. The aim of the intervention seems in each case to have been to give the group-as-a-whole a reasurring experience of active support and clear acceptance of their guilt-provoking feelings and impulses. This reduced anxiety in the groups, and enabled the members to pull back their projections from the scapegoat. The energy hitherto expended on defence against anxiety and guilt was thus liberated for use on the maturational or other tasks of the group. The former scapegoat also clearly gains through relief from the pressure of the group's projections and punitive drives, being both less manipulated by the group, and more able to find relationships and a role in accordance with his more mature wishes and growth needs.

Both the scapegoat and the group are also helped in the context of their relationship with the worker. The latter, by avoiding playing in to the group's defences, helps them through their identification with himself to develop a reality-oriented approach to their problems, and to develop a less anxious and a better informed attitude towards both their own impulses and those of others. All three examples were from groups of young people. In being the non-judgemental parent-authority figure, the social worker leading youth groups also provides a valuable adult image to counteract the condemning uncomprehending stereotype of the adolescent's fantasy—and, sometimes, of his experience.

Where the scapegoat has a pathological need for this role, the withdrawal of the group's projections provides new problems for him. Within the context of social-group work—with its often limited opportunities for taking up and interpreting such material in the group—this will involve, as in the case of Anne, a need for individual help outside the group situation, preferably by some other worker. In some other group work situations, the worker might of course take the problem up in the group in some appropriate way, if doing so is consistent with the aims of the group and with the sanctions—implicit or explicit—of the worker/individual/group relationship.

Status

THE NATURE AND SOURCES OF STATUS

Status has been simply defined as "position in a social system" (Parsons, 1951). Benoit-Smullyan (1944) defines it as "relative position in a hierarchy'. He states that position is determined by varying degrees of prestige, or of political or economic potency, or combinations of these factors. The concept of status is frequently met in everyday life. People seem on the whole to be preoccupied with status phenomena. This preoccupation is also found among those with a more scientific interest in group processes, since very extensive group dynamics research has been addressed over the years to the manifestations, implications and sources of status. It is a fascinating aspect of group life, and is important to us all.

It is interesting to note that the term "status" is usually equated in everyday speech with "high status": "He has status", usually means "He has *high* status". This common distortion of the concept already suggests both the nature of our ambivalent interest in it and our awareness of its implications for social potency and success. There is a tendency to strive for high status, but not without a certain embarrassment on account of its association with self-interest and desire for power.

It is often contended that capitalistic Western societies, whose economy is built on competition, are particularly prone to status struggle, and that they are for this reason both spiritually and culturally impoverished. A popular sociological analysis of contemporary America, which develops this theme, is significantly entitled "The Status Seekers" (Packard, *op.cit.*). There is much truth in this contention. However, while comparative politics are outside both our scope and competence, it is our impression that the socialist and communist states are also not without their status problems. These may give rise to struggle which is often quite ruthless, though based upon quite other philosophical premises and rationalisations than in capitalist societies.

Our point is not a political but a behavioural one. Status is an important aspect of *all* human interaction. Indeed it pervades the whole animal world. The clarification of status in terms of leadership and territorial rights is the only motive for violence, other than predatory behaviour necessary for survival, in the much-maligned animal kingdom. There is both lethal and ritualistic battle for the leadership of herds of various species. Status in the herd, once defined, then involves different degrees of privilege in such matters as choice of mate, pasture or prey. High status (leadership) frequently implies responsibility for decisions on behalf of the herd in such matters as fight, flight, conflict-resolution or migration. Well-known experimental observations have shown how the pecking order among farm-yard hens is very precisely defined, a status distribution which carries with it important privileges or disadvantages for the individual birds, depending upon where they are placed in the hierarchy (Scheldrup-Ebbe, 1922). No doubt the unusual success of Adams' saga of the rabbits of Watership Down (*op. cit.*) derives from our preparedness to believe that also among the bunnies life *is* like that, not least in regard to the continuing and diverse attempts to find viable ways of organising societies and groups and of according, retaining and using status. In short, social living and status differentiation seem to be inseparable.

There are a number of important concomitants of status in human groups. The first of these is the amount of *power and influence* which is invested in people of given status. The higher the status, the greater the power, and vice versa. This power may be acknowledged and formalised, status being indicated by some kind of official ranking. Where this is so, there is clear understanding of the extent and limitations of power, influence and decision associated with such formally designated statuses. Examples of this would be committee chairman, ship's captain, shop-steward, foreman, drill-sergeant, secretary, etc. It is important to note that these titles indicate both status and role, the interdependence of which is a vital aspect of group structure. The various roles filled by different members are rarely regarded as being equally important for the group. Certain roles are therefore accorded higher status, provided the member filling such a role performs it adequately. Conversely, we may see members placed in certain roles precisely because of the degree of respect and influence with which the group already regards them, or because of their popularity. These observations remain true also in groups where status is not specified and reflected in a formal title. Status may be more informally acquired as an emerging product of the group process, and does not lead to any specified ranking.

People who have higher status, however acquired, have greater influence over others' behaviour, attitudes and perceptions than those of lower status. Numerous experiments and clinical reports as well as everyday observation, show how readily many of us suspend our capacity for rational opinion and objective judgement in order to ally ourselves with the views, attitudes and behaviour of high-status persons (see, *inter alia,* Ramsøy, 1964; Harvey and Rutherford, 1960; Horowitz *et al.,* 1951).

Status and *initiative* are also closely related. People of high status take the initiative more often than those of low status. Their initiative has also greater chances of success. Furthermore, there is a certain circularity in this, since those who take the initiative tend to be accorded high status by the groups in which they do so. In social-work groups we see frequently how initiative takers are accorded a high regard, which, because of this circularity, tends to persist. For example, a group may meet for the first time, and find it difficult to overcome their initial discomfort. A tense silence may develop. Or a group which is already in progress may meet obstacles which frustrate or confuse them. In these and similar situations the member who first speaks, or suggests an approach to the problem, performs a function which wins gratitude and regard. Thereafter, members will tend in similar situations to turn to this member, and, in general, will reflect their partial dependence upon him by according him power and respecting his views. Thus, initiators are often able to exert considerable influence for better or for worse, according to the appropriateness of the views and solutions which they propose. (There are exceptions to this, of course, since initiative by unpopular or marginally-placed members may be regarded as inappropriate, striving or impertinent, and may therefore depress rather than enhance status.)

Status is also related to what we might term the *privilege of deviance.* The relationship between them is, however, not entirely clear, as we will show. Since higher-status people participate actively and are deferred to in their groups, it would seem reasonable to assume that they manifest high degrees of both functional and normative integration, to use Feldman's terms. However, while there is agreement on their being highly orientated towards group aims, there is some dispute as to the extent of their conformity to its norms. We have already quoted Sherif and Sherif, who suggest that the latitude of acceptance of deviance is inversely proportional to members' status. Dittes and Kelly (1956) describe an experiment which, on the contrary, implies that higher-status members are freer to deviate from group norms than those of lower status. Sherif and Sherif, (1964), and elsewhere, Thibaut and Kelley (*op.cit.,* p.179) modify these propositions. They suggest that the latitude of acceptance is also related to the importance to group members of the behaviour concerned. Deviance by high status members in highly significant activities is unacceptable, although in less significant areas they may be permitted greater freedom to deviate than lower status members. This interpretation is still incomplete, and it is also somewhat inconsistent with a well-regarded proposal put forward by Hollander (1958), who suggests that it is precisely in areas significant to the group that high-status members' deviance may be most acceptable. This is predicated on the belief that their presumed superior resources in significant areas qualify them for more experimental behaviour. Their behaviour, though deviant, is a product of superior judgement and may lead the group into more fruitful avenues of action. This concept is called the "earning of idiosyncrasy credit". The picture is a confusing one. A recent hypothesis by Shichor proposing further clarification is introduced on p. 217 in our discussion of leadership. At this point we simply wish to draw attention to the fact that varying degrees of concern are shown by groups about the conformity or deviance of members of different status, although no conclusive observations of the intensity and quality of that concern as yet exist.

The sources of status, whether formally or informally acquired, are many. They include, according to the group and its situation, such factors as organisational ability, wealth, courage, seniority, verbal fluency, and degree of skill in the group's central activity, whether that be football, negotiation, crime, or surgery. These criteria will usually relate fairly directly to the group's expectations of the persons filling the various positions. They will therefore reflect the members' criteria for prestige, their values, and to a large extent their objectives and perceived needs at any given time. It is for this reason that the understanding of status phenomena is so informative a component of group diagnosis for the social worker, group therapist, teacher or indeed anyone attempting to work purposefully with groups.

Status distribution in social-work groups may be either formally or informally determined, according to the type of agency and group concerned. In such settings as youth clubs, clubs for the elderly or for discharged psychiatric patients, or treatment agencies where clients are both democratically and therapeutically involved in the milieu, a number of positions may be determined formally and specified as ranks. This is usually achieved by some kind of elective procedure. In other groups, where common problems are to be solved or clarified by some kind of counselling process, statuses will emerge informally. In the informal, and occasionally chaotic, milieu of some social-work groups, status may simply evolve, although the group aims may necessitate some formal recognition of the higher status roles, as in the following case.

Example 34. Setting: a municipal hostel for homeless men in a northern city. Some have lived there many years, some only during winter months, and others are transients. Average age about 50 years. The residents are physically, psychically and intellectually reduced by many years of vagrancy, malnutrition, imprisonment, alienation and alcoholism. They are "derelicts", with the lowest possible self-evaluation, and chaotically disorganised lives. Unlike residents in a similar setting described in the literature (Shapiro, 1966 and 1971), these men are markedly isolated from each other, as well as being collectively withdrawn from all but essential contact with the hostel staff.

Two social-work students took the initiative of introducing group work in the hostel, with the aim of reducing social isolation. It was hoped to develop a sense of community, and of personal worth, and to improve relationships and mutual understanding between clients and permanent staff. Much emphasis was placed on sharing pleasant activities— coffee and sandwiches, film shows, bingo and other games, for which the members took increasing responsibility. The group later moved into more externally directed activity, aimed at effecting change in their milieu. (A similar parallel project at another hostel culminated in a deputation meeting with the City Treasurer, which received considerable supportive publicity.)

Initially the group was quite unable to achieve any formal organisation, although this would have had advantages in organising activities, sounding opinions, making representations, etc. After some unsuccessful attempts, it became customary for younger, less-damaged members, with higher capacity for self-presentation, to "assume" chairmanship and membership of the committee, whereupon they were accepted as if they had been elected to these roles. Similarly, when a "committee member" had alcoholic episodes or journeyed on, some relatively capable member would step into his place. This informally assumed status would thereafter become formally recognised.

(This material is abstracted from a dissertation at the Norwegian State School of Social Work, Oslo, and from discussion with its authors, Skjaelsbak and Lundblad, 1972.)

With the exception of certain clearly apparent statuses at the extremes of the range, status usually tends to appear somewhat unclearly distributed within groups. The common image of typical status distribution as some kind of lineal spectrum from lowest to highest is an oversimplification. Rather, with the exception of the extremes, one sees a series of overlapping clusters of people with similar statuses. Only with time and careful observation may individual differences in the middle range be perceived. Sherif and Sherif (1964) have noted this in their study of adolescent reference groups. Their observation seems applicable to all groups within our experience.

Golding, in *The Lord of the Flies* (1954), describes the development of a group in which this aspect of status distribution, among other group processes, is vividly depicted. In this well-known story of a group of refugee children, isolated following the Third World War, we see two members almost immediately accorded high status. Each of these has his particular gifts and directions of leadership, and each his limitations. Equally early, we see one member become isolated and scorned for his particular characteristics. He is clearly, and at once, placed at the bottom of the status spectrum. Differentiation among the remaining members occurs only slowly. The group structure does not become further refined until the growing conflict between the two potential leaders leads to the formation of two separate and competing sub-groups, each of which requires a re-defining and clarification of structure below the leader level, with lieutenants, advisors and obedient followers all taking positions of more clearly defined prestige and function.

A MULTI-FACTORIAL APPROACH

We have already implied that several factors infuence the status which is achieved by the individual members of groups. Experience with social-work groups strongly suggests that status is determined by the interplay of individual predelictions, group needs and environmental pressures, in much the same way as role assignment, which we have earlier discussed. This is not surprising, since role and status are so closely related. We have seen that while "role" refers to the functions and behaviour of group members, "status" refers to the approval and influence accorded to members acting in their various roles. Status, like role, is therefore basically determined by the priorities arising from the group's perceived needs and the varying abilities of the individual members to act in accordance with these priorities. This includes behaviour in both the external and internal systems of the group, and functioning in both task and group-maintenance roles, according to the group's major concerns at any given time. These impressions from practice are to a large extent confirmed by a number of propositions and findings of group theorists and researchers. Jennings (1943), Gibb (1947) and others to whom reference will be made have also demonstrated that status-assignment is strongly influenced by the interaction of these various forces.

This multi-factorial approach to status calls into question the notion of "the born leader". It has long been popularly held that certain individuals carry with them a charisma compounded of gifts, persuasiveness, inherent power and high self-evaluation which almost predestines them for leadership. This, however, is an over-simplification.

Whether a particular member may acquire or be awarded the leader role is as much determined by the group's perception of needs as by the nature of that member's charisma.

We are again tempted to illustrate from secondary groups engaged in political struggle. Castro has been regarded as such a charismatic leader. But it was Batista before him, cynical, corrupt and brutally repressive, who aroused the needs among the people which could be met by the idealistic, puritanical, stern-father kind of leadership which Castro offers. Churchill has been regarded as another such charismatic leader. During the 1939-1945 War he was certainly a remarkably effective and highly acceptable leader, regarded with gratitude and awe, often approaching love, the errors and arrogance of pre-war domestic politics forgotten or forgiven. But his gifts were those of Mars, and immediately the war was over the British public chose others with other gifts and values to lead them in tackling the new problems of peace. Group needs change. The criteria for prestige therefore change, and the group may reject its leader if he is not able to adjust to the new expectations.

The group may at any time confer or withdraw leadership by choosing whether or not to follow. Despite the wide difference in the remedies which they propose, the revolutionary teachings of Mahatma Ghandi and Mao Tse-Tung have in common the basic truth that oppressors remain in power only as long as the people find the discomforts of accepting their leadership less burdensome than the discomforts of revolution.

From these general observations of status development in secondary groups (from which many relevant political arguments have consciously been admitted) we will now return to the small group. We will draw attention to two contrasting studies, discuss their findings, and again illustrate from similar observations in social-work groups.

A study by Borgatta, *et al.* (1954) found with "emphatic significance" that certain so-called "Great Men" retained top positions in a number of groups of different composition, and that the groups led by these Great Men were particularly productive and harmonious. This interesting study, whose methodology included both interaction process analysis and sociometric measurement, might at first sight seem to support the notion of the charismatic leader and to refute our multi-factorial approach to status distribution. However, this would be a misinterpretation of the study. This is partly because of the arguments put forward by Talland (*op.cit.,* see chap. VI), but mainly because the Great Man concept as defined by Borgatta, *et al.* (1954), includes by implication the element of the needs perceived by the group members. It does not confine itself to the personal charisma of the leader. Their definition of Great Men was not limited to individual assertiveness, but also included ability to facilitate the group tasks (a task, determined by the investigators, but also accepted by the group) and "social acceptability", that is popularity among co-members. This study, then, far from refuting a multi-factorial approach to status differentiation, emphasises the importance of the conjunction of task ability, acceptability and individual assertiveness in determining leadership.

Feldman (1969, *op.cit*), whose research on group cohesion was mentioned earlier, has studied the opposite end of the status spectrum. He used the concept of "intense personal dislike" to denote the feelings with which certain groups regard the member who is accorded lowest status and who is subjected to isolation and rejection. In the groups studied, he found that such "intensely disliked persons" contributed negligibly, if at all, to the attainment of essential group goals. They also expressed or demonstrated low commitment to the norms espoused by their fellow group members. They were little involved in intra-group communication and interaction, and they expressed little liking for their co-members. In Feldman's terms, they demonstrated low levels of functional, normative and inter-personal integration. That is to say, in addition to their personal idiosyncracies, their extremely low status was related to their lack of involvement in both group-task and group-maintenance behaviour, and to their apparent indifference to the group's attempts to deal with both its external and internal problems.

Of the numerous studies of status which might be cited, we have selected the above for brief comment since they are concerned with opposite extremes of status. They both support our general proposition, derived from social-work practice, that the whole range of statuses is determined by interplay between environmental, intra-group and individual personality forces.

The two following examples, which concern low and high status respectively, illustrate briefly something of how this complex interplay may be manifested in social-work groups.

Example 35. A group of parents of handicapped children were formulating an open letter to the authorities responsible for provision of treatment and educational facilities. The letter was to be signed by all members, and sent to several major newspapers. One member repeatedly suggested more diplomatic and circumlocutory formulations, advocating caution for fear of official resentment. "We must not tread on the authorities' toes." We do not know whether her placatory behaviour was due to a general anxiety about aggression, or to her fear that certain assistance she had recently applied for might be refused if she became publicly associated with a "troublesome" group. But whatever the explanation of her behaviour, she was rapidly accorded low status in the group, her comments first being rejected and then either ignored or ridiculed. Her position can only be understood in terms of an interaction between environmental, group and individual factors.

Example 36. In Example 30 on page 153 we referred to a group of cardiac failure patients, in which a particular member became central person. He was also accorded high status, because of the advantages to the group-as-a-whole of his being placed in a position of informal leadership. The fact of sickness, the need for subsequent social readjustment, and the hospital milieu itself aroused certain group needs. These were primarily of acquiring knowledge and attitudes to cardiac conditions conducive to appropriate co-operation with medical advisors and, implicitly, dealing with the anxiety and shock aroused by traumatic illness and sudden hospitalisation. While these problems are, with fatal frequency, "solved" by denial or regressive over-dependence, the group cited was fortunate in including a mature and articulate member who had already learned to manage them very well indeed. External conditions (both present and future), the group's perceived needs and this member's personal resources combined to determine both his role as central person and his status as leader. (These, as we earlier have noted, are not always synonymous.)

Where, as in this group, members are concerned with the solution of problems arising from their common situation, higher status will be given to the member or members whose resources or behaviour tend to promote problem-solution, and low status to members whose behaviour inhibits such problem-solution. The published case report to which this material refers (Goldner and Kyle, *op. cit.*) focuses, not upon the central person, but upon another member. His role is described as that of "problem-finder", in that his highly defensive behaviour and attitudes help the group to locate the issues which are most important for them to work on. In a group where environmental factors and group perceptions resulted in more intense and self-destructive defence against recognising problems, such a member might well be accorded high status, precisely because his own defensive behaviour aids the group in avoiding confrontation with painful common problems.

ASCRIBED STATUS

We have so far presented a tidy picture of status distribution as a purposive process achieving balance between the needs of the group and the individual and the demands of the environment. The process is by no means always so purposive and rational, however.

Benoit-Smullyan (1944) points out that persons of high prestige may be objects of admiration, or deference, or imitation, and may be sources of suggestions and centres of attraction.

> Admiration may or may not be based on objective characteristics or personal achievements. Deference is the symbolic expression of another's priority, manifested in the presumptive right of another to take the initiative. ... With regard to imitation we may say that the behaviour of the person of high prestige becomes a model and is deliberately or unconsciously reproduced by others. Deliberate imitation may be intended to create a favourable impression upon the one imitated, but in many cases some mechanism like identification will probably be required to account for the imitative behaviour. . . (Such persons) are sources of suggestion, in that the ideas they express are accepted more readily than the same ideas expressed by others.

Clearly, these are not processes which are always dominated by reasoning and rationality. We are by no means always conscious of our deference, our imitative behaviour or of the springs of our admiration. These often arise in the world of symbol and fantasy. Echoes of earlier experiences distort our current perceptions and evaluations and cause us to imbue both situations and other people with characteristics which they may not possess. Status-assignment is thus not always rationally and appropriately related to the realities of the group situation and to the members' needs, nor are a member's real qualities and capacities always reflected in the status which the group affords him. A common example of this merits special mention.

Our perceptions of others—at Goffmann's non-focused interaction level—may cause us to "defer to and imitate" people in a given situation simply because they possess high status in some other setting. They may respond to our assumptions of their authority, or we to their own expectations of high status, or both, even though they may not be at all equiped for leadership in the actual context. Numerous generals have become Presidents of the U.S.A., although military skills are of dubious relevance to the resolution of internal racial strife, intricate questions of social, economic and environmental planning, or delicate and subtle questions of foreign policy and relations. A medical doctor, as member of a child care committee, could hardly avoid becoming its chairman even if he wished to do so. But we must search very hard indeed in the medical training for content which gives insight into family dynamics, into appropriate dispositions in questions of psycho-social conflict and deprivation, or into the administrative problems of social services and institutions. Our point is not that other members of such committees are necessarily better qualified, but that both they and the appointing executive assume that the doctor is. The process is one of habitual deference. People are appropriately accorded high status in situations where they have special competence or high formal rank, and then dependence upon them spills over into situations where their competence or rank have little or no relevance.

This so-called "halo effect" is one example of what has been called "ascribed" as opposed to "achieved" status.

In social-work groups, the phenomenon of ascribed status is also frequently encountered, although the criteria on which it is based are less obvious than in our examples of generals and doctors. Observations from practice suggest some common dynamics. The member who is ascribed status, rather than achieving it, often seems by his self-presentation, attitudes or appearance to expect a particular status. Again, this is more readily apparent at the extremes of status. A member is likely to be ascribed high status if his bearing or dress imply a higher socio-economic background. He may emanate a real or pretended confidence in a new group situation which others find threatening and inhibiting. It may be known, or he may make it known, that he has a background and experiences which are ascribed high prestige either by that particular group or by society at large. He may simply take the initiative and assume leadership functions, in a manner implying both that he is accustomed to doing so and that is is advantageous to the group.

But clearly the perceived needs of the group also enter this picture, though perhaps at a less rational level than in the situations previously discussed. There is a common tendency in situations of uncertainty to invest hope in the seemingly strong man. By becoming dependent upon his apparent strengths the group reduces its anxiety and relieves the demand upon members for appropriate and effective functioning. Whether his strength is real or an over-compensated response to insecurity is not at that point relevant, although it may later become a critical question. Indeed, the greater our uncertainty, the more we seem to wish to imbue our potential leaders with illusionary but extra-ordinary powers. This is one of the aspects of charisma which enables the dictator to emerge from the confused mass, or the self-assertive and immature client to dominate for a time a small group of others in a painful and threatening situation.[4] Thus, such factors as low self-evaluation, insecurity, dependence and immaturity may initially predispose members of a client group to ascribe status in this manner. Persisting role traditions are also relevant, causing members to ascribe high prestige to people imbued with authority and responsibility, such as the worker himsef, or to fellow clients who are members of high-status professions, trades or other groups.

It is important to add that an unconscious manipulative element may also be present when group members seem willing to abrogate responsibility and (ambivalently) to idealise a strong leader. The defeated client, experiencing his own inadequacy as painful, often by his very dependence manipulates the worker or other members into authoritarian responses, such as taking decisions, ignoring, rejecting, giving directive advice, or making provisions which the member could make himself. The dependent member is then, in his fantasy, no longer responsible for what has happened in the group or for the consequences of accepting the leadership, which has been passively manipulated. Both present and future failures thus becomes less painful, since others are responsible for them. "If only I had not taken your advice. ... " Further, these others are thereby shown to be less than omnipotent, since they share the defeated member's inability to "solve" his problem. This again serves the purpose of increasing his self-evaluation, although the reality of his situation is in no way changed.

Whether or not group members ascribe status in this way, and how far they persist in doing so, may be a valuable indicator of such factors as members' growth potential and resources, their self-evaluation, their possible reistance to change, and ambivalence about problem-solving. It may therefore bring into focus appropriate areas for such intervention as support, invitation to group reflection, confrontation, or interpretation.

Social workers, who are also fallible human beings with problems, share very many attributes with their clients, including the tendency readily to ascribe status to others, particularly high status. The professional team is also a group in which the social worker is involved, and many of our comments on the manifestations and motivations of ascribed status in client groups are equally relevant to team situations. Our impression is that the social worker's struggle for professional recognition is an ambivalent one, for we often see that when confronted with opportunities for the exercise of professional skills, initiative and decision, many social workers are lamentably ready to thrust responsibility onto team colleagues who represent the better-established professions.

Lawyers, teachers, doctors, political scientists, architects who look to the social worker for his contribution are often met by power-laden preconceptions of their own role. The social worker inappropriately ascribes to them status in his own field, as well as appropriate status in their own. Because of the reciprocal nature of role-behaviour—each social role involving interaction, and therefore calling forth complementary role-behaviour—these colleagues may then behave with authority and assumed expertise. The dynamics of this distorted and unproductive interaction resemble those of the client groups earlier discussed. Insecurity leads to the surrender of autonomy and thus to dependence. Earlier role models cause certain kinds of people to become the targets and recipients of dependency needs. Abrogation of professional responsibility causes reduced self-evaluation, which in turn gives rise to externally displaced aggression, and thus to diffuse tension and perhaps manipulation in the team. Loeb (*op.cit.*), applying role theory to interdisciplinary practice, describes a typical situation, here paraphrased:

> A (the social worker) and B (the psychiatrist) co-operated for the first time in a professional task, both contributing their insights and skills in the exploration of a problem. At the close of the discussion, in which agreement was reached, B remarked, "Well, that's that". This was intended to express satisfaction and recognition of shared accomplishment. A, investing B with authority, interpreted this as dismissal.
> A's next moves reflected his response to this distorted perception of the situation, not to reality. He moved into the roles of placator, suppliant for help and direction, and maintainer of continuity of this new-found relation, which he found fying. B then shifted into the roles of supervisor and director.

ver, is only one side of the coin. Not only high status

may be ascribed rather than achieved. Low status, accorded in one situation, also tends readily to be transferred to new situations without the person concerned having acted in a manner in itself conducive to being regarded with low prestige. The proverb "Give a dog a bad name ... " has its roots, like many cliché's, in valid everyday observation.

Such ascribing of low status may have several causes. Perhaps the person involved expects low prestige, owing to the accumulation of earlier experiences. He may, therefore, consciously or unconciously, signal these expectations to others, thereby ensuring that he is ascribed low status. The social worker in Loeb's study did this. Many of our clients find themselves trapped in this web of self-fulfilling expectations and rejecting experiences. For example, a discharged prisoner who is being interviewed for a job, in anguish because of his need and anxiety, may behave apologetically, or defiantly or untruthfully. Thus his presentation of his case militates against equal treatment and respectful regard. (Green's group of unemployed ghetto-dwellers to which we referred earlier was occupied with this kind of problem, and used role-play of work-application interviews as one means of drawing members' attention to their own contribution to the problem.)

Or the needs in a group which have led to their ascribing low status to a given member may be particularly inflexible. Thus the group continues to need an object to deride so that they may assert, by negative example, their perceived standards, values and aims. In some groups this serves the additional purpose of giving some relief from the emotional pressure of repressed wishes. People who have earlier suffered low prestige, whether they are in the group or outside it, are readily available targets. For example, while the Good Citizen's own restrained impulses to occasional irresponsibility and asociality gain some measure of satisfaction by vicarious participation in crime and errant eroticism (TV, book's, cinema, newspapers, etc.), the need to assuage guilt for these fantasies remains. The actual perpetrators must therefore be punished and ostracised. Thus, our discharged prisoner mentioned above, no matter how well he handled the situation, would automatically be ascribed very low status in most social settings other than his peer-group. Mrs. Green, in e.g. 25 (p. 111), representing the "bad woman" for her community, was similarly ascribed a low status because of the submerged emotional conflicts of the group. This, however, was diametrically opposed to the status which would have resulted from a rational evaluation of her potential contribution to that particular group!

Inter-group factors may also determine the low status ascribed to an individual. He may belong to some secondary group, perhaps a racial or religious minority, who are stereotypically imbued with certain common and prejudicial characteristics. His potential value to the new group, and therefore his status, is often defined by the prevailing attitudes to the secondary group with which he is associated, rather than by what he could potentially contribute and achieve. Economic, political or sexual anxieties seem to provide the bases for this kind of status ascription. Since we "know" that our coloured brothers and Southern Europeans are less energetic, less disciplined and less well educated than Northern Europeans it is not discriminatory but merely good sense to restrict immigrant foreign workers as long as possible to employment in routine manual work subject to close supervision. At another level the argument is advanced that they are accustomed to much lower living standards and, given the opportunity, would under-cut wages in better-paid areas of employment. Short-term work contracts are the obvious answer to this, adding the stigma of transience and impermanence to their existing disadvantages. They are thus compelled into the suspicion-laden status limbo occupied for generations by the gypsy, the itinerant and the nomad. At yet another level, though less frequently articulated, lies the threatening fantasy of the darker man's greater sexual prowess and his almost legendary penis. "Half of them only come here for our light-skinned Northern girls, anyway." Stereotypes flourish in this atmosphere of irrational fear and prejudice, walling round the individual's capacity for self-realisation by limited and limiting preconceptions of what he is capable of performing.

This process is highly relevant to the kinds of problems which may give rise to social action, and also to the obstacles met when implementing purposive programmes. Two episodes related to the same tragic incident may illustrate this.

Martin Luther King was assassinated during the course of demonstrations which were ostensibly concerned with wage and other claims of coloured workers who held certain badly paid jobs. Specht (1969), in an important paper on "disruptive tactics", discusses the situation thus.

> Memphis, Tennessee, in the events preceding the assassination of Martin Luther King, was not confronting a simple question of the redistribution of resources as in an ordinary labor dispute. That the striking workers recognised the question of status was quite evident in their signs that read: "I Am a Man!" for indeed it was their manhood they perceived to be at stake. That the Mayor of Memphis saw it the same way is clear from this statement that he would be damned if he would be the first southern mayor to bargain collectively with a black union.

Dr. King's mantle is now ably born by Jesse Jackson. This brilliant young man, theologian, orator and expert community organisor, who may yet become one of the most influential American politicians of our time, approached the Mayor of Chicago offering his services in the attack upon racial strife. The Mayor offered him work—sweeping up. That, after all, is the kind of work which negroes do (Jackson, 1969).

Both of these episodes show us that vitally important positions may be taken on questions of status because of inflexible needs in the group, and because evaluations of individuals may be determined by stereotypic perceptions of their sub-cultural groups, rather than by their resources and self-presentation as unique individual human beings.

We will briefly mention one further aspect of ascribed status which merits attention by social workers. This concerns the observation that prestige is contagious. That is to say, the status of people with whom we have contact becomes in some strange way extended into and partly determinant of our own status. We "participate in the prestige" of people with whom we have contact, "at least to the extent of raising or lowering our own". Benoit-Smullyan (*op. cit.,* p.157) observes: "... even menial services rendered to a king tend to ennoble, and the servants of the great assume a supercilious demeanor. Per contra, close association with those of markedly lower prestige status tends to degrade. ... " We suggest that particularly the latter part of this observation is of interest to the social worker, for two reasons.

In the first place, it refers to one important determinant of the status accorded to many clients, both by other clients in groups and by the organisations which impinge upon their lives, including the welfare services. The social worker, too, must exercise great care to avoid ascribing regard and assessing potential resources in this kind of way. But how difficult it is! From tenement-block X one has encountered and attempted to help five families, all characterised by marked immaturity, poverty, improvidence and instability. When a sixth couple from the same block apply for help it is difficult to avoid colouring one's initial expectations of them by earlier experiences of their neighbours. Were they to enter a client group, it is highly likely that their status as group members would also there be ascribed in this way.

Such so-called "prestige contagion" is also of interest since it may well in another context influence the position of the social worker himself. The profession has so far been conspicuously unsuccessful in influencing the situation in which its preventive and treatment functions are performed. We have been virtually impotent in affecting social legislation. We have been only spasmodically effective in contributing to appropriate change at the local and agency level. In innumerable agencies the social worker remains subordinate to others, with or without alternative training, who are charged with directing the social worker's efforts, and who feel themselves quite competent to do so. Even the training of new members of the profession is a function in which social workers often have only a subordinate role. Perhaps this may be connected with the fact that most practising social workers are engaged daily in direct work with low-status people. Our hypothesis is that the low status of social work among the professions is partly attributable to our "participation in the (low) prestige" of those people with whom we "regularly associate". Some evidence supporting this may be found in the increased influence of those colleagues who enter the academic field or social planning and administrative positions which involve little or no direct contact with low-status clients. This hypothesis is not in conflict with our earlier suggestion that the social worker's low self-evaluation contributes to his being ascribed low professional status. In a multi-factorial model, these hypotheses are complementary.

CHANGES IN THE STATUS STRUCTURE

We have seen that group needs are important contributory determinants of the criteria for high or low status. Every group, however, is a dynamic entity, steadily undergoing change. The needs which members perceive, or to which they give priority, therefore, also change. Some implications of this for role-assignment have already been touched upon. Equally important are the re-adjustments of status structure consequent upon such developments as maturation or problem-solving by members, change in the relationship with the immediate milieu, successful completion of tasks, or more appropriate identification of group objectives.

Again, the impact of these changes seems to be more readily apparent at the extremes of the status range. Changes in perceived needs may cause change in leadership, perhaps in its occupancy and style as well as its direction. But new grounds for rejection and isolation may equally well arise from such developments, producing status changes at the lower end of the range which are also more visible than the adjustments and re-alignments of the middle range.

These issues arise in the following case extract:

Example 37. (This example is taken from a similar setting and the same period as example 3, p. 29. Also in discussion of group work method the two examples may profitably be compared.)

A penal institution commenced a scheme of group counselling as a well-intentioned step in the direction of a treatment orientation. The social worker, among others, was to have a series of problem-centred open groups of prisoners. At that early and tentative stage, there had been only minimal investment in motivating the prisoners to participate, and the objectives of the groups were equally unclear for all concerned.

The social worker had one group consisting of eight clients, all of whom had extensive criminal records and had served several periods of imprisonment. Most, if not all, had established defensive, suspicious and oppositional attitudes to authority in general, and to prison and police personnel in particular.

At the first meeting, there were long periods of strained and hostile silence. This was first relieved when a member exploded into an angry expression of suspicion about the group programme. The worker's rather passive acceptance of this seemed to provoke this member into yet further and more scornful rejection of the proffered "treatment" and of the social worker's person. The other members remained silent, but with occasional brief comments and signs they expressed their agreement and support of the active member.

This pattern was sustained during several subsequent meetings. The group-as-a-whole remained passive, still uncertain and suspicious but, by their silent consensus in this less inhibited member's continued attack, gave vicarious expression to their own aggression and their anxiety about being further manipulated in the group. The active member's role was that of spokesman for group attitudes and feelings. Through his performance of this role he was accorded highest status in the group.

With time, however, members experienced the group situation as less threatening. The worker's reaction to the earlier testing out was reassuring. They gradually changed their perception of him. He was no longer regarded as some kind of spy or agent provocateur for the Governor, but rather as a somewhat naîve, optimistic, but decent-enough type who perhaps really and truly wished to help them.

"... Not that we need any help, of course, but. ... " The group's aggression and suspicion was greatly reduced. It was not a long step from this to a relatively positive attitude towards the meetings, and to the awakening of ability to invest something in them. In consequence, they no longer needed a member to express their own earlier guarded feelings of resistance and suspicion. But the earlier spokesman for these feelings was too well established in his role to change. He was "stuck with his role", both because of his insensitivity to change in the group atmosphere and needs, and no doubt also because of his own high personal aggressivity and anxiety. He thus hindered the group in their attempts to use the meetings constructively. Their irritation with him grew to such an extent that the group eventually collectively proposed that he withdraw from membership.

The perceived needs of the group had changed. A member who had earlier performed an important role for them no longer did so. On the contrary, he restricted the group in their attempts to satisfy newly perceived needs. As his role changed from the most central to the most peripheral, his status also changed from the highest to the lowest. Yet he and his behaviour were entirely unchanged!

In this case, change in a member's status resulted from change in group needs brought about by an improved relationship to the immediate environment and by perceptual changes in the members. The perceived need swung from that of ventilating suspicion and aggression to that of discussing common psycho-social problems. This kind of process could equally well be illustrated by other common changes in perceived needs. Our earlier discussion of the "clown" role and some common dynamics of that role assignment could well be included here, for example.

It is important, however, to take note that we must not *always* assume that prominent high-status members necessarily reflect and express group needs and attitudes by their behaviour, although they very often do so, as in Example 37. There is a current tendency, however, to somewhat facile group diagnosis which assumes that all dramatic or assertive individual behaviour which is not opposed by the group is vicarious communication by the group-as-a-whole. This may only be assumed, and then only tentatively, if the worker's observation of the group's relationship to its environment, of the intra-group processes and of the individual members' needs support such an assumption. The issues of differentiation and integration are again raised here.

Such behaviour is often simply individual role behaviour (in Benne and Sheats' sense) which the group passively accept because of indifference, anxiety about the assertive member's possible reaction to attempts at group control, or because of their need for help in locating and expressing more relevant comment and behaviour. Indeed, a part of group work method consists of examining the extent to which individual comment or behaviour is idiosyncratic, or to which it may provide an opening enabling the group-as-a-whole more clearly to manifest their shared problems, attitudes and perceptions.

Change in the status structure of the group may also result from the social worker's interventions. Several models of social group work method implicitly or explicitly refer to influencing status criteria and distribution as one of the worker's tasks. While discussion of such models is outside the scope of this volume, we may briefly illustrate this kind of change in status distribution by referring yet again to Example 25, which referred to a group of parents of pre-school children who had been advised to postpone commencement of school attendance. The parents whom we called Mr. and Mrs. Brown initially had very high status. The single mother whom we called Mrs. Green had very low status. The worker's concern for the Browns was to enable them to experience, and then to work on, the sense of failure which caused their angrily defensive behaviour. His concern with Mrs. Green was not only that she should gain the clarification and information which she sought, but that her open, undefended and relevant contributions should be better used by the group-as-a-whole. The worker's interventions also had the secondary effects of reducing the intensity and frequency of the Browns' contributions, and thereby their status, and of arousing the group's interest in Mrs. Green's points, thus implicitly emphasising their value and relevance, and increasing her status. This case extract, therefore, shows us status change in opposite directions and from both extremes as a result of social work intervention.

TYPES AND STYLES OF LEADERSHIP

No matter how brief our discussion of status phenomena, we may hardly conclude without some comment on the ways in which the status structure manifests itself in the exercise and acceptance of various types and styles of leadership. While we have earlier mentioned the popular tendency to confuse "status" with "high status", there is little doubt that this end of the status spectrum is the one which is most decisive for the group's functioning. It is also perhaps the most informative area of study for the observer who, for whatever professional reasons, wishes to understand the needs, aims and problems of the group.

Democratic, authoritarian and laissez-faire leadership

A much-quoted series of studies conducted by Lewin, Lippitt and White (1938, 1939, 1953) investigated three alternative styles of leadership. Their findings have important consequences for group leaders in many varieties of group, including social workers. Lewin, Lippitt and White distinguish between authoritarian, democratic and *laissez-faire* leadership. They were able to show that authoritarian leadership produced more work over a short period of time, but engendered aggression, competitiveness and hostility, both within the group and in relation to leadership. Further, orginality was inhibited, while dependence was stimulated. Democratically-led groups were initially less productive, but became more productive as they learned how to co-operate, and as members developed positive relationships with each other and with the leader. Motivation and satisfaction remained high, and participants used their resources well. *Laissez-faire* groups were less productive than either of the above, spending a disproportionate amount of time in discussing their tasks, and—probably because of frustration—engendered more aggression than the democratic groups, though less than the authoritarian groups. (These findings may also remind the reader of some of Leavitt's observations on the consequences of patterns of communication mentioned in Chapter 5.)

These styles of leadership may be exercised in a number of ways. Macarov (*op. cit.*) divides authoritarian (autocratic) leadership into the styles of the bully, the example, the manipulator, the exploiter, the briber and the sacrificer.[5] Common to all is that the leader is primarily concerned with his own objectives and needs, and only incidentally with those of the group. To the autocrat, the group is a tool. Many forms and formulae are also possible where democratic leadership is concerned, but common to all truly democratic groups is the recognition of the individual's ability to contribute and of his right to differ—also from the leader. The leader in his turn, although obtaining personal satisfaction from leadership, does not exploit the group by manipulating it to meet his own needs.[6] *Laissez-faire* leadership seems to arise either where the group is very vague about its objectives—perhaps because of a very heterogeneous membership or of ambiguity in the initial offer of group service—or where it is denied the opportunity to develop a more purposive internal structure because "responsibility" for the group is regarded as being a function of an authoritarian environment.

While we attempt in this book to avoid discussion of social-work method, we are compelled to indicate that these studies have important practical implications concerning the worker's own role as formal leader of client groups, the indigenous leadership style which is most profitable for the members, and, finally, the understanding of some of the tensions and problems of social-work agencies and other institutions.

Mature and immature leadership

Related psychoanalytical observations by Freud (1950) and Alexander (1942) are discussed by Scheidlinger (1952, *op. cit.*) in the context of "mature and immature leadership". Freud described a personality type which readily assumed a constructive and democratic leader role in an acceptable way. Such persons were described as being independent, active, relatively free of internal conflict, and as tending to "give" emotionally rather than to "take".

Such people impress the observer, and as leaders they tend to give fresh stimulus to cultural development and to be orientated towards change. With the sensitivity to others' feelings and needs arising from their own freedom from conflict, such "mature leaders" may truly represent their groups and thus use the influence inherent in high status in the service of group goals. Scheidlinger sees the relative degrees of emotional independence and dependence, i.e. security and insecurity, as decisive personality factors in the emergence of leadership or of readiness to be led.

"Immature leadership" corresponds closely with what we have discussed above as "authoritarian" or "autocratic" leadership, in that primacy is given to the satisfaction of the leader's needs rather than those of the group. Such role behaviour may serve compelling needs for power and control over others. This kind of exploitation, in addition to its possible tangible and conscious gains for the leader, also permits a symbolic or actual living out of anxieties and conflicts, the immature leader often being, unlike the mature leader, deeply conflicted. Scheidlinger reminds us how frequently delusionary ideas or other pathological conditions have been evidenced by dictators throughout history. Very commonly, immature authoritarian leadership is in fact a compensatory defence against repressed feelings of inadequacy and impotence, or fears of inability to deal with potential competition or hostility in the environment or group. Rigidity of behaviour and attitudes will therefore also tend to characterise immature leaders. Very many cases could be quoted here, but the point probably does not need illustration.

The impact of immature leadership on the group is to foster immature behaviour among members, with regression to earlier levels of behaviour. Members manifest dependence and either passive receptivity or diffuse aggression. At the same time, efforts at individual problem-solving, growth and environmental mastery are again suspended, as in earlier life situations when subject to authoritarian and dependency-producing control.

We may wonder why some groups accept such leadership? The tidy and rational pattern of status distribution and leadership choice described earlier seems to suffer a setback where an immature leader is accepted. We have seen that fear may be one factor explaining this, and also that the group may be unable without external help either to depose the autocrat or to locate the needs which call for a more mature and democratic leader. We will also return in Chapter 8 to the suggestion that authoritarian leadership may in fact represent and meet the survival needs of the group during the uncertainty and ambivalence of group formation, although this need will typically decline as such initial problems are solved.

Another important point here is that the immature leader may well succeed in "getting things done", but it is always a critical question whether what they choose to "get done" coincides with the needs of the groups concerned or only of the leader. However, given that a group accepts an immature leader's interpretation of their needs, it may occur—as in the Lewin, Lippitt and White studies—that group goals are rapidly achieved. The price paid for this, however, is that members become increasingly dependent and gain little satisfaction from achievement. Since they are less identified with what has been achieved, they may also readily return to the situation and attitudes which prevailed before membership. Where the members reject such a leader's interpretation of their needs, but are not able to mobilise opposition, they tend strongly to develop internal conflicts, verbally to express conformity but behaviourally to deviate surreptitiously, and when outside the group will minimally identify themselves with its norms and values. The behaviour of long-term prison inmates or hospital patients comes readily to mind.

Finally, there may be an unexpressed coincidence of aims, perhaps even verbally denied, between the dependent group and the immature leader where the latter's manifest aims and values are open to popular disapprobation. To return to secondary groups for an example, it is surely no coincidence that ambitious, immature and brutal dictators such as Hitler and Mussolini were able to gain support and control at a point in their respective countries' histories when the populace were depressed, poor, divided and aimless, and in the case of Germany were shamed by recent defeat and the loss of the dream of dominion over Europe. They needed someone to blame, and they needed ego-building experiences. Their new-found leaders offered them both—on the one hand the Jews, and on the other, new conquest.

There is an analogy here to the social work situation. Many clients suffer feelings of defeat, inadequacy, guilt and disorientation on account of their problems. They may therefore be prone as a group to accept the authoritarian leadership of immature members. This is both because of the dependent feelings generated by their own inadequacy, and because the immature leader often offers invitingly simplistic approaches, including projective defence, to what are assumed—perhaps quite accurately—to be common problems.

This is a recurring situation in group-work practice, which the worker approaches at two levels. According to the extent of pathology or immaturity in the leader, the worker has more or less possibility of helping him to modify his leadership style. At the same time, members may be helped by supportive techniques to increase their self-esteem and to locate in themselves alternative resources to those apparently represented by the leader.

Examples 25 and 37 (pp. 119 and 179) may serve again to illustrate immature leadership, as well as appropriate and inappropriate social-work intervention in dealing with it. *The Lord of the Flies,* so rich a source of illustrative material, shows how an immature leader, Jack, narcissistic and dictatorial, was able gradually to gain dominance over the group as members' increasing fear, impotence and disorientation caused them to regress to a stage of extreme dependency. Golding's observation of this boy's motivation for dominance is also well in accord with group theory. Jack's arrogant assumption of leadership, coincident with his inability to meet the real needs of the group, reminds of the proposition by Sternback (1947) that "some narcissists need to be leaders in a group, or else they become too anxious if confronted with a reality that does not correspond to their inflated self-estimation".

Instrumental and integrative leadership

Other distinctions between types and functions of leadership have also been made. We have seen that Bales distinguishes between task-centred and socially emotionally centred interaction. Similarly, Benne and Sheats differentiate between task-centred and group-maintenance role-functions. This kind of distinction is met again in leadership theory.

Bales (1955), using the terminology of systems theory, distinguishes between the "instrumental-adaptive" leadership function and the "integrative-expressive" function. Verba (1961), making a similar distinction, also uses the term "affective" to denote the latter aspect of leadership. Whatever terminology may be used, there is considerable agreement among observers of group behaviour about the duality of the task of leadership. On the one hand, leadership must serve the purposes of goal-attainment, problem-finding and decision-taking or decision facilitation. No matter how democratically conducted, this is a structuring and directive activity. This is the instrumental-adaptive function. (While "instrumental" is in this context self-explanatory, perhaps we should mention that "adaptive" here refers to adaptation to the group environment. The implication is that instrumental-adaptive leadership is particularly involved in the external system of the group.) Leadership must, however, also ensure that the atmosphere and relationships in the group are at least sufficiently positive to enable the group to survive and to wish to continue the common task. This is the integrative-expressive, or affective, function of leadership.

These are not alternative leadership styles, but are mutually supplementary functions. Since both group-task and group-maintenance roles are necessary in every group, it follows that both instrumental and affective leadership are always present. This fact partly explains how rarely we can point to any one person as *the* indigenous leader of his group. More usually we find a small cluster, often more than two members, who seem collectively to share the leadership function. Slater (1955) found that differentiation and specialization of leadership occurred in widely varying degrees in different groups. Some degree of specialization of leadership function was, however, always present within this cluster of high-status members.

Instrumental leadership is oriented towards achievement, mobilisation and change. It therefore induces resistance, tension and some loss of popularity. This was already indicated in our earlier discussion of interaction phenomena. However, where one member can be identified as integrative-expressive leader, he is usually also the most popular member of the group. This is not surprising, since affective leadership—unlike instrumental leadership—tends to support existing ideas and relationships, and aims at maximising mutual attraction and the lessening of tension.

It is clear that different personality characteristics are involved in these two leadership functions. While both are probably present to some extent in most people, it is rare indeed that they are equally apportioned and one or other tends to dominate in each individual. It is mainly for this reason that specialisation occurs. Nevertheless, there tends to be duality rather than a dichotomy of leadership. The rather contrasting personalities which express themselves through these different leadership functions seem on the whole to co-operate in achieving satisfactory leadership. Bales (1955) makes an interesting observation about this. He suggests that:

> . . . a kind of "coalition" exists between the top instrumental-adaptive leader and the best-liked man. They suspend their status struggle and "tacitly agree", as it were, not to undercut each other, which is to say, not be "seduced" into attempting to form a coalition with lower status members in order to displace each other. If such a coalition can be formed, it becomes quite difficult for lower status members to revolt, unseat the top men, or develop the norms of the group in any different direction.

In the context of social work with groups such differentiation certainly occurs. However, one or other of these aspects of leadership seems to predominate according to the major preoccupations of the group. The supplementary function sometimes becomes so recessive that it is barely observable. In a group of clients, sharing some urgent and compelling problem, perhaps meeting frequently over a brief period, the instrumental function is dominant in leadership and the maintenance role is less important owing to the high motivation and is not accorded such high status. Nevertheless it will at times, even in short-term groups, affect the group's ability to progress in problem-solving. (Certainly it will have played an important role in ensuring the group's survival at the time of formation.)

Conversely, some clients are in situations of protracted and unalleviated dependence upon each other, where the group is not merely a transitory expedience, but provides their life-milieu. The residents of an old people's home provide a case in point. In such groups the affective element in leadership—the maintenance function—is usually dominant, except in brief periods of engagement in particular tasks. High status will tend to be accorded to the people best able to "keep the group going".

These concepts may also illuminate a problem which has already been mentioned, namely the confused issue of group response to non-conformity on the part of high-status members. Shichor (1970) suggests that the "latitude of acceptance" of deviance by leaders is primarily determined by whether they derive their high status from instrumental or integrative functions, and in which of these areas they exhibit deviance.

> Therefore, it is suggested that the possible fields of nonconformity for the instrumental leader will be in the integrative dimensions of group life, and the possible fields of nonconformity of integrative leaders will be in the instrumental dimensions. . . .
>
> As a word of caution, it must be stated that these leeways of conformity for the different types of leaders must be within certain boundaries, that they will not cause serious damage to group life, because if they exceed these boundaries, it could cause the disintegration of the group. . . .

Some of the apparent disagreement in the literature may be resolved by Schichor's reasoning, although as yet his propositions have not to our knowledge been subjected to empirical research. However, they do appeal to reason, and arouse associations from one's practice. Thus, the cheerful and popular "Life of the Party" in the old people's home may not necessarily lose esteem if he disagrees with the majority about, for instance, a new disposition of accommodation or proposed common purchases. But if, during the argument, he becomes querulous and therefore disintegrative, he must anticipate a loss of prestige. Conversely, the instrumental leader of a treatment group may lose much influence and regard if he misses meetings, or exhibits defensive attitudes at a time when other members have become able to approach their problem less defensively. But provided he does not deviate in such important instrumental areas he may well, unlike most other members, be allowed to make irreverent jokes or sarcastic remarks now and then, or to dress bizarrely, without loss of status.

This duality of leadership is yet another area of group dynamics which presents analogies with the nuclear family. While many writers have observed the similarities between father/family and leader/group relationships, others regard this as an over-simplification, and have asserted the leader's ability to represent both Father and Mother images. Discussions on this theme (Money-Kyrle, 1950; Schilder, 1940; and others) propose that such parental roles arise mainly from the fantasies, displacements and transferences of the subordinate members. This is an important and acceptable notion. However, it is also interesting to reflect that the instrumental and integrative functions of leadership coincide closely with what have traditionally been thought of in Western culture as paternal and maternal role-behaviour respectively.

Thus we may view the differentiation of leadership in familial terms, and describe the high-status cluster as consisting of members who, irrespective of sex, may be separately performing paternal or maternal leader roles, as opposed to a situation where one high-status member alone is imbued by others' fantasies with both father and mother qualities. While we may well object today to the stereotypes of Father as dominant, doing and directive, and of Mother as submissive, caring and affective, they are in practice still sufficiently familiar for the analogy to have relevance. Very many parental couples have a distribution of labour which roughly corresponds with Bales' concepts of instrumental and expressive leadership functions. Even where some modification, or even reversal, of these traditional sex-roles occurs, the parents must jointly in some way ensure that both functions are carried out if the family is economically, culturally and emotionally to survive. It is highly unlikely, all personalities being unique, that parents will share equally in both functions. Thus, there must be specialisation, whether in the most traditional or the most advanced and experimental of family constellations. The question of who tends to specialise in which functions is a matter of personalities, resources and values.

Another aspect of this analogy is the similarity between Bales' "coalition" concept and the emphasis placed by so many parents on the desirability of solidarity. Common views must be demonstrated about matters which may in fact be issues of disagreement between them, but it is believed that the children should not experience conflict between the parents. While the avoidance of open conflict can be justified as contributing to the children's sense of security, the avoidance of disagreement, which is not necessarily the same thing as conflict, also serves the purpose indicated by Bales of maintaining joint parental power. "United we stand . . .".

We have drawn this analogy since every small group has some echoes of familial configurations for its members and leaders. While the fantasy elements in this situation are certainly very important, both the practice and literature of group treatment, in paying so much attention to these, seems to have overlooked certain relevant realities. The analogy briefly discussed here served to remind us that the actual behaviour of the worker or other leaders, in this context their leadership style, may have maternal or paternal components and therefore influence the nature of other members' fantasies and transference. This reality is more amenable to control and modification than members' fantasy; this is another reason for drawing attention to it.

GROUP CONTAGION

Another leadership phenomenon, which at first seems somewhat irrational, and which certainly relates to unconscious or defended areas of the members' emotional lives, is that of *group contagion*. This concept is different from that of "prestige contagion" earlier mentioned. It refers to the sudden manifestation of intense feelings or dramatic behaviour on the part of a hitherto controlled and tranquil group. Such unexpected group behaviour is triggered off by an initiating act by one member who, for various reasons, is less able or willing to control impulses which the group has been dealing with by denial and repression. The initiating act brings such impulses to the surface, and so becomes "contagious". Our experience suggests that this is in fact a further, though indirect, example of how group needs influence group structure. Group contagion seems clearly to exemplify the important point that the same dynamics underlie status and role distribution, even where the group needs concerned are unconscious or suppressed.

We have observed the waiting room at an ear, nose and throat clinic. Awed and still, the children sit on each their parent's knee, encapsulated in silent fear. Their tears and their wish to protest against the horror of it all are blocked by the combined forces of the transparent parental attempts at distraction (carrying the latent message "Please do not cry"), by the receptionist's bright smile, with its continual invitation to collude in her own denial, and—above all—by the silence of the others. Even the grown-ups only whisper. Then a new Mum struggles in, dragging her screaming and protesting 4-year-old, who has had his sinuses "looked at" before. In no time at all, the children are all crying and heading for the door. Such is group contagion. The protesting child's behaviour harmonises with and triggers off the suppressed, though conscious, feeling of the others. We may regard him as being in that instant a leader who enables a group to meet their perceived needs, hitherto inhibited by both external and intra-group controls.

The dynamics of group contagion may become yet clearer if we consider in some detail a case resumé from social work in the Probation setting, and so will its connections with earlier formulations on role theory.

Example 38. John. *Five boys, all aged 16 years, were charged as co-defendants with malicious damage, warehousebreaking, and a series of car-thefts. This caused general surprise, for they were found to be "decent, intelligent, obedient lads" whose parents were "respectable hard-working church-going folk, well able to control their children".** With one exception, John. John had not previously associated with the co-defendants, but he alone had been in trouble several times before. His parents were divorced, and he lived with his mother and three sisters in a crowded terrace-house in a poor district with high criminality.

John was said to have led the gang, and this was well borne out by the facts. As leader, he was regarded as responsible for misleading the others, for initiating them in and inspiring them to crime. This view appealed not only to John's co-defendants and their parents, but also to the Court, which sentenced him to a detention centre, giving the others a conditional discharge.

Taking into consideration earlier criminal history, apparent degree of responsibility, and likelihood of further offence, this may well juridically speaking have been a sensible and just disposal. But a closer look at the dynamics of the group compels one to raise certain questions pertinent to our theme of group contagion. "Who really led whom?" "Who manipulated and misused whom?" and "why?"

John was by no means imposed upon the group; indeed, his friendship had been actively pursued by the others. They were in no sense compelled to follow him—he was physically weaker, less intelligent, and possessed fewer social skills—yet he rapidly became their leader, an honour for so under-privileged a boy with such a group. But there seem to have been certain expectations of him, and he was required to pay a certain price.

The other boys were highly conforming with parental and community norms and expectations. They had apparently never shown any sign of rebellion or protest, always "obedient" to the parents who were so "well able to control them". Conforming, and socialised to "respectability", they had not been able to express the adolescent wish to reject parental control and to experiment with other assumptions and standards. Their growing need to assert their individuality had been blocked, and under pressure had given rise to aggressive and anti-social wishes. Nor could these be independently expressed without the

*Extracted from previously published paper (Heap, 1966 *op. cit.*)
**From Probation Officer's report.

help of a leader of another type. A known delinquent, John, was drawn into the group and assigned the role of leader. He was flattered and encouraged in his exhibitionistic behaviour and stimulated to show his daring in delinquent escapades. The group "went along" with these, so that under his leadership they were at last able to give expression to their aggressive wishes and thereby obtain relief. Guilt and responsibility were then projected onto John. In this defence they were well supported by their parents, the Court, the newspapers and each other.

This reminds us strongly of Redl's (1942, *op.cit.*) proposition that the initiator in acts of group contagion has also a "guilt-bearing" function. "Who started all this?" is one of the most common questions asked by the teacher returning to the noisy classroom, by the prison governor in the aftermath of a riot, by the angry parent and many others. The ringleader having been identified and dealt with in some repressive way the "problem" is then also presumed to have been dealt with. No one else is to blame, since the initiator's apparent responsibility acts as what Redl desribes as a "magical exculpation" for the others.

Punitive or other repressive reactions to the initiator will in many cases return the group to their earlier stage of inability to express their real feelings and needs, thus keeping these safely under the rug. Removal from the hospital ward of the tearful child who "makes the others cry" may re-create a controlled and controllable situation in the ward. But the protest and despair of the children, with which they need help, is no longer available. On the contary, their renewed withdrawal into tranquillity and denial, which may bear seeds of permanent emotional damage, may be welcomed by the overworked and anxious medical staff, whose limited resources compel them to give priority to other (somatic) problems and probably therefore to defend themselves against experiencing the children's feelings.[7] But in other settings, where the infectious behaviour has had a releasing effect, the group are now free of the tension of repressed wishes and also experience the immediate advantages of freedom from responsibility. How far this serves the long-term ends of social and emotional growth is, however, open to question.

Group contagion also exemplifies the scapegoating phenomenon, and illustrates further the Type 9 central-person role, namely the "bad influence". It is a curious but not uncommon combination of the roles of leader and scapegoat, usually played consecutively.

The relevance of the individual's personality dynamics to such status and role assignment can also be demonstrated if we return to Example 38.

> John's early life experiences were of constant inter-parental strife, of vacillating brutality and reparation from his father, and of an intense, mutually dependent relationship with his mother, leading at the age of 12 years to his present position of "man of the house". He seemed to be manipulated by both parents—by mother to express her aggression against father, and by father to express his guilt and to perform his reparations after a bout of drinking, beating, or absence. ("Give your mother this blouse/brooch/perfume for me, John, and tell me how she takes it.")
>
> John thus grew up confused, insecure, labile, and with no consistent sense of personal identity. His ego-weakness permitted unmodified acting-out of his anxiety and confusion, and the diffuse anger he felt against his parents found generalized expression in his spasmodic destructive delinquency.
>
> John's unresolved identity problems and his very necessary survival-orientation enabled him to adjust superficially and briefly to the demands of most groups he had known. He pleased them with a brief surrender to group norms and expectations because of his anxiety to please and be accepted, but was never able to make meaningful and lasting relationships with his peers. In the episode described we have seen John being manipulated, accepting the roles of delinquent leader and then of scapegoat assigned him by the group, and thus satisfying both his own neurotic needs and theirs.
>
> John exhibited his customary agility of adjustment in the detention centre, and was regarded as a "model detainee". Six months after discharge he was sentenced to Borstal training; his further experiences in Borstal are unknown.

These observations on group contagion are mainly derived from diagnostic hypothesis and reflection in social group-work practice and supervision. Surprisingly little empirical research has been addressed to this aspect of group processes. It has therefore been encouraging to find a number of collaborative studies conducted during the 1940s by Polansky, *et al.* (1950, 1951, and others) which support our interpretation of group contagion. We wish briefly to draw attention to one such study.

Polansky (1952) describes research into the dynamics of group contagion in which the subjects were mainly disturbed children and teenagers in summer camps, with a smaller number of "normal" children also in camp. Data was gathered on thirty-two such groups, which were systematically observed over several weeks during the whole day from rising to retiring, as well as in a number of tests designed to produce motivation for completion of set task, conflict, frustration and contagion. The study was particularly concerned with the relationship between the initiator and the group, with the prestige of the initiator for the group, and with his impulsivity. The hypothesis that members of high prestige would be the most frequent initiators was disproved. Prestige was shown to affect the situation only indirectly, by determining which children were likely to act frequently and thus to provide acts which could be contagious.Impulsivity was more relevant. While the impulsive members were not observed during daily life to have contagious influence, they were shown to have significant initiatory power in experimental situations where the group experienced both frustration and social restraints. It was shown to be "the act itself rather than enduring relationship with the initiator (which) produced contagion". In situations calling for delay and frustration tolerance they "broke through their own or adult-imposed controls" and, "by clearly and spontaneously expressing needs which the other children were also feeling. ... (carried) them along into uncontrolled episodes by acting as triggers setting off the group".

All the findings of this study point to suppressed group needs as a major determinant of what kind of behaviour is initiated and what rejected. Klein (1963) states that " ... leadership must always remain a situational and not a personal variable", while Gibb (*op.cit.*), yet more accurately, explains that, "Leadership is both a function of the social situation and a function of personality, but it is a function of these two in interaction". This general proposition appears to have particular relevance to group contagion as a specific case of leadership.

These observations have several applications in the practice of social work with groups. They help us to see that whether or not the impulsive behaviour of the initiator implies that he needs limits and control, the fact of its contagion gives us unambiguous information about the feelings and needs of the group-as-a-whole and their inability to express them. This is useful in direct treatment of small groups, in dealing with certain administrative problems, and not least in work at the community level. Further, awareness of the dynamics of group contagion may help the worker to avoid playing into other members' manipulation of the initiator into a scapegoat role. It may, for example, be appropriate, as the impulsive or high-prestige member moves into this position, to stimulate members to ventilate the feelings they share with the budding initiator. By thus declaring their commonality with him they must as a group jointly face the reality which has emerged, rather than evading it by subsequent defensive projection on to the initiator.

(As a case in point, the prisoners' group in Example 37 (p. 179) would probably have developed quite differently had the social worker registered earlier the emergence of this pattern and the associated need for the kind of intervention which we have just mentioned.)

Relationships and Sub-Groups

In addition to status and roles, the concept of group structure embraces the relationships existing between the members of the group. Both implicitly and explicitly, the factor of affective relationship has already been introduced at many points in the preceding pages. It could perhaps be claimed that the entire study of groups is a study from different viewpoints of multiple-relationship phenomena. In the context of group structure, however, we are particularly concerned with the *patterns* of the relationships which occur in small groups. Every group develops a certain network of personal relationships. This is sometimes referred to as the "informal structure" of the group, since it arises spontaneously out of the affective responses of individual members to each other and to the group situation.

THE INFLUENCE OF DISPLACEMENTS AND TRANSFERENCE

Where individual factors are concerned, informal structure is determined by the personality dynamics of the individual members, their capacities for forming and sustaining relationships and their varying degrees of emotional maturity. These factors determine who relates to whom, how and on what basis.

We have already remarked that our ability to form relationships, and the nature of the relationships which we form, is to a considerable extent determined by early family experiences. In so far as our basic emotional needs have been satisfactorily met in earlier life, and our relationships to certain vital persons have been warm, consistent and satisfying we will in later life be able to relate to other people as they really are, rather than as we need to see them. But if early emotional needs have not been satisfactorily met, we may perceive certain other people as if they were parts of our earlier frustrating life experiences. Thus we involve them, possibly against their wishes and their knowledge, in our continuing struggle for identity and self-esteem, for freedom from emotional turmoil and from social anxiety. We do this either by attempting to manipulate others into meeting our unmet needs and/or by reacting to them as if they were extensions of the people who earlier frustrated, or over-protected or frightened us. This is to say that we distort such relationships by displacement, by projection and by transference.

The primary family group of our childhood nurtures in us a repertoire of feelings, emotional resources, attitudes and behaviour which profoundly influence all our later social relationships and performance. These attributes are not merely established and thereafter produced on demand, as it were, but become both modified and extended as adulthood makes new adaptive demands and requires us to learn new role behaviour. Nevertheless, these extensions and adaptations all contain the elements of the "self" whose nucleus was developed in the family group. The nature, harmony and intensity of relationships in the social-work group, as in other groups, will depend on whether members' early experiences have enabled them to relate in rewarding and appropriate ways to the reality of others' personalities and qualities, or whether life experiences have left them frustrated, conflicted and self-negating and therefore prone to distorted perceptions of others.

In all kinds of groups, with members of all ages, we witness both negative and positive transference relationships, as in the following example. During a training experience the author observed a nursery play-group. One little girl, whose mother had recently "presented" her with a baby brother, was seen first to put the dolls one by one into the stove and thereafter, following a brief but thorough temper-tantrum, to vomit explosively in the nursery teacher's lap. (Concurrently in individual therapy, she was at this point also most concerned about how often and for how long the therapist—a young woman—saw the other patients.) But in the same group we saw a little boy who, owing to his parents' divorce, was separated from his younger sister. His relationship to a little girl in the group of about his sister's age was one of protective love, and at times almost overwhelming concern.

In work with the elderly, whether in clubs, old people's homes, or geriatic wards, it is frequently noted that their dependence upon the group leads to relationships of considerable intensity. Even at this late stage in life such relationships are often shown to be coloured or distorted by their symbolic and surrogate connection with earlier life experiences. Both the richness and the apparent pettiness of many relationships between aged people who are forced into continual intimacy have their source in transference phenomena. Thus Laverty (1962) described the interaction of certain members of the group in an old people's home as reflecting "re-activation of sibling rivalry". Schwarzmann (1966) reporting on work in weekly group meetings of eleven elderly clients (average age 72 years) also notes: "The transference situation in such a group can be complex. One member remarked: 'We feel like a family now—we're so used to each other'. This re-creation of 'family' re-activated sibling rivalries and rejections. ... I found it necessary to intervene when one member attacked another. . ."

But here, too, positive transferences are also important determinants of the relationships in the group and between group members and the worker. Wasser (1966) describes the relationship between a social worker and a patient in a nursing home—Mrs. M., 82 years, a childless widow, approaching death.

.... and Mrs. M. developed a strong positive transference to her, both as mother and daughter. Mrs. M. and the worker repeatedly discussed the deaths of Mrs. M.'s grandmother and mother, and the possibility of her own death. The worker, moreover, spoke of many of Mrs. M.'s fears and feelings about the approaching unknown of death.

In a sense the worker psychologically took Mrs. M. into her arms in her dying, as Mrs. M. had actually done with her own mother. The client, as a dying person who felt forgotten by family and friends, accepted the caseworker as a substitute.

THE INFLUENCE OF MATURITY LEVELS

The maturity or immaturity of members is another important factor in shaping the informal structure of the group. By "maturity" and "immaturity" here we refer to members' behaviour and attitudes in relation to their age. Thus, "immaturity" refers to behaviour and attitudes characteristic of any stage of development which we might expect individuals to have outgrown. It is, for instance, perfectly "normal" for pre-school children to be dependent and self-centred, to be little involved in the needs and rights of others, and for their behaviour to be determined by impulse and the need for immediate satisfactions. For adults or adolescents to behave in this manner is immature, just as behaviour characteristic of adolescence is immature in an adult.

Immature behaviour may be seen at both individual and group levels, for it is clear that the immaturity of individual members must in some way be reflected in group behaviour and performance. Isaacs (1933), in what has virtually become a classic study of social development in young children, saw this very clearly, when observing children in a nursery and infants' school. She was struck by the extreme egocentricity of the younger children. Although it seemed important to them to be in the presence of their peers, and although there was a considerable amount of both friendly and hostile exchange, the group and its interaction seemed to be perceived by each member as existing exclusively for the satisfaction of his or her particular needs. From such a viewpoint fellow members are regarded as objects to be used and manipulated in one's service, to the extent that they will permit this. Perceptible change occurred, according to Isaacs' observations, after about the age of 4. There was a gradual increase in co-operative rather than parallel activities, and a growing readiness to make at least some concessions to others. This was reflected in group structure first by the fleeting establishment of small sub-groups. Later, towards the age of 7, the group had a more stable and defined structure. While a considerable degree of egocentricity still remained, together with a high rate of sub-grouping, there was increasing orientation towards the group-as-a-whole, towards "others". Such developments in social life, she concluded, are necessary and normal consequences of the continuing personality development and maturation of the individuals concerned.

But in social work we frequently meet the adult who in these respects functions at a level appropriate to such earlier stages of development.

He may do so consistently, in which case we may think of him as having a generally immature level of emotional development, or he may merely regress to immature behaviour levels—as we all may at times— under the pressure of some kind of crisis or stress. Any of us may regress to dependency during a crisis involving loss. Or we may regress to indiscriminate and misplaced aggression when we are afraid, to take but two examples.

The presence of marked degrees of persisting immaturity among some or all members of a group will clearly influence the patterns of relationships which are formed and the uses made of those relationships. Since relationships will tend to be more exploitive and role-behaviour more "individual-centred", as in Isaacs children's groups, a lower level of group functioning will necessarily result, and the development of a viable group situation will be slower.

These observations have important consequences for the worker's role in social work and other forms of group treatment or learning. Where the maturational, and therefore group-functioning, level of members is low, the social worker, therapist or teacher finds it necessary to engage himself more directly in leadership functions (decision-facilitation, planning activities, enabling interaction, setting limits, etc.). Wilson and Ryland (1949, *op.cit.*) have constructed a model relating a descriptive scale of group-functioning criteria to a scale representing the social worker's varying degrees of engagement in leadership. These scales proceed respectively from "out of touch with reality" (lowest social health) to "eager and competent to participate in group" (highest social health), and from "controller" (most active in leadership) to "enabling observer" (least active). They depict graphically an inversely proportional relationship between these variables; that is to say, the higher the social health of members, the less structure from the worker; the lower the social health, the more structure from the worker.

While maturity is only one element of Wilson and Ryland's "social health" concept, it is a major one, so their proposals seem to be particularly applicable to groups where immaturity is an issue, and where maturational development is a goal of treatment. An implication of their model is that as group functioning improves during treatment, the worker may—indeed should—engage himself decreasingly in direct leadership functions. We have elsewhere described this process as "giving up the role of central person" (Heap, 1968, *op. cit.*). This is a vital process in both social group work and community work.

A number of difficult evaluations are involved here, however, and there are grounds for caution.

In the first place it would be a mistake to regard the maturity of an individual or a group as being fixed at a certain level at a given time, so that relationships and behaviour in all situations at that time reflect that level of maturity. On the contrary, there is much to suggest that maturity is to some extent also a situationally determined attribute. If we are infantilised, we may readily regress. The compliant and dependent passivity with which many of us take on the patient role when placed in hospital is a common example of this. If we are treated as responsible and autonomous adults we tend, on the other hand, to behave as maturely as we are able within the limits of our personality resources. This may further be exemplified by the remarkably independent and courageous behaviour of many of the students who have accepted (or fought for) the opportunity of involvement in decision-making in their schools and universities. A seriousness, a concern, and not least an organisational and political skill far beyond expectations have sometimes been demonstrated during these first years of school and university democracy. Only a few years ago the student was not regarded as sufficiently mature for such involvement: ergo, he was not in fact mature enough. He stuck to his books and cricket, and accepted what came his way of wisdom and decisions from on high.

In this context we may note the interdependence of the component aspects of group structure. Relationships, and the maturity which they reflect, are in this way clearly related to role. In our earlier discussion of role we may not have sufficiently emphasised that one person may play many different roles at the same period of his life, each characterised by its particular range of attitudes and behaviour. We each occupy numerous positions in various patterns of social relationships—in our families, studies, work-places, organisations, etc. Occupancy of these positions places us in reciprocal relationships which give rise to many different mutual expectations of behaviour and attitudes, i.e. of role. Our point here is that where role expectations demand little of our social skills and personality resources, the maturity we demonstrate in our relationships and behaviour may be relatively low. Where another part of what Merton (1957) calls our "role-set" presupposes responsible and "other-directed" behaviour, we tend to behave and to relate to other participants at a higher level of maturity.

This interdependence of relationships, role and environmental influences is well observed by Robertson (1954). In his account of a joint Scottish and Norwegian whaling expedition, he remarks the contrast between the behaviour and relationships manifested by the whalers on shore and when exposed to the rigours and hazards of the whaling-grounds. On shore they appeared intemperate, improvident and impulsive. While whaling they were serious, industrious, responsible and engaged over protracted periods—very successfully indeed—in complex and demanding co-operative effort. Many other observations suggesting similar conclusions could be mentioned.

In brief, the evidence suggests that a favourable and ego-supportive situation in the group's environment, with expectations or demands of responsible social behaviour, may not merely hinder regression, but may promote maturity in relationships and behaviour. This provides a major argument for group and therapeutic community methods of treating delinquency and other forms of asociality and immaturity. Instead of hoping that externally derived control will produce maturation through some vague process combining indentification, fear and moral awakening, group treatment builds upon internally derived group control and the influence of an environment which assumes the group's inherent potential for more mature behaviour.

Here again, however, an important cautionary note must be added. Where expectations of mature behaviour are unrealistic, feelings of anxiety, frustration and inadequacy will be generated, and may find expression either in withdrawal into further dependence, or in aggression. This may be either inwardly directed and self-destructive, or outwardly directed. In the latter case, it may be released on to chance targets, leading to damage to property, hostility to other members, etc. Alternatively it may be more appropriately directed towards the source of the anxiety-provoking demands—namely the worker, therapist or teacher. This is a point of considerable current relevance. Some contemporary group treatment, not least within allegedly therapeutic milieux, appears to be based on a total rather than a partial abdication of professional authority and expertise. In our view this commonly reflects a serious mis-understanding of the group therapist's function. To interpret psychotic patients' wishes for some degree of clarification and help from the therapist, and their concern that he is still only a student as "the group's problem of dependence, which you will have to do something about" (*sic*), is to stand the problem on its head, and to use the group as a receptacle for the projections of the therapist's own inadequacy. Group treatment is not a means of abrogating professional responsibility; it is a way of co-operating with patients/clients which is predicated on two assumptions. One, that the clients have resources which they can mobilise in their own treatment, and which can be both reinforced and made more readily available by the use of a group setting. Two, that the worker's presence has a purpose, namely to aid the group in their work by such stimulation, clarification, resource provision, confrontation, support and interpretation as may be diagnostically indicated and consistent with the group's objectives. To reduce the therapist's involvement to some sterotype of profound passivity, with the occasional grunt, or a continual evasive, "well, that depends on how the group sees it, doesn't it?", is to place new burdens upon the already burdened, and to make demands of social health which only the exceptionally mature and psychically well adjusted can be expected to meet. Thus, regressive and defensive responses are often invited from people for whom quite other objectives are manifestly held. This particular suit of cheaply produced emperor's clothes is currently hanging in many a clinical wardrobe. No least for this reason the present trend for increased research into the assumptions and practices of group treatments of many kinds is particularly timely.

ALLIANCES AND SUB-GROUPS

We have so far observed the importance of residual problems from early life-experiences in influencing relationships in small groups, and the manner in which members' current extra-group relationships may be reflected in the group situation. We have also discussed the impact of members' maturity levels on the informal structure of the group, and have briefly considered some implications this may have for treatment.

These factors of transference, displacement and maturity in relationships influence who relates well or badly to whom in the group, and are therefore reflected in patterns of alliance and rejection. But many other factors also influence this aspect of the group process.

In any group we will find that some individuals are more attracted to certain fellow members than to others. All our lives we have for various reasons moved into relationships with some people and avoided relationships with others, and the relationships concerned have been either sustained or avoided for very different periods.

In any group, therefore, such an informal structure quickly begins to develop as the members are more or less attracted to or repelled by each other. Much of this will be due to spontaneous attraction between individuals, which defies more than speculative explanation. A vague and comforting feeling of being similar perhaps, or in some way complementary as in so many relationships. Inexplicable and instant antagonisms are perhaps equally common. Transference undoubtedly plays an important part in such initial feelings about each other, but so do more tangible factors such as recognisable signs of commonality—manners of speech, dress, bearing, etc. As time goes on, members gain increasing experience of each other. Their feelings of mutual liking and disliking become more refined and are more related to the realities of others' self-presentation. This will, however, still depend upon the extent to which perceptions of others are distorted by the residual and unresolved problems mentioned earlier. But with time, relationships in most groups are mainly influenced by shared or competing interests and attitudes, values, problems and behaviour.

Explicable or not, rational or not, the network of relationships develops. It influences our security and satisfaction in the group, the extent and nature of our participation, and to a large extent the effectiveness with which the group functions.

The informal structure effects the group's efficiency because it may at any time either reinforce or compete with the formal structure. An important consideration here is the unstable correlation between leadership and popularity. We have seen that leaders are usually chosen on other grounds than popularity. Choice of leader may be determined by, for example, organisational ability, verbal facility, or freedom with aggression—none of which are particularly endearing traits. Thus, there may be a conflict between the self-interest and group objectives which might best be served by following a certain leader, and loyalties or liking for other members of the group. "I don't care much for Smith, although he is usually right. At least, we end up following his suggestions most of the time. But I am glad that Jones is sticking up to him, even if I don't altogether agree with him. I like Jones, he's helped me a lot. He should not stand alone on this one. I'll support him against Smith, although Smith may be right". It is a common observation that people who like each other tend to agree with each other, even against objective evidence and their own better judgement.

In fact a number of studies suggest that while the most popular member always has high status, the highest status member usually ranks second or even third in degree of popularity. The most popular member may sometimes be, for example, the "clown". But a group with any discriminatory ability will hesitate to adopt him as leader for any length of time. "Fools rush in . . .". Further, when members are accorded leadership *because* of their popularity, there is a tendency afterwards for their popularity to decline. This had doubtless much to do with the functions of leadership. Conflict, compromise, confrontation and cajolery are at different times unavoidable activities for leaders, and must inevitably involve some decline in personal popularity.

The reverse of this also illustrates the potential conflict between informal and formal structure. Where a group is avoiding its problems by scapegoating, the unfortunate scapegoat will be the least popular member, having few positive relationships in the group or none. He is the "rejected isolate". But he may have become scapegoat precisely because he possesses the experiences, traits, or insights which the group needs in order to achieve its goals. The group's inability to accord him status appropriate to his attributes and potential, involves the rejection of a valuable resource.

These various degrees of attraction and rejection result in the formation of clusters of members having closer relationships to each other than to the group-as-a-whole. These are sub-groups, an inevitable aspect of group life.

Earlier social group work literature spoke of "the problem of sub-groups" as if they were in some way malign and we would sooner or later learn to eradicate them. Some of today's more far-out "human potential" groups also seem to assume that the members of virtually any chance-composed group can learn to love each other, can become all-embracing, egalitarian, totally democratic, without these tiresome alliances between individuals—if only we could get the technique right. But it is not so. Sub-groups must exist.

Members will always like some fellow members more than others. A commonality of ideas and attitudes will bring some members of the group closer to each other than to others. Variations in expectations of the group and in motivation for joining it will also cause sub-grouping. In social-work groups, one sees repeatedly how clients also form sub-groups on the basis of common approaches to problem-solving or problem-avoidance. One sub-group may be open to express concern and feeling; another is busy projecting blame for the problem on to others outside the group; another is denying or minimizing the problem; yet another is defeated and attempts to enter into passive dependence upon the worker, and so on. Differences in interests will also naturally lead to the development of sub-groups. Youth groups, in clubs, for example, often divide into sub-groups pursuing various interests—some play table-tennis, others work on the wall newspaper, others improve the stereo system, etc.

Far from being a problem, this diversification of group life may enrich the group experience, and be an important factor in tempering the demand for group conformity. Further, many people who are too uncertain to express their particular views and needs without support, seem to gain confidence from awareness of fellowship with a sub-group. Thus, the sub-group is a potential source of strength for such members and helps to ensure more comprehensive exposition of the problems and feelings present in the group-as-a-whole.

A period of membership in a sub-group also provides an opportunity to observe and evaluate life in the larger group, and seems thus to provide a "stepping-stone" into the more challenging situation. New members of open groups are often seen to place themselves thus. Silverstein (1973) made use of this observation in her waiting-room groups at an adolescent out-patient psychiatric clinic serving "hard-to-reach'' ghetto families. She initiated a variety of small-group activities in the waiting room, including discussion groups, arts and crafts, and so on. This protected transitional experience with its immediate satisfactions and reassuring atmosphere was instrumental in increasing clients' readiness to commit themselves to the clinic's therapy groups, and other features of its service.

Sub-grouping only becomes a problem when the members' identification with their sub-group becomes so intense that it detracts from their identification with the group-as-a-whole. This kind of exclusive sub-group is sometimes referred to as a *clique,* although consistently defined distinctions between these two kinds of aggregation do not seem to exist. In such cases the sub-group becomes in some way a separate social entity for its members, rivalling the group-as-a-whole, with which they identify and communicate less and less. They may also begin to see other sub-groups as rivals, or even enemies. In many contexts involving larger and more heterogeneous groups—for example the university campus, political organisations, industry—this may be a reasonable consequence of the emergence of new ideologies or objectives which may not be satisfied within the parent group. The emergence of such sub-groups, with increasing self-awareness and developing identity differentiated from that of the inclusive parent group, occurs frequently and almost inevitably involves some degree of conflict between the parent system and the sub-system. However, further discussion of this manifold relationship is outside the scope of this introductory book. The reader is referred for further study to the wide-ranging and insightful discussion of this theme by Ramsøy (1962).

In the context of social work with groups, however, where groups are usually small, where membership is based on common need, and where resources for mutual help and enrichment are believed to be present, this kind of fragmentation would be a regrettable consequence of sub-grouping. Group energy and time would be dissipated in unfruitful strife, and resources needed by all members would become concentrated in a sub-group rather than being available to the group-as-a-whole. In the atmosphere of social work groups which is often laden with anxiety and guilt, the resultant conflict might also readily be interpreted as confirmation of others' rejection and contempt. While viewing sub-groups as an integral part of all group life and as a potential enrichment, today's social worker therefore invests some of his energies in stimulating interaction across the boundaries of sub-groups, keeping alive the identity and cohesion of the group-as-a-whole, in order to help all members attain their objectives. Both appropriate programme activities and such discussion techniques as reflective observation, "linking", and interpreting associations to the common group problem may be helpful here.

There is both clinical and experimental evidence in support of this approach to sub-groups.

Sherif *et al.* (1961), in an experimental study of inter-group conflict, showed how readily sub-group identification could be manipulated into feelings of pride, leading to competitiveness and then to conflict with another sub-group, despite similar composition and circumstances. Their experiment is of particular interest to the social worker since it gives strong experimental support to an aspect of established practice. The investigators showed how members could be diverted from their sub-group allegiances to identification with and investment in a combined "super-ordinate" group, by sharing the satisfactions of successfully completed co-operative tasks which were meaningful to them. Both at the neighbourhood and small-group level this has important implications for selection of activities and goals in social-work practice.

The position of the dyadic sub-group—the pair—has been given much attention. Bion (1961) sees "pairing", in the context of analytical group psychotherapy, as one of the less mature mechanisms for preserving the group and for sustaining membership in it. In so far as it is also essentially defensive, it inhibits the group from engaging in the "work" of therapy. The "pair" are ambivalently tolerated by the group, their greater intimacy being experienced as threatening and as having sexual overtones. A recent empirical study has been addressed to the processes of acceptance, adjustment and integration between the pair and the group of which they are a part (Merei, 1971). Among several interesting findings of this study are two rather surprising observations, which we will state somewhat simply. Firstly, members of pairs are in fact more lonely than other members. They participate in less interaction, viewed totally. Secondly, when members of such a pair are able both to retain their own dyadic traditions and to accept the traditions of the group-as-a-whole (the so-called "double-tie" relationship), they manifest "emotional impoverishment" rather than enrichment. This was indicated by the significant decrease within double-tie relationships of mutual intimacy and aggression, as well as a decrease in the general level of activity.

A NOTE ON SOCIOMETRY

Clearly an overview of this network of relationship is essential for the group worker. The questions arise as to how this may be obtained and how systematically it may be described. In social-work practice one can usually do no more that recognise the importance of these relationship patterns, train oneself to observe and register them as sensitively as possible, and to try to take such observation into account when participating in the group. In certain other contexts, however, (and in social work very occasionally) the device of *sociometric measurement* is available for more precise deliniation of the informal structure.

Sociometry is a technique devised by Moreno (1953) for measuring and graphically depicting the network of likes, dislikes and indifferences which characterize groups under investigation or treatment. Jennings (*op.cit.*) has conducted major work on the inter-relation of social structure and personality, using sociometric techniques. Many of the studies mentioned in the present book have consisted either wholly or in part of sociometric investigation.

The technique consists basically of asking group members to name one or more people with whom they would most wish to carry out some specified activity—to work with, share room with, spend leisure time with, etc. An addition of the results of this questionnaire will clearly show who is most, next most, . . . and least *popular* in the group. These findings can then be expressed in a diagram, called a sociogram, which gives a readily interpreted graphic representation of the attractiveness or isolation of each member of the group at a given point in time, and of the direction of each member's preferences. This is done simply by drawing a line between each member and the persons he has chosen. Arrowheads are drawn indicating the direction of choice. By these means popular "stars", rejected or withdrawn isolates, mutual or unilateral relationships, sub-groups, etc., may be seen at a glance.

Similarly, negatively slanted questions may be asked and transferred to a sociogram. "With whom would you *least* wish to share a room, a task, etc.?" On the basis of such inquiry an even clearer picture of the patterns of rejection and isolation may be obtained.

We will illustrate this briefly with a hypothetical group consisting of Black, White, Red, Blue, Brown and Green, each of whom are invited to choose two persons on the basis of some appropriate positive criteria. We might find that Red is chosen four times, Black and Green are both chosen three times, White and Brown are both chosen once, and Blue is not chosen at all. Transferred to a sociogram these choices would look as shown here (Fig. 3).

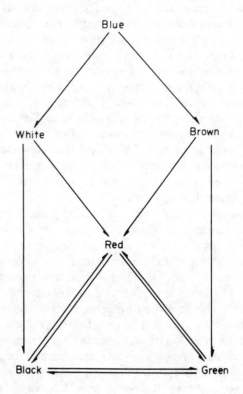

We see that Red is the "star", the most popular. Black and Green tie for second place, and also have reciprocal choices with Red and with each other. Thus, the informal structure is clearly characterised by strongly cohesive central sub-group or clique. White and Brown are more peripheral. No one in the central sub-group chooses either. Nor do they choose each other, although they both subscribe to Red's popularity. Both make second, but different, choices within the central clique. Despite their own lack of popularity in the group, they may therefore be tentatively assumed to subscribe to the behaviour and attitudes of the most popular members and thus to group values. Perhaps they are rather unimpressive neutral people—followers, anxious conformers? Blue, however, is in a very different position. Not only is he not chosen by anyone, but he directs his own choices to the two other most peripheral members. He is not attracted by any of the members who are central to the group's informal structure, so it may be tentatively assumed that he is least identified with the group values and behaviour. Perhaps he is a rather tragic figure? Rejected, low self-esteem, naturally attracted to other isolates, who may be companions in distress? Or perhaps something quite different? A rebel, antipathetic to Red and orientated towards Brown and White as the most likely potential members of a sub-group which might be persuaded to compete with the present central alliance?

With a group of six members, making two positive unrated choices each, we have gained both some overview of the pattern of attraction and isolation in the group, and some working hypotheses about certain members' roles and status. Larger groups, with perhaps more choices per member, including popularity ratings, immediately present material which is more difficult to analyse but which, in compensation, generates a greater wealth of facts and hypotheses. It is proper to mention that sociometry has developed into a highly refined method of investigation to which we can offer only the most cursory introduction.

However, our example, despite its simplicity, demonstrates both some uses of the sociogram and some of its limitations. We see that the interpretation of sociograms, beyond the membership of sub-groups and the ratings and direction of attraction and isolation, can only be speculative. Unless other kinds of supplementary observation and test are brought into play, the very important factors of emotional content, the qualitative aspects of the relationships depicted and their causative explanations cannot be deduced. As hinted above, however, some clues to further inquiry may be found.

Because of these limitations, and the possible exposure of hurtful material, sociometry has become primarily—but not entirely—a tool for research. Sociometric techniques have been used to inquire into the widest imaginable range of group phenomena where informal structure is a relevant variable. Much of this, including many findings we have mentioned, is of relevance and value to social work with groups.

More practical applications have included the use of sociometry in establishing cohesive work teams, for example in industry, since it is known that morale and efficiency are increased where team members are attractive to each other, and have to some extent chosen each other. (Such use, however, always raises the ethical and therapeutic problems of not only placing but also helping the person or persons now unambiguously shown to be unpopular.) Therapeutic use has also been made of sociometry in residential treatment institutions. The emphasis here has been on the best possible placement of rejectees, ensuring if possible some degree of friendship and support for *all* members in the numerous group activities which are inseparable from residential treatment. (See Leonard (1974) for an example of sociometric analysis of treatment indications and social structure in a group treatment home for disturbed children, and Grundy and Wilson (1973) for its use in the diagnosis and planning of a community residence for discharged long-term psychiatric patients.) Sociometric techniques are from time to time also employed in various types of sensitivity and leadership training, to provide control for participants' own assumptions about how others perceive them. Members might, for instance, first rank themselves on the basis of their own perceptions of their place in the group, and later compare this with the sociometrically determined factual situation. But all such applications of the method raise unavoidable ethical questions, including those germane to sensitivity training of all persuasions and purposes: namely, does the trainer knowingly or unknowingly run the risk of precipitating social or emotional crisis in the trainee, does the trainee know this, and is the trainer competent to deal with such a crisis or assured of access to someone who is?[8]

In social-group work, however, sociometric *method,* in the strict sense of the term, has little place. On the other hand, many social workers, in search of diagnostic clarification and/or as an illustrative tool in supervision, construct what we might term "sociogrammatic sketches", based simply upon observations during work with the group and not upon questionnaires. Such sketches lack precision but are nevertheless useful aids in maintaining the worker's awareness of the current informal structure, in the ordering of impressions, and not least—if sketched periodically—in focusing attention on changes over a period of time. Social work with groups is in its very essence orientated towards various forms of change, including changes in the group itself during treatment. The worker may easily be pressured into moving with the group from crisis to crisis, from decision to decision, without, as it were, standing off from time to time to see what is happening in terms of group development and to evaluate the relevance of that development to group objectives. Periodic sociometric sketches are a useful aid here.

Notes to Chapter 7

1. Some group dynamics research suggests that group structure is in fact little subject to change. We submit that while this may be true of the transient and artifical laboratory group it is by no means a valid generalisation for small groups in life situations. (See Riecken and Homans (1954) for a review of pertinent studies.)

2. Readers who find this kind of concept helpful, may be orientated towards an important theory of group dynamics developed by Kurt Lewin (1938, 1951) which is recommended for later study. It is a very technical approach. Lewin's "Field Theory" uses mathematical models in its approach to the understanding of group phenomena. It is postulated that any group at any point of time exists in a psychological field which is in certain ways analogous to an electromagnetic field. The analogy is based on the notion that the group field consists of a number of forces, which affect the behaviour of the members. The development, direction and efficiency of the group-as-a-whole is a product of the resolution of all these forces and may be examined and expressed mathematically.

   An impression of the "flavour" and complexity of this kind of approach may be gained from the more recent "Vector Model" of small-group study by Rabinovich *et al.* (1973), whose brief exposition concludes with the printout of the computer program used in the model.

3. Wissler (1912) and Lincoln (1935) describe a culture where such scapegoating has been formalised. The Sioux elders interpret the dreams and visions of adolescents. Certain "deviant" dream patterns cause them to ordain that the boy or girl concerned shall lead a deviant life—as homosexual, prostitute, clown, or artist. Erikson (1963) in drawing our attention to this, comments that " . . . . The Sioux deals with its deviants by giving them a secondary role. . . . Without, however freeing them entirely from the ridicule and horror which the vast majority must maintain in order to suppress *in themselves* (writer's italics) what the deviant represents."

4. This point reminds us of a fascinating paper by Appelbaum (1967), who reflects upon an analogy between small sensitivity-training groups and the populations of nations in terms of their attitudes to leadership. Commitment to these two kinds of group, the frustrations of membership, sources of power, alliances between membes, and both competition for and hostility to the leaders are among the themes discussed.

5. With reference to the styles of "example" and "manipulator", Macarov draws our attention to a paper by Halleck (1963). This discusses the impact on certain client groups of the social worker's possible exercise of these inappropriate leadership styles. The prevailing student concern about manipulation in social work suggests that this paper should currently arouse interest.

6. Both the results of these contrasting leadership styles, and group reactions to conflict between leaders who represent different styles, are powerfully conveyed by Kesey (1962) in his novel *One Flew over the Cuckoo's Nest*. The smiling, manipulative and subtly tyrranical Big Nurse and the extroverted, life-loving, rebel patient McMurphy in "her" ward of psychiatric patients represent polarised styles of leadership. Their impact on the patient group of, respectively, dependence, inertia, diffuse anxiety and lack of solidarity and stimulation, activation of resources, increased self-esteem and hope, come over with dramatic clarity. The fear-borne resistance of the pacified group to involvement in a more democratic and fertile organisational form is also a well-perceived conflict, having many parallels in social work both where client-treatment and social action are concerned. (Since this manuscript was written, Kesey's novel has been well filmed, exciting considerable attention.)

7. This hypothetical example refers to certain disturbing phenomena which have emerged from research into small children's experience of hospitalisation. Robertson (1958), a British social worker and psycho-analyst, has over many years studied the impact of in-patient experience on young children. He has been particularly concerned with the significance of the enforced separation from parents. This separation is usually the first and occurs at a time of great anxiety and also, possibly, of physical discomfort or pain. Inescapable conclusions from Roberton's studies are: (1) that there is compelling need for change in both the regulations and the structure of hospitals such that maximum contact between patient and parents is enabled, preferably by rooming-in for a parent; and (2) that serious obstacles exist to the implementation of such arrangements, these obstacles being caused primarily by adults' needs to defend themselves against experiencing the importance and intensity of the child's separation anxiety. "Adult" here refers not only to medical personnel and administrators but also to many parents. Such defences usually take the form of rationalisation or denial.

    Our text above uses terminology derived from Robertson's studies. "Adjustment" to hospitalisation is seen as occurring in three successive phases. These are the phases of *protest, despair and denial*. The third phase is likely to occur under long-term stay and with too little parental contact. It consists of a defensive withdrawal from own need for the unattainable affection, and may seriously impair the child's emotional health. Ironically, children at this stage are undemanding, "relate" easily to all the staff, and are not distressed by the end of visiting time. Thus they appear "settled", manifesting a behaviour which the staff, understandably, may welcome if they have not been assisted to gain insight into its underlying meaning.

(While, as indicated, these problems must mainly be solved or prevented at the administrative level, it is interesting in the context of this book to note the use of social-group work as an ameliorative measure. One example of this is the "Talk Time" programme for hospitalised children (Sheridan, 1975), which stimulates discussion on the ward, encouraging the patients to share their fears and fantasies and to ventilate their feelings about being "deserted" by their parents.)

8. Current unease about these and related questions is reflected in such papers as Crawshaw (1969), who puts the T-group and its siblings to the test of the Nuremberg Rules. The T-group alas, is found wanting! Crawshaw's paper is frankly polemic, but demands a rebuttal, which to our knowledge has not yet appeared. His paper may be obtained in a symposium of informative and thought-provoking papers on "T-groups and the Laboratory Movement" (see references).

Recent years have, of course, witnessed a great deal of research on sensitivity-training, T-groups, etc. Much of this does seem convincing. But Wahrman (1974)—who clearly enjoyed getting something off his chest—points to weaknesses in this research, not least the fact that it is research *by* the trainers, about *their* particular methods, based on *their* clients' reported evaluations. So you pays your money, and . . . .

Somewhere between the trainers' enthusiasm, Crawshaw's indignation, and Wahrman's scepticism lies the truth!

One of the most balanced discussions of this increasingly important activity—its potential and problems—is provided by Parloff (1970). We draw attention to these papers since we assume that most readers will have participated in some kind of group-training experience and will find the issues raised of interest. They are not in any other sense necessary supplementary reading to the present volume.

CHAPTER 8

Group Development

Regularities in the Development of Small Groups

We have referred several times to the impermanence and fluidity which characterise some aspects of group processes and to certain changes which usually occur over time. The general picture is one of a dynamic relationship between people, their milieu, their perceived needs and their aims. Change in any one of these factors leads to change in the others, as satisfaction and harmony are continually sought. There are many examples of this, some of which the reader has already encountered.

The change phenomena we have touched upon include changes in status and role distribution. We saw that status and role-assignment relate closely to the needs perceived by the group, but we saw also that these needs and perceptions change, thus inducing change in structure. In introducing Bales' studies, we noted a general tendency for the leader's popularity to decline, which often results in the leader role becoming more diffused throughout the group. We have seen that the style, content and level of communication and interaction are all subject to change. We have also hinted at the existence of a critical stage in group development at which disagreement between subgroups about group objectives may cause the fragmentation of the group. The list could go on.

These are not mere theoretical constructs. In social-work groups, the practitioner is confronted with the reality of this shifting scene. Sometimes change is rapid, even dramatic. At other times, more commonly, change gradually evolves. Much of the social worker's thinking and activity has to be directed towards understanding and meeting the new demands and needs suggested by changes in the dynamics of the group. One has not worked with many groups before it becomes evident that they must all, like individuals, deal sequentially with a series of problems involving dependency, identification, relationships, values and goals. As with the individual, these maturational tasks generate internal tension, conflict and defence; the resolution of these is decisive for the group's harmony and efficiency—perhaps for its survival. The practitioner is virtually compelled by such observations to raise the questions: "Are there recurrent phases or cycles in small-group development? Some predictable patterns which the social worker may recognise, prepare for and try in some way to influence in the service of the group? Or does each group develop in an entirely idiosyncratic manner, quite unlike all others?"

Relatively few scientific studies have been addressed to these questions. Some of those which have, such as Bales and Strodtbeck's study mentioned above, are dubiously applicable to treatment groups, as opposed to laboratory groups. The investigation of regularities in the overall development of group behaviour in treatment situations presents a challenge which research methodology has until recently been unable to meet without some surrender of scientific standards. The sheer number of interdependent factors involved is a major obstacle. Further, it is not possible to standardise chosen factors in order to facilitate reliable and valid inquiry into other variables, since the overall picture would then be lost. Even more important is the objection that in social-work practice the "variables" are people and their resources, their feelings and their problems, all of which must be allowed to come freely to expression, rather than be restricted and controlled for purposes of research.

The possible existence of patterns of group development remains, however, even if they are not readily accessible to research. The importance of this possibility to practitioners with groups of various kinds has been reflected in recent years in a number of attempts to describe developmental sequences which seem to have emerged in practice. Group psychotherapists, social workers and, not least, practitioners of human relations training have all made contributions.[1] These have necessarily been mainly based on accumulated impressions rather than vigorous scientific study and seem at first sight to vary widely. A number of factors contribute to this impression.

Some Differences Between Proposed Models
of Group Development

As with theories of individual personality development, the various observers' frames of reference substantially influence the shaping of the models proposed. The behavioural science or clinical orientation to which the observer has been most exposed influence both his outlook and terminology. Thus, some differences are simply semantic, the same or very similar phenomena being named quite differently.

A more important point is that theory affects perception. Different observers therefore focus on different features of the group process. This is, however, also influenced by the method and setting of the group practice which provides the framework for observation. Thus, Scheidlinger, *et al.* (1959), writing on activity group therapy for children, describe a pattern of development in which the children's changing patterns of play and use of media are emphasised. Austin (1957), writing on detached group work with street-corner gangs, is involved in a setting where the delicately balanced and challenging relationship between the worker and the group is necessarily in the forefront of the worker's concern. It is therefore not surprising that in the sequence of developmental steps which he briefly sketches, he emphasises changes in that relationship and their implications for the group. Standish and Semrad (1951) base their model on groups of psychiatric patients in a mental hospital. Their observations focus on changes in attitude to the hospital environment, changing degrees of inhibition and freedom in expressing anxiety-laden material, and the development of re-orientation towards society outside the hospital and the group.

Garland, *et al.* (1965), introducing their very creative formulation, recognise this problem and comment:

> Since the construction of our model was based primarily upon observation of formed club groups, whose members had not been closely associated prior to formation, its applicability may be limited to groups of this general type. A question may be posed as to whether this model would apply to other kinds of groups, such as already-existing friendship groups that come into agencies ... or to committees and other task groups. ... It remains for practitioners who are working with various types of groups to test the model to see where it does or does not apply.

Not only the agency setting but also the clinical method employed with the group observed has bearing on this question. Formulations developed from practice necessarily relate to groups which are influenced by some kind of formal leadership. The aims and styles of leadership vary greatly, however. This also causes some variation in the sequential patterns which emerge. For example, Thelen and Dickerman (1949) and Bennis and Shepard (1956) are interested in group development phenomena in T-groups. The leadership style of such groups is, however, so different from that of most social-work groups that we would expect it to give rise to some differences in development patterns. The literature on marathon group therapy also includes several observations of developmental process (Rogers, 1967; Stoller, 1968; Schwartz and Schwartz, 1969, and others). These all focus on changes in such central features of marathon therapy as the arousal of defences against self-confrontation, and various responses to the increasing pressure to expose conflicts and problems and to give more open and genuine expression of inter-personal feelings.

Theories of group development also vary widely in degree of refinement or differentiation. Some formulations suggest that three phases of group development may be discerned. At least one proposes as many as eight recurring stages (Bugental and Haigh, 1965). There are numerous formulations between these extremes, and some observers do not perceive group development as occuring by "phases" at all, but rather by cycles—as in a life cycle, or by progressively deeper repetition of similar patterns of work with the central group problem. (In particular, the formulations by Schutz (1958), and Mills (1964) represent the latter type of conceptualisation).

Some Areas of Similarity Between Models
of Group Development

Are there, then, so many differences between these various formulations that a generally applicable model of group development must be regarded as unattainable? Such a view would be too pessimistic. Careful study of existing formulations shows that extensive areas of similarity and accord are concealed by the differences in emphasis, focus, terminology and degrees of refinement which we have mentioned.

We shall give three, out of many possible examples of such areas of similarity.

1. An early developmental feature which is included in most formulations is the initial tentative behaviour of members. Members of newly formed groups tend to be preoccupied with locating themselves in the group, finding out what the expectations are, getting feedback on their first self-presentations and testing the possibilities of forming relationships on the basis of some common characteristics, needs or interests.

This stage in development is similarly perceived, though differently described, in most formulations. For example, Maier (1964), who presents a four-phased developmental model, draws attention to this tentative and exploratory behaviour in his first phase. He refers to it as "locating commonness".[2] Hartley and Hartley (1961), who present a six-phased model, include this element as a feature of both their first and second phases, known as the Phases of Exploration and of Identification, respectively. Garland, *et al.* (1965), who present a five-phased model, include this element in their first phase which is called the Pre-affiliative—approach/avoidance—Phase.

2. Testing-out of the worker and/or agency occurs so often that it, too, is included in most formulations. Many qualities on the part of the worker may be tested—his understanding, his consistency, his ability to accept, his possible investment in established views of moral and social behaviour, his tolerance of provocation and his freedom from authoritarian attitudes, among others. Most writers who mention this testing-out behaviour observe that it is usually most prominent during the early life of groups. Indeed in some formulations it is included in the initial exploratory phase referred to above.

In the context of group psychotherapy, Mann (1955) perceives the uncertainty and defensive hostility underlying such testing-out as a critical feature of the group situation. He points out that unless it is appropriately dealt with members may never achieve a therapeutically meaningful involvement in the group. Austin (1957), in the contrasting setting of detached social work, includes "varied and often intense testing" in the third of his six phases. Standish and Semrad (1951), during treatment of hospitalised psychotic patients, discerned four phases of group development. The first of these was characterised by a hostile and suspicious testing out of the institution, which necessarily occurred mainly through the medium of the worker. Mintz (1967) sees the development of marathon group therapy as occurring in four stages. In the second and third of these, particularly the second, attacks on the therapist's competence usually occur and attempts are made to unsettle him by expression of futility and boredom. Schwartz and Zalba (1971) present an anthology of group work in a broad range of settings. While no model of group development as such is offered, testing out is reported in the first meetings of a number of groups in settings which vary from a hospital ward for paraplegic adults to a treatment home for children with severe emotional disturbances.

3. Many formulations refer to a stage of group development characterised by competition for the more dominant roles in the group. Bales (1953, *op.cit.*) describes the frequent and early occurrence in small groups of a phase of agitation and conflict, which he sees as reflecting a struggle for high status. Thelen and Dickerman (1949) refer to the first stage of their four-phased model as the "Individually-centred, Competititve Phase". In their study of eight groups, each of three weeks' duration, they found repeatedly that members were engaged at an early stage in establishing themselves in the leadership hierarchy. (Commonly, the T-groups studied seemed to want a strong leader to take over and accept responsibility. This reminds us that although the leader may assume his role or achieve it by struggle, he may also have it thrust upon him.) Garland *et al.* (*op.cit.*) see status struggle as the most salient feature of their second phase, which they accordingly call the "Phase of Power and Control".

At Attempt at Unification

We have tried to show that both differences and similarities exist in observations and theories about the ways in which small groups develop, but that the apparent differences in fact cloak a good deal of similarity.

Some of the differences noted arise from the varied nature of the groups observed and of their leadership. Certain formulations may perhaps be valid only in the setting concerned. However, the areas of similarity—only a few of which have been touched upon here—are very extensive, and relate to phenomena of such importance in group life that they compellingly invite the group worker or group theorist to attempt to unify them into a single model of more general applicability.

In this regard we are indebted to two American social workers, Rosemary Sarri and Maeda Galinsky (1967), who have formulated such a general "conceptual framework for group development". Their attempt is based on an extensive literature review, from which they have abstracted the regularities which most consistently appear. Findings from a wide range of practice descriptions and experimental studies are included. Their formulation is intended to relate to all groups, "regardless of their objectives, composition and environmental location, or whether or not they are served by a professional or other type of worker". To our knowledge no thorough scientific study of this rather bold contention has yet taken place. In the absence of such testing we must take a position based upon our observations and opinions.

In the attempt to construct a generally applicable model, Sarri and Galinsky have been compelled to adopt a somewhat unspecific formulative style. However, it seems to us that their formulation does indeed describe regularities met by social workers in a wide variety of settings, *mutatis mutandis.*

Sarri and Galinsky relate their observations to their own extensive and varied social group-work experience. On this basis they have also proposed a treatment-sequence model which suggests appropriate intervention by the social worker at each stage of the group's development. (This will not be described here, as this is not a publication on group-work method.)

We shall now present a resumé of Sarri and Galinsky's model. We shall indicate the main changes in group structure, group culture and "group operating procedures" (i.e. activities, tasks, and decision-making) which run through this formulation.

It will be seen that a seven-phased pattern of small-group development is proposed, composed of the Phase of Origin, the Formative Phase, the First-intermediate Phase, the Phase of Revision, the Second-intermediate Phase, the Phase of Maturity, and the Phase of Termination. The authors stress, however, that all seven phases will not be experienced by every group, since some will circumnavigate certain of the proposed phases. This is particularly the case with the Phase of

Revision and the Second-intermediate Phase. It will be seen that these phases have no relevance if the Formative Phase has resulted in a structure which already serves the long-term goals of the group. Other groups may need to go through these phases several times, particularly where there is conflict or uncertainty about group aims, where there is protracted status struggle, or where members are markedly immature and lacking in social skills. Changes of sequence might also occur. Overlapping between phases will always occur, the divisions into discrete phases being only an arbitrary device to aid clarity of formulation. Group development is a continuum of evolving behaviour, rather than a series of abrupt and separate steps. It is also evident that different groups will need very different periods of time to resolve the problems of each phase. Phase II may last for one hour in one group, and several months in another. In short, no group will tidily demonstrate all the phenomena described according to some prescribed plan, but it is suggested that every group will demonstrate enough of them for this model to provide a useful developmental frame of reference for the social worker.

Parallel with the resumé of Sarri and Galinsky's model, we also present an illustrative case record, which describes social work with a group of refugees. It is intended to show the manifestations in practice of some of the phenomena to which these authors refer. This case has been chosen since it represents the "middle range" where duration of group life is concerned. The events recorded occurred over a period of three to four months; a sufficient length of time for a great deal of process to become evident, but not so long that it is difficult to gain an overview.

From Phase II onwards each separate component point in the resumé of the model will be numbered, and each illustration in the case material will be related to the appropriate point by the corresponding number.

Sarri and Galinsky's Model of Group Development and a Case Illustration

MODEL

EXAMPLE

PHASE I

The Phase of Origin

This refers to the pre-formation situation of members and the composition of the group at time of formation. It does not include any activity from time of formation onwards. While not a phase of group development in a strictly logical sense, it contains vital preconditions for the development which will follow.

Sarri and Galinsky emphasize here the relevance of such factors as members' personal characteristics and problems, their initial orientations towards the group and group service, the size of the group, and its environmental location (including the functions and philosophy of the agency).

Agency. Board of Refugees of a West European Country.

Members of group. Male East European refugees, some of whom are already acquainted. Two nationalities represented. All are handicapped in various ways. Ages range from 21 to 55 years, and periods spent in refugee centres in Southern Europe vary from 2 to 15 years. Several members have earlier been unsuccessfully placed in other countries and returned to refugee centres. Members arrive together. They and the social worker are to live together for three to four months as sole residents of a privately owned hostel a few miles outside an industrial city.

Size of group: Twelve members; a size considered optimal for proposed purposes. Low enough to enable participation by all in various group tasks. Interpersonal ties and interaction within the whole group are theoretically possible, as well as identification with group conducive to group support. Number is, however, high enough to allow some constructive sub-group formation.

Assumed problems. Language. Needs for medical, rehabilitation, job placement, and industrial training service. Identity conflicts arising from cultural disorientation and from fantasies (or reality) of rejection by country of origin. Fear of inadequacy engendered by movement towards independent living, following lengthy period of institutionalisation (apathy and dependence are common in

226

these groups).

Ambivalence and aggression towards the "generous host" country which may be seen as expecting gratitude and idealisation.

Function of worker

(A) To assist members with their psycho-social problems, so that the best possible adjustment to their transition crisis occurs, with a view to best possible solution of relocation-problems.

(B) To arrange language training and orientation on the host-country's culture, laws and way of life. To arrange relevant excursions and meetings with the local population.

(C) To assist the members to find suitable accommodation and employment, or employment-training. To introduce case-workers who will provide supportive individual help after termination of the group, if this is not also to be given by the present worker.

(D) In general to use professional skills, knowledge and relationships so that this group experience maximally contributes to the above objectives and to the harmony and enrichment of the members' life-situations, widely conceived.

MODEL

PHASE II

The Formative Phase

1. Members seek similarities in background, in personal values and attitudes in expectations of the group and attempt generally to establish areas of compatibility.

2. The tentative relationships which begin to emerge already give rise to a partial, and usually transient, structuring of the group. This is called the "quasi-structure".

3. The emergence as leader of a member

First hours. Tentative and exploratory behaviour. Contacts briefly established, by reaffirming earlier acquaintance, or by asking about time spent as refugee, which refugee centre, nationality, whether previously placed, etc. (see 1 in model). Four members quite inactive. Three of these seem anxious, particularly in relation to social worker, whilst one of them, Stefan, seems secure in his silence, aloof (see 2 and 8).

MODEL   EXAMPLE

who has assertive and aggressive character traits.[3]

4. He receives deference, however, because of the order and direction which he gives the group.

5. The "search for commonality" causes the tentative emergence of norms based on common values and attitudes.

6. These become further clarified in terms of acceptable forms of behaviour within the group. In this, the initial leader has considerable influence.

7. It is necessary for the group's survival that it should be found more attractive than unattractive at this stage.

8. Testing-out of the worker frequently occurs at this stage, trying his understanding, acceptance, concern and reliability.

(Stefan—40 years old. His wife and only child killed in Budapest in 1956. Alcoholic. Partially sighted. Eight years as refugee. Not previously placed.)

First day. Sharing some necessary tasks produces more interaction and spontaneity. Members more freely mix languages, signs and interpreters' assistance in attempts to communicate (see 1 and 7). Occasional bubbles of something like gaiety occur, usually surrounding Luvac (see 2 and 7).

(Luvac—42 years old. Unmarried. Epileptic. 10 years as refugee. Placed once previously (in France). Returned by French authorities to refugee centre because of offences committed while drunk. Luvac denies both that he was drunk and that he committed offences, contending that he had an epileptic attack. "But it's all the same to me. I'll survive anyway." An expansive extroverted, attention-seeking man. Physically impressive. Charismatic. Focal already first day. Says with a grin, "Don't look so glum, you lot. Life isn't so difficult" (see 2, 3, 4 and 6).

Towards social worker some members display rather exaggerated interest in building-styles, textiles, terrain, etc. This seems artificial and placatory, being the "appreciative tourist" (see 7 and 8). Others carefully make only necessary remarks and questions, otherwise remaining quiet. Little ability to decide and organise, group being dependent upon or cautious about social worker, with exceptions of Stefan, Luvac and Anton (see 2 and 8).

(Anton, 55 years old. Machine-tool cutter. Political activist when younger. Lost arm in accident during rail-movement of political prisoners. Mature, independent, quiet but not uncommunicative.)

MODEL

EXAMPLE

PHASE III

The First Intermediate Phase

9. Interpersonal ties increase, thus introducing a moderate level of group cohesion. Having experienced events in common also contributes to this.

10. Cliques and sub-groups may now begin to form as a result of a successful "search for commonality".

11. Additional norms and values are acquired which specifically relate to group functioning.

12. Social control in the direction of conformity develops as a result of this. It may be harsh.

13. Norms and values in favour of attitudinal expression are rarely arrived at by this stage.

14. There is increasing clarity and consensus about the objectives of the group.

15. Thus activities tend to be more goal-directed.

16. This in its turn necessitates role-differentiation, which now becomes more apparent.

17. In particular, task and socio-emotional leaders may be more clearly seen.

18. Where the quasi-structure has given status to a leader who serves only short-term objectives of the group, conflict will necessarily arise from the group's increasing orientation towards its long-term objectives.

19. This may be a causative factor in the "honeymoon" phenomenon described at this stage; the tendency to idealise the group and its leader, and to "keep things as they are". This may serve, among other purposes, those of avoiding confrontation with underlying problems, as well as the difficulties of resolving the structure conflict mentioned in 18 above.

At three weeks. Group has become active in language study, questions to orientation speakers, visits of interest, etc. (see 11, 14 and 15)—and in their interactions with each other (see 9). Domestic and other tasks are fairly shared, following a rota arranged by the group members (see 11). Different potentialities for learning and adaptation already becoming clear, but this factor is not a basis for selecting associates. Overall level of interaction is high, relationships generally are positive (see 7 and 9). Members are mobile. Sub-groups form transiently on basis of common nationality, age group, previous acquaintance or common handicap (see 1 and 10) without becoming crystallized into cliques. The embarrassing failure of a "social evening", organised by a local chapel, seems to have intensified group identification and cohesion (see 9). The group were not able to use this experience also as a manifestation of a major problem, namely culture-conflict, calling for ventilation and working through (see 13 and 19).

Only two members, Stefan and Luvac, are seen to belong to all sub-groups. They now occupy polarised roles in the group, and are accorded contrasting statuses.

Stefan speaks rarely, sitting quietly and listening critically to the others' discussions. His contributions are, however, disturbing. He interposes short, pessimistic, disillusioned comments which often silence the group. "It's all hopeless, and you know it" ... The food in this country isn't fit for pigs" ... "People here use us to ease their social conscience, contributing their pennies in World Refugee Week, but in fact they couldn't care less about you and me" ... "Don't

EXAMPLE

expect any real help. You're not welcome" ...

The members, with the notable exception of Anton, have begun to avoid Stefan. They defend themselves against identification with his views by ridiculing and rejecting him. ... "Our little ray of sunshine ... etc. " (see 12 and 13). Luvac has become a highly influential and central figure. Highest status. Talks constantly. Invests intensely in "keeping up the atmosphere". His only apparent source of displeasure is Stefan, whom he regards as a depressing and disturbing influence. ... "He spoils things every time we get into a good mood and begin to enjoy ourselves. To Hell with him. ... " Stefan appears indifferent to Luvac's opinion. This intensifies the tension between them, which finds expression in Luvac's, and therefore the group's increasing isolation of him (see 6, 12 and 16—19).

In their acceptance of Luvac's leadership, with its reliance on defences of denial and over-compensation, the group is establishing norms (see 12 and 13) which prevent clarification and solution of painful problems (see 19). The tensions arising from helplessness, dependence and anxiety are relieved instead by projection into the one member able to experience and express these feelings (see 12, 16 and 19).

At three to five weeks. In these weeks no change in structure of group has occurred, although both Anton and social worker have intervened in various ways with the respective aims of protecting Stefan and of gradually enabling the group to recognise in themselves the fears and feelings to which only Stefan gives expression. The group's activity pattern, however, has undergone some change, in that there is less investment in learning and in sharing tasks. There is a developing apathy or depression, as if members are becoming increasingly preoccupied, perhaps with the problems hitherto unsuccessfully dealt with (see 18 and 19).

MODEL   EXAMPLE

PHASE IV

The Phase of Revision

20. This phase consists primarily of a revision of leadership. It occurs either where leadership has been invested in one who does not serve the group's objectives, or in one who is so authoritarian that he excludes other members of the group from the leadership function.

21. Increased role-differentiation can be expected, with more members assuming leadership functions in their particular areas of competance.

22. Security in new roles, increased interdependence and interaction and the growing possibility of task satisfaction have two consequences:
(a) the likelihood of positive feelings between members is increased, and
(b) members are freer to express negative reactions.

23. This increased safety and cohesion results in a reduction—not a strengthening—of the rigidity of group behaviour and controls.

24. Norms and values of the group will usually undergo some modification. If not, they will be reinforced by further clarification.

25. Further clarification of group purposes can be expected, both during the following revision.

During the sixth week. One rather passive member, Jan, 46 years old, a former school teacher with alcohol problems, has been placed in a mental hospital following a psychotic episode. This event, and increased contact with the outside world, including potential employers, have reinforced the attempt of both the social worker and Anton to demonstrate the reality in much of Stefan's anxiety and pessimism. While Luvac continues to be well accepted in his role of social-emotional leader his influence on attitudes and approach to group task is declining. Anton—serious, mature and reflective—is now more deferred to (see 17, 20, and 21). Anton's relationship to Stefan has also helped the group to acknowledge the feelings they share with Stefan. He is for the first time offered acceptance and respect (see 21-24). Interestingly, he now presents a more balanced view of their situation, mentioning resources and sources of hope, as well as bluntly stating the harsher realities (see 15, 22 and 23).

PHASE V

Second Intermediate Phase

26. Many earlier problems are now solved. Group resources are therefore now readily available for co-operation in specific goal-required activities.

27. This involves a continuing increase in role-specialization and diffusion of leadership.

Seventh to tenth week. Structure stabilised as described in sixth week, except for more clearly defined sub-groups (see 26 and 28). Sub-groups now and for remainder of group life consist of stable friendship relations along axes of intellectual capacity, cultural interests and

MODEL

EXAMPLE

28. Equilibrium is fairly quickly restored following revision, resulting in a high level of group cohesion, identification and stability of structure.

29. The group's influence upon individual members may now be very high. More "traditions" and both clearer and purposive norms exist.

maturity levels, rather than the more visible and superficial criteria of the Formative and First Intermediate Phases (see 28, 31 and 33). Group-as-a-whole well able to tolerate this (see 23), not least since sub-group membership does not hinder contribution to task of group-as-a-whole (see 25 and 26). For example, a sub-group of four members (including Anton) spend free time playing chess, and through one member's contact with a local widow have also begun to spend some evenings with local people in the village (see 24, 25, 27, and 30). Nevertheless, this sub-group, all of whom are intellectually well endowed, give much help to others with language study, discussion of problems, local orientation, etc. (see 26, 27 and 29). By this time the group-as-a-whole is "looking outwards", so that this sub-group gives the group-as-a-whole very relevant help indeed (see 26, 29 and 31). The approaching transition to life outside the group has made relevant a great deal of work with releated fear and feelings. The group is now moderately well able to undertake this (see 24, 26, 30, 32). Luvac, having become somewhat isolated, is in need of considerable support from the worker. His continued dependence upon defence by denial is too well established to justify any attempt to modify this in the present situation (or perhaps at any time?).

PHASE VI

The Phase of Maturation

30. A high level of group functioning with consensus on and mobility towards objectives.

31. Well-developed and accepted structure with clear ranking, specialized and interdependent roles, sub-groups and proliferated interpersonal ties.

32. Patterns of problem-solving decision-making and implementation well established.

Tenth to fifteenth weeks. During eleventh week, first member, the 25 year-old Bela, an unskilled worker, now leaves the group to work in an hotel in a nearby town. Returns on his free days for the next two weeks, but not thereafter. During twelfth week two more leave; Josef, 36 years, to work in his field as an engineering draughtsman, and Anton to enter a Rehabilitation Centre for training in use

MODEL

EXAMPLE

33. Relatively stable relationships exist at levels of both internal and external system, but effective procedures for achieving and/or adapting to change exist. It is a state of "dynamic equilibrium". This phase is rarely experienced in social work, both because the individual clients will have achieved their goals by the time this stage is attained, and because a group which is able to function at this level has little need for professional service.

of his artificial limb and in certain industrial skills. ... All are placed by the fifteenth week. This final period, with its emphasis on gradual dissolution, militates against a high degree of group identification and support, and weakens structure. Members seem to withdraw somewhat from each other, as if consciously preparing for independence. Processes of differentiation seem to dominate. Much social work is now at an individual level, concerned with individual problems of work placement, training, housing, transfer to local caseworkers, etc. Group activity centres mainly round the daily life of the hostel, free-time activity and language training. Members are again reluctant to take up personal problems at group level.

PHASE VII

The Phase of Termination

Sarri and Galinsky see the termination of groups as resulting from one or more of four general conditions.

1. Goals are attained and the group has no reason to continue in existence.

2. Groups are established for definite periods of time, specified at time of group formation.

3. Group terminates through lack of integration, as when its members are unable to agree about goals, or because it is for other reasons unable to provide satisfaction to members.

4. Groups may terminate because of "maladaptation", usually where groups have not developed effective means for responding to needs for change.

Termination of this group results from both conditions 1 and 2. A flexible time-limit was imposed, but it was assumed within three to four months the members should be able to live and work away from the group. Within the range of reasonable expectations consistent with that time limit, it may be contended that group goals have been attained.

It will be noted that the group has not attained the very high degree of functioning which characterised the Phase of Maturation, Phase VI. »

Although the case material approaching termination occasionally exhibits some traits of this phase (which are noted) we cannot contend that the group established itself at this level. Whether it would have done so with more time is a matter for speculation. The group may have been too heterogeneous to attain any higher degree of cohesion and maturity of functioning than that reflected in this record.

The above presentation has attempted both to introduce Sarri and Galinsky's model of small-group development and to exemplify it by means of a case resumé. Consistent with the practice and purpose of this book we have not referred to the social worker's treatment interventions, and have limited the material to the sequence which Sarri and Galinsky claim to be typical for small groups "with or without formal leadership". Where groups "with formal leadership" are concered, which of course includes social-work groúps, we wish finally to make a cautionary comment.

The case material in this chapter has been selected from an unusually extensive record. Nothing, however, really guarantees that the material chosen is truly representative of the group, according to stringent scientific standards, nor that other phenomena than those selected were not more germane to the group's development. The possibility always exists in this kind of observation that we have become committed to the theories and models which stimulate us, and that this causes us unknowingly to limit our perceptions to the phenomena to which they refer. This in turn may in pratice have the effect that we influence the direction the group takes, perhaps quite unconsciously, in order that it better accords with our theories and preconceptions. This is the problem of "self-fulfilling prophecies", whose relevance extends far beyond that of group development theory.

Our attitudes to both knowledge and to people enter in here. Knowledge of human behaviour and emotions cannot and must not be regarded as an accumulating store of immutable rules and laws. It is true that it consists of systematised and sensitive observation and testing. But it is equally true that it is open, like all knowledge, to modification in the light of new learning and evidence. Our present knowledge is limited and much of it tentative; much of it will be modified or discarded in the future, so that commitment to any model as if it were unassailable truth is grotesquely inappropriate. The infinite complexity of any one man, not to mention a group, demands an approach to understanding which is continually open to modification and new thinking, and which is always prepared to see and consider perspectives which have not earlier been registered. The good scientist has regard for open and rigorous methods of inquiry and therefore for new impulses and questions, and has humility in the face of the extent of his own ignorance. The social worker, whose "material" is other human beings, must not have less humility, nor less regard for the importance of pursuing understanding on the basis of sensitive observation, disciplined method and readiness to be wrong.

We hope that the introduction to group theory in the foregoing pages, among its virtues and faults, reflects these qualities, as well as providing an introduction to basic concepts in the field which, hopefully, will be of interest and use to the begining group worker.

Notes to Chapter 8

1. In the preamble to their model of developmental phases, Garland *et al. (op.cit.)* present an incomplete but informative review of these studies, which is recommended, as is that by Douglas (*op. cit.*). The review by Tuckman (1965) is perhaps more extensive. It, too, is now incomplete, however, mainly because of the recent resurge of development studies which make use of the Hill Interaction Matrix, (*op.cit*).

2. Henry Maier, who is Professor of Social Group Work at the University of Washington, is one investigator who has for some years been engaged in rigorous scientific study of group development. He proposes that group members' qualitative involvement with each other as expressed through their problems of interaction tends to occur in four different levels, and that these consistently follow a similar progressive pattern in *all* primary groups. While no conclusive material has yet been published, many progress reports are of considerable interest. See, for example, Maier (1964, *op.cit.*), Maier and Crawford (1972) and Crawford (1972).

    While I have the opportunity I would like to thank Prof. Maier for an encouraging and informative correspondence.

3. Sarri and Galinsky derive this from Theodorson (1953). I question the universality of this. It does seem to be true where the group feels manipulated, guilty or very insecure, or has aggressive feelings towards the agency, the worker or others. Such situations are, of course, frequently met in social work. But it is also common that a conciliatory person, a smooth diplomat or "The Life of the Party" emerges as the initial leader. In a group of mature people, well able to discriminate and evaluate, it is also probable that the initial leader will be a mature person who possesses those qualities which are most relevant to the group's main purposes.

    In a model aiming at general applicability it would probably be more appropriate to emphasise that the leader who emerges initially is able to meet the needs most acutely experienced at the Formative Phase. Sarri and Galinsky's important main point then holds good, namely that these needs are not necessarily the same as the long-term ones. (Hence, the Revision Phase.) Thus, the "assertive and aggressive" leader is a special, but common, case exemplifying this general observation.

References

Alphabetically by authors.

The following abbreviations are frequently used:

C.G.S.	=	*Comparative Group Studies* (Sage Publications).
S.C.	=	*Social Casework* (published by Family Service Association of America).
S.W.	=	*Social Work* (published by National Association of Social Workers).
Small Groups	=	*Small Groups: Studies in Social Interaction,* Hare, P., Borgatta, E.F. and Bales, R.F. (eds.); Knopf, New York, 1955.

Abramson, M (1975) "Group treatment of families of burn-injured patients", *S.C., vol. 56, no. 4, April, 1975, pp. 235-241.*

Ackley, E.G. and Fliegel, B.R. (1960) "A social work approach to street-corner girls", *S.W.,* vol. 4, no. 4, pp. 27-36.

Adams, R. (1974) *Watership Down,* Penguin, London.

Alexander, F. (1942) *Our Age of Unreason,* Lippincott, Philadelphia, pp. 253-255.

Appelbaum, S.A. (1967) "The world in need of a 'leader': an application of group psychology to international relations", *Br.J. Med. Psychol.,* vol 40, pp. 381-392.

Argyle, M. (1967) *The Psychology of Interpersonal Behaviour,* Penguin, London.

Argyle, M. and Dean, J. (1965) "Eye-contact, distance and affiliation", *Sociometry,* vol. 28, pp. 289-304.

Asch, S.E. (1951) "Effects of group pressure upon the modification and distortion of judgements", *Groups, Leadership and Men,* ed. Guetzkow, H., Rutgers University Press, Pittsburgh.

Asch, S.E. (1956) "Studies of independence and confirmity: I. A minority of the one against a unanimous majority", *Psychol. Monographs,* vol. 70, p. 416.

Austin, D. (1957) "Goals for gang workers", *S.W.,* vol. 2, no. 4, pp. 43-50.

Bach, G.R. (1966) "The marathon group, intensive practice of intimate interaction", *Psychol. Reports,* vol. 18, pp. 995-1002.

Bales, R.F. (1956) *Interaction Process Analysis,* Addison Wesley, Cambridge, Mass., p. 9 (N.B. A revised and extended presentation of this method is included in Bales', *Personality and Interpersonal Behaviour,* Holt, Rinehart and Winston, N.Y., 1970.)

Bales, R.F. (1955) "The equilibrium problem in small groups", in *Small Groups,* pp. 424-456.

Bales, R.F. and Borgatta, E.F. (1955) "Size of group as a factor in the interaction profile", in *Small Groups,* pp. 396-413.

Bales, R.F. and Strodtbeck, F.L. (1951) "Phases in group problem solving", *Abnorm. Soc. Psychol.,* no. 46, pp. 485-495.

Barclay, L.E. (1969) "A Group Approach to young unwed mothers", *S.C.,* vol. 50, no. 7, pp. 379-384.

Bateson, G. *et al.* (1963) "A note on the double bind", *Family Process,* no. 2.

Bateson, G., Jackson, D., Haley, J. and Weakland, J. (1956) "Toward a theory of Schizophrenia", *Behav. Sci.*, no. 1, pp. 251-264.

Benington, J. (1970) "Community development project", *Social Work Today*, vol. 1, no. 5, pp. 5-14.

Benne, K.D. and Sheats, P. (1948) "Functional roles of group members", *J. Social Issues*, vol. 4, pp. 41-49.

Bennett, E. (1955) "Discussion, decision, commitment and consensus in group decision", *Human Relations*, vol. 8, pp. 251-273.

Bennis, W.G. and Shepard, H.A. (1956) "A theory of group dynamics", *Human Relations*, vol. 9, no. 4, pp. 415-457.

Benoit-Smullyan, E. (1944) "Status, status types and status inter-relations", *Am. Sociol. Rev.*, vol. 9, pp. 151-161.

Berne, E. (1964) *Games People Play*, Grove Press, New York.

Bernstein, B. (1960) "Language and social class", *Br. J. Sociol.*, vol. 11, no. 3.

Bernstein, B. (1964) "Social class, speech systems and psychotherapy", *Br. J. Sociol.* vol. 15, no. 1.

Bettelheim, B. (1950) *Love is not enough*, Free Press, Glencoe, Illinois.

Bettelheim, B. (1955) *Truants from Life: the rehabilitation of emotionally disturbed children*, Free Press, Glencoe, Illinois.

Bettelheim, B. (1960) *The Informed Heart; autonomy in a mass age*, Free Press, Glencoe, Illinois.

Bion, W.R. (1961) *Experiences in Groups*, Tavistock, London.

Borgatta, E.F., Couch, A.S. and Bales, R.F. (1954) "Some findings relevant to the 'Great Man' theory of leadership", *Am. Sociol. Rev.*, vol. 19, pp. 755-759, also in *Small Groups*, 1955, pp. 568-574.

Bovard, E.W. (1952) "Experimental production of interpersonal effect", *J. Abnorm. Soc. Psychol.*, vol. 47, pp. 521-528.

Brown, D. Elizabeth (1960) "An experiment in mental health consultation", *Ventures in Professional Co-operation*, ed, Irvine, British Association of Psychiatric Social Workers, London.

Bugental, J.F.T. and Haigh, G.W. (1965) *Residential Basic Encounter Groups*, Psychological Service Associates, Los Angeles.

Caplan, G. *Concepts of Mental Health and Consultation*, Washington, D.C., Children's Bureau Publication, no. 373.

Caplan, G. (1961) *An Approach to Community Health*, Tavistock Publications, London.

Caplan, G. (1970) *The Theory and Practice of Mental Health Consultation*, Tavistock, London.

le Carré, J. (1964) *The Spy who came in from the Cold*, Pan, London, p. 48.

Cartwright, D. (1957) "Achieving change in people: some applications of group dynamic theory", *Human Relations*, no. 4, pp. 381-392.

Cattell, R.B. (1955) "Concepts and methods in the measurement of group syntality", *Small Groups*, pp. 107-126.

Cattell, R.B. Saunders, D.R. and Stice, G.F. (1955) "The dimensions of syntality in small groups" *Small Groups*, pp. 305-330.

Champion, B., Fein, A. and Samson, M. (1963) "Group meetings for mothers on ANC as preparation for employment", *Group Methods in the Public Welfare Program*, ed. Fenton, N. and Wiltse, K.T., Pacific Books, Palo Alto, pp. 104-110.

Cooley, C.S. (1909) *Social Organisation*, Scribner, New York, p. 23.

Crawford, K.B. (1972) *Testing a Theory of Group Development: a progress report*, School of Social Work, University of Washington (Master Thesis).

Crawshaw, R. (1969) "How sensitive is sensitivity training?", in Special Section Supplement, *Am. J. Psychiatry*, vol. 126, no. 6, pp. 136-141.

Deasy, L.C. (1964) *Social Role Theory: its component parts, and some applications*, Catholic University Press, Washington.

DeLong, A.J. (1971) "Dominance—territorial criteria and small-group structure", *C.G.S.*, vol. 2, no. 3, pp. 235-266.

Dinges, N.G. and Weigel, R.G. (1971) "The Marathon Group: a review of practice and research", *C.G.S.* vol. 2, no. 4, pp. 339-458.

Dittes, J.E. and Kelley, H.H. (1956) "Effects of different conditions of acceptance on conformity to group norms", *J. Abn. Soc. Psychology*, vol. 53, pp. 100-107.

Dittmann, A.T., Parloff, M.B. and Boomer, D.S. (1965) "Facial and bodily expression: a study of receptivity of emotional cues", *Psychiatry*, vol. 28, no. 3, pp. 239-244.

Docker-Drysdale, B.E. (1960) "The outsider and the insider in a therapeutic school", *Ventures in Professional Co-operation*, ed. Irvine, British Association of Psychiatric Social Workers, London.

Douglas, T. (1970) *A Decade of Small Group Theory, 1960-1970*, Bookstall Publications, London. 1970.

Durkin, H.R. (1964) *The Group in Depth*, International Universities Press, New York.

Eisen, A. (1958) "Group work with newly arrived patients in a mental hospital", *Social Work with Groups*, N.A.S.W., New York.

Eisenstein, F. (1959) "Life enrichment of the seriously handicapped through the group work process", *Social Work with Groups*, N.A.S.W., New York, pp. 30-40.

Ekman, P. (1964) "Bodily position, facial expression and verbal behaviour during interviews", *J. Abnorm. Soc. Psychol.* no. 68, pp. 295-301.

Erikson, E.H. (1963) *Childhood and Society*, W.W. Norton, New York, pp. 149-153.

Esser, A:H. (1973) "Cottage Fourteen: dominance and territoriality in a group of institutionalised boys", *S.G.B.*, vol. 4, no. 2, pp. 131-146.

Euster, G.L. (1972) "Social learning in school groups", *S. W.*, vol. 7, no. 5, pp. 64-70.

Exline, R.V., Thibaut, J. *et al.* "Visual interaction in relation to Machiavellianism and an unethical act", *Am. Psychol.*, vol. 16, p. 396.

Ezriel, H. (1950) "A psychoanalytic approach to group treatment", *Br. J. Med. Psychol.*, no. 23, pp. 59-74.

Feldman, R.A. (1967) "Determinants and objectives of social group work intervention", *Social Work Practice*, N.C.S.W., Columbia, New York, pp. 34-55.

Feldman, R.A. (1969) "Group integration, intense interpersonal dislike, and social group work intervention", *S. W.*, vol. 14, no. 3, pp. 30-39.

Fendrich, J.M. (1967) "A study of the association among verbal attitudes, commitment, and overt behaviour in different experimental situations", *Social Forces*, vol. 64, pp. 347-335.

Fenton, N. and Wiltse, K.T. (1963) *Group Methods in the Public Welfare Program*, Pacific Books, Palo Alto.

Fischer, P.H. (1953) "An analysis of the primary group", *Sociometry*, vol. 16, pp. 272-276.

Foren, R. (1954) "On not grunting", *Case Conference*, vol. 1, no. 4, pp. 19-20.

Foulkes, S.H. (1964) *Therapeutic Group Analysis*, Allen and Unwin, London.

Foulkes, S.H. and Anthony, E.J. (1965) *Group Psychotherapy; the psychoanalytic approach*, Penguin, London.

References 239

Freese, A.L. (1972) "Group therapy with exhibitionists and voyeurs" *S.W.*, vol. 7, no. 2, pp. 44-53.

Freud, S. (1955) *Moses and Monotheism,* (first published 1939), Random House, New York, p. 170.

Freud, S. (1950) *Collected Papers,* vol. V, Hogarth Press and Institute of Psychoanalysis, London, pp. 248-250.

Freud, S. (1921) *Group Psychology and the Analysis of the Ego,* Hogarth Press, London, pp. 6-9.

Frey, L. (1962) "Support and the group: a generic treatment form", *S.W.*, vol. 7, no. 4 pp. 35-42.

Frey, N.C. and Pizzitola, D. (1973) "Group therapy with schizophrenics", *S.W.*, vol. 18, no. 4, pp. 94-95.

Garland, J.A., Jones, H.E. and Kolodny, R. (1965) "A model for stages of development in social work groups", in *Explorations in Group Work,* ed. Bernstein, S., University of Boston.

Gibb, C.A., "The principles and traits of leadership", *J. Abnorm. Soc. Psychol.,* vol. 42, pp. 267-284; also in *Small Groups,* N.Y., 1955, pp. 87-95.

Ginott, H. (1965) *Between Parent and Child: new solutions to old problems,* New York.

Goetschius, G.W. and Tash, M.J. (1967) *Working with Unattached Youth,* Routledge and Kegan Paul, London.

Goffman, E. (1961) *Encounters,* Bobbs Merrill, New York.

Goldberg, E.M. (1968) "Working with the family in the child care field: concepts, methods and practice", *Social Work, the British Qu.Jnl.,* vol. 25, no. 1, pp. 9-19.

Golding, W. (1954) *The Lord of the Flies,* Faber and Faber, London.

Goldner, R. and Kyle, E.H. (1960) "A group approach to the cardiac patient", *S.C.,* vol. 41, no. 7, pp. 346-353.

Green, P.S. (1970) "Group work with welfare recipients", *S.W.*, vol. 15, no. 4, pp. 3-4 and 121-122.

Gross, E. (1956) "Symbiosis and consensus as integrative factors in small groups", *Am. Sociol. Rev.,* vol. XXI, pp. 174-179.

Grundy, D. and Wilson, S.F. (1973) "Diagnosis and planning of a community residence— A sociometric study" *S.G.B.,* vol. 4, no. 2, May 1973, pp. 206-226.

Gump, P. and Sutton-Smith, B. (1955) "Activity-setting and social interaction: a field study, *Am. J. Orthopsych.,* vol. 25, no. 4, pp. 755-760.

Halleck, S. (1963) "The impact of professional dishonesty on the behaviour of disturbed adolescents", *S.W.*, vol. 8, no. 2, pp. 48-56.

Hallowitz, E. and Stephens, B. (1959) "Group therapy with fathers", *S.C.,* vol. 40, no. 4, pp. 183-192.

Hare, A.P. (1952) "Interaction and consensus in different sized groups", *Am. Sociol. Rev.,* vol. 17, pp. 261-267.

Hartley, E.L. and Hartley, R.E. (1961) *Fundamentals of Social Psychology,* Knopf, New York, pp. 389-405.

Harvey, O.J. and Rutherford, J. (1960) "Status in the informal group: influence and influencibility at different age levels", *Child Development,* vol. 31, pp. 377-385.

Heap, K. (1966) "The scapegoat role in youth groups", *Case Conference,* vol. 12, no. 7, pp. 215-221.

Heap, K. (1968) "The social group worker as 'Central Person' ", *Social Work, Brit. Qu. Jnl.,* vol. 25, no. 1, pp. 20-29.

Heap, K. (1974) *Om prosessen i sosialt arbeid med grupper,* Munksgaard Publications, Copenhagen.

240   Group Theory for Social Workers

Heap, K. (1977) *Noen Malsettinger for ikke-verbale aktiviteter i sosialt arbeid med grupper,* Diakonhjemmets Sosialskole, Oslo.

Heap, K. and Killén-Heap, K. (1969) "Utredning og forslag til innhold av videreutdanning i individuelt sosialt arbeid og sosialt gruppearbeid", *Utredning om videreutdanning av sosionomer,* Norwegian Council of Social Work Education, Oslo, pp. 26-78.

Heinicke, C. and Bales, R.F. (1953) "Development trends in the structure of small groups", *Sociometry,* vol. 16, pp. 7-39.

Henry, J. (1963) *Culture Against Man,* Random House, New York.

Heymann, D. (1971) "The community: a function for the social worker in the antipoverty program", *The Practice of Group Work.* ed. Schwartz, W. and Zalba, S.R. Columbia Univ., New York, pp. 157-176.

Hill, W.F. (1966) *Hill Interaction Matrix (HIM),* monograph, Youth Studies Centres, University of Southern California, Los Angeles.

Hoffer, E. (1951) *The True Believer,* Perennial Library, Harper and Row, New York.

Hollander, E.P. (1958) "Conformity, status and idiosyncrasy credit", *Psychol. Rev.,* vol. 65, pp. 117-127.

Homans, G.C. (1951) *The Human Group,* Routledge and Kegan Paul, London.

Horowitz, M.W., Lyons, J. and Perlmutter, H.U. (1951) "Interactions of forces in discussion groups", *Human Relations,* vol. 4, pp. 57-76.

Irvine, E.E. (1963) "Transference and reality in the casework relationship", *Relationship in Casework,* Association of Psychiatric Social Workers, London, pp. 53-66.

Isaacs, S. (1933) *Social Development in Young Children,* Harcourt Brace, New York.

Jackson, J. (1969) Interview, *Playboy Magazine,* Chicago, Nov. 1969.

Jehu, D. (1969) *Learning Theory and Social Work,* Routledge and Kegan Paul, London.

Jehu, D., Hardiker, P., Yelloly, M. and Shaw, M. (1972) *Behavioural Modification in Social Work,* Wiley, London.

Jennings, H.H. (1950) *Leadership and Isolation,* 2nd ed., Longmans, Green, New York.

Joselyn, I.M. (1952) *The Adolescent and his World,* F.S.A.A., New York, pp. 39-40.

Kangas, J.A. (1967) "Self-disclosure in small groups as a function of structure, leadership, and sex", Master's thesis, Washington State University.

Kangas, J.A. (1971) "Group member's self-disclosure: a function of preceding self-disclosure by leader or other group member", *C.G.S.,* vol. 2, no. 1, pp. 65-70.

Kendon, A. (1965) *Some Functions of Gaze-direction in Social Interaction,* report to Science Research Council.

Kesey, K. (1962) *One Flew over the Cuckoo's Nest,* Signet Books, New York.

Klein, J. (1963) *Working with Groups,* Hutchinson University Library, London, p. 95.

Knapp, V.S. and Hansen, H. (1973) "Helping the parents of children with leukemia", *S.W.,* vol. 18, no. 4, pp. 70-75.

Knowles, M. and Knowles, H. (1959) *Introduction to Group Dynamics,* Association Press, New York.

Konopka G. (1970) "Our outcast youth", *S.W.,* vol. 15, no. 4, pp. 76-86.

Laing, R. (1960) *The Self and Others,* Tavistock, London.

Laing, R. and Esterson, A. (1964) *Sanity, Madness and the Family,* Tavistock, London.

Lambrick, H.M. (1962) "Communication with the patient", *The Almoner,* vol. XV, no. 7k, also in *Social Work and Social Values,* ed. Younghusband, pub. Allen and Unwin, London, 1967, pp. 191-200.

Lavin, A. (1970) "Simultaneous groups as a means of treatment in a child guidance clinic", *Social Work Today,* vol. 1, no. 7, pp. 5-11.

Laverty, R. (1962) "Reactivation of sibling rivalry in older people", *S.W.*, vol. 7, no. 1, pp. 23-30.

Leary, T., (1957) *Interpersonal Diagnosis of Personality: a functional theory and method for personality evaluation,* Ronald, New York.

Leavitt, H.J. (1951) "Some effects of certain communication patterns on group performance", *J. Abnorm. Soc. Psychol.,* no. 46, pp. 38-50.

Le Bon, G. (1895) *Psychologie des foules,* F. Olean, Paris, Trans. *The Crowd,* Fisher Unwin, London 1896.

Leonard, P. (1966) *Sociology in Social Work,* Routledge and Kegan Paul, London, pp. 61-63.

Leonard, W.M. (1974) " A sociometric analysis of a group treatment home" *S.G.B.,* vol. 5, no. 3, pp. 274-288.

Levinson, H.M. (1973) "Use and misuse of groups", *S.W.,* vol. 18, no. 1, pp. 66-73.

Lewin, K. (1938) *The Conceptual Representation and Measurement of Psychological Forces,* Duke University Press, Durham, N.C.

Lewin, K. (1951) *Field Theory in Social Science,* ed. Dorwin Cartwright, Harper and Brothers, New York.

Lewin, K., and Lippit, R. (1938) "An experimental approach to the study of democracy and autocracy: a preliminary note", *Sociometry,* vol. 1, pp. 292-300; also in *Small Groups,* 1955, pp. 516-523.

Lewin, K., Lippitt, R. and White, R. (1939) "Patterns of aggressive behaviour in experimentally designed social climates", *J. Soc. Psych.* vol. 10, pp. 271-299.

Lincoln, T.S. (1935) *The Dream in Primitive Cultures,* Cresset Press, London.

Lippitt, R. and White, R. (1953) "Leader behaviour and member reaction in three 'social climates' ", in *Group Dynamics,* ed. Cartwright and Zander, Row, Peterson; Evanston, Ill., chap. 40.

Loeb, E. (1960) "Some concepts for interdisciplinary practice", *S.W.,* vol. 5, no. 4, pp. 83-90.

Loeser, L.H.(1957) "Some aspects of group dynamics", *Int. J. Group Psychotherapy,* vol. 7, pp. 5-19.

Macarov, D. (1964) "Introduction to Group Processes" (mimeo), Hebrew University, Jerusalem.

McCulloch, M. (1954) "The 'grunting method' and matrimonial conciliation", *Case Conference,* vol. 1, no. 4, pp. 18-19.

McCulloch, M. and Ely, P. (1968) *Social Work with Groups,* Routledge and Kegan Paul, London, pp. 33-34.

Maier, H.W. (1964) "A Model of Phases of Group Development" (mimeo.), School of Social Work, University of Washington.

Maier, H.W. and Crawford, K.B. (1972) "A Model of Group Development" (mimeo.), School of Social Work, University of Washington.

Mann, J. (1955) "Some theoretical concepts of the group process", *Int. J. Group Psychotherapy,* vol. 5, no. 3, p. 236.

Matsushima, J. (1962) "Group work with emotionally disturbed children in residential treatment", *S:W.,* vol. 7, no. 2, pp. 62-70.

Matthews, J. (1964) "Social group work in youth clubs", *New Society,* 9th Jan. 1964.

Matthews, J. (1966) *Working with Youth Groups,* Univ. of London Press, London.

Mead, G.H. (1934) *Mind, Self and Society,* Chicago University Press.

Merei, F. (1971) "The pair and the group: experiments in group dynamics with children",

242 Group Theory for Social Workers

C.G.S., vol. 2, no. 1, pp. 17-24.

Merton, R.K. (1957) *Social Theory and Social Structure,* Free Press, Glencoe, Ill.

Middleman, R. (1968) *The Non-Verbal Method in Working with Groups,* Association Press, N.Y.

Mills, T.M. *Group Transformation. An analysis of a learning group,* Prentice Hall, N.Y.

Mintz, E.E. (1967) "Time-extended marathon groups", Psychotherapy: Theory, Research and Practice, 4, pp. 65-70.

Money-Kyrle, R. (1950) "Varieties of group formation", in *Psychoanalysis and the Social Sciences,* ed. Roheim, G., II, pp. 313-329.

Morales, A. (1971) "The collective preconscious and racism", *S.C.,* vol. 52, no. 5, pp. 285-293.

Moreno, J.L. (1953) *Who Shall Survive?* (revised ed.), Beacon House, New York.

Morris, D. (1967) *The Naked Ape,* Jonathan Cape, London, pp. 13-49.

Newcomb, T.M. (1952) "Attitude development as a function of reference groups: The Bennington study", *Readings in Social Psychology,* ed. Newcomb, T.M. and Hartley, E.L.; Holt Publ. Co., New York (2nd revised ed.).

Newson, J. and Newson, E. (1963) *Patterns of Infant Care in an Urban Community,* Pelican, London.

Newson, J. and Newson, E. (1970) *Four Years Old in an Urban Community,* Pelican, London.

Nursten, J. (1965) "Social work, social class, and speech systems", *Social Work, Brit. Qu. Jnl.,* vol. 22, no. 4.

O'Connor, A.L. (1970) "A creative living centre for the mentally ill", *S.C.,* vol. 51, no. 9, pp. 544-550.

Packard, V. (1959) *The Status Seekers,* McKay, New York, pp. 87-88.

Park, R.E. and Burgess, E.W. (1924) *Introduction to the Science of Society* (2nd ed.), University Press, Chicago.

Parker, T. (1970) *The Frying-Pan; a prison and its prisoners,* Hutchinson, London.

Parks, J.C. and Antenen, W. (1970) "A modified marathon with voluntarily institutionalised alcoholics: an interaction process analysis", *C.G.S.,* vol. 1, no. 4, pp. 357-372.

Parloff, M.B. (1970) "Group Therapy and the Small Group Field: an encounter" (mimeo.), Nat. Inst. of Mental Health, Bethesda, Maryland.

Parsons, T. (1951) *The Social System, London.*

Pentony, P. (1970) "Persons as teams: an analogy", *C.G.S.* vol. 1, no. 3, pp. 211-268.

Perlman, H.H. (1961) "The role concept and social casework: some explorations; I; the 'social' in social casework", *Social Service Rev.,* vol. 35, p. 378.

Perls, F.S. (1969) *Gestalt Therapy Verbatim,* Lafayette, Calif., Real People Press.

Polansky, N. (1952) "On the dynamics of behavioural contagion", *The Group,* April 1952; also in *Group Work; foundations and frontiers,* ed. Trecker, Whiteside-Morrow, New York, 1955, pp. 109-122.

Polansky, N., Lippitt, R. and Redl, F. (1950) "An investigation of behavioural contagion in groups", *Human Relations,* vol. III, pp. 319-348.

Polansky, N., Lippitt, R. and Grosser, D. (1951) "A laboratory study of behavioural contagion", *Human Relations,* vol. IV, pp. 115-142.

Psathas, G. (1960) "Phase movement and equilibrium tendencies in interaction process in psychotherapy groups", *Sociometry,* vol. 23, pp. 177-194.

Purcell, F.P. and Specht, H. (1965) "The house of Sixth Street", *S.W.,* vol. 10, no. 4,

p. 69-76.

Query, W.T. (1964) "Self-disclosure as a variable in group psychotherapy", *Int. J. Group Psychotherapy,* vol. 14, pp. 107-115.

Rabinovich, H., Hislop, D.H. and Derbyshire, R.L. (1973) "A vector model of small group behaviour", *S.G.B.,* vol. 4, no. 2, pp. 163-176.

Ramsøy, O. (1962) *Social Groups as System and Sub-system,* Scandinavian University Books, Oslo.

Ramsøy, O. (1964) "Rang og oppslutning: sammenhenger mellom en forslagstillers rang og forslagets skjebne", *Tids. for Samfunns Forskning,* Oslo, vol. 4, pp. 205-219.

Redl. F. (1942) "Group emotion and leadership", *Psychiatry,* no. 5, pp. 573-596, also in *Small Groups,* 1955, pp. 71-87.

Reese, W.H. (1961) "Relationship between self-acceptance and sociometric choices", *J. Abnorm. Soc. Psychol.,* no. 62, pp. 472-474.

Richards, L.D. and Lee, K.A. (1972) "Group process in social habilitation of the retarded", *S.C.,* vol. 53, no. 1, pp. 30-37.

Riehman, L. and O'Brien, C.F. (1973) "Project in apartment group living", *S.W.,* vol. 18, no. 3, pp. 36-43.

Robertson, J. (1958) *Young Children in Hospital,* Tavistock, London.

Robertson, R.B. (1954) *Of Whales and Men,* Knopf, New York.

Robinson, M.B. (1970) "A Study of the effects of focused video-tape feedback in group counselling", *C.G.S.,* vol. 1, no. 1, pp. 47-75.

Robson, R.A.H. (1966) "Group structure in mixed sex triads" (mimeo.), 1966, Referred in Argyle (1967, *op. cit.*).

Rogers, C.R. (1967) "The process of the basic encounter group", in *Challenge of Humanistic Psychology,* Bugental, ed., McGraw-Hill, New York, pp. 260-276.

Rogers, C. (1970) *Carl Rogers on Encounter Groups,* Harper, N.Y.

Riecken, H.W., and Homans, G.C. (1954) "Psychological aspects of social structure, in *Handbook of Social Psychology,* ed. Gardner, Lindzey; Addison-Wesley, Camb., pp. 786-833.

Sanges, K.B. (1962) "The group approach in a general hospital, part 2: a geriatric counselling group, *S.W.,* vol. 7, no. 4, pp. 61-65.

Sarbin, T.R. (1954) "Role Theory", in *Handbook of Social Psychology,* ed. Gardner lindzey; Addison-Wesley, Cambridge, Mass., pp. 223-258.

Sarri, R. and Galinsky, M. (1967) "A conceptual framework for group development", *Readings in Group Work Practice,* Campus Publishers, Michigan, pp. 72-94.

Satir, V. (1967) *Conjoint Family Therapy,* Palo Alto, Calif.

Saul, S., Segal, A. and Saul, S.R. (1962) "The use of the small group in orientating new residents to a home for the aged: the admissions group", *J. Jewish Community Service,* Spring 1962.

Schelderup-Ebbe, T. (1922) "Beiträge zur Socialpsychologie des Haushuhns", *Zeitchr. Psychol.,* vol. 88, pp. 225-252.

Scheidlinger, S. (1952) *Psychoanalysis and Group Behaviour; a study of Freudian group psychology,* Norton, New York, 1952.

Scheidlinger, S., Douville, M., Harrahill, C., King, C. and Minor, J.D. (1959) "Activity group therapy for childen in a family agency", *S.C.,* vol. 40, no. 4, pp. 193-201.

Schilder, P. (1940) "Introductory remarks on groups", *J. Soc. Psychol.,* vol. 12.

Schulman, L. (1971) "Program in group work: another look", in Schwartz, W. and Zalba, S.R., eds., *The Practice of Group Work,* Columbia, N.Y., 1971.

244   Group Theory for Social Workers

Schutz, W. (1958) F.I.R.O., *A 3-dimensional Theory of Interpersonal Orientation*, Holt, Rinehart and Winston, N.Y.

Schwartz, R. and Schwartz, J. (1969) "Growth encounters" *Voices* (Spring), pp. 7-16.

Schwartz, W. and Zalba, S.R. (1971) *The Practice of Social Group Work*, Columbia University, New York.

Schwarzmann, B. (1966) "Observations on the dynamics at play in a group of older people", *Medical Social Work*, vol. 19, pp. 159-165.

Shapiro, J. (1966) "Single-room occupancies: a community of the alone", *S. W.*, vol. 11, no. 4, pp. 23-33.

Shapiro, J. (1966) "Single-room occupancies: group work with urban rejects in a slum hotel", *The Practice of Group Work*, ed. Schwartz, W. and Zalba, S.R., Columbia Univ. Press, New York, pp. 25-44.

Sheridan, M.S. (1975) "Talk-time for hospitalised children", *S. W.*, vol. 20, no. 1, pp. 40-47.

Sherif, M. *et al.* (1961) *Intergroup Conflict and Co-operation: the Robbers' Cave Experiment*, University of Oklahoma Inst. of Group Relations, Norman, Oklahoma.

Sherif, M. and Sherif, C.W. (1964) *Reference Groups*, Harper and Row, New York, p. 166.

Shichor, D. (1976) "Noncomformity patterns of different types of leaders in small groups", *C.G.S.*, vol. 1, no. 3, pp. 269-274.

Silverstein, S. (1973) "The adolescent waiting room" *S. W.*, vol. 18, no. 6, pp. 105-107.

Singler, J.R. (1975) "Group work with hospitalized stroke patients", *S.C.*, vol. 56, no. 6, pp. 348-356.

Skjelsbaek, H. and Lundblad, L.G. (1972) *Et gruppearbeid med alkoholskadde menn*, Joint dissertation, Norwegian State School of Social Work and Municipal Administration, Oslo.

Sklar, A.D., Yalom, I.D., Zim, A. and Newell, G.L. (1970) "Time-extended group therapy: a controlled study", *C.G.S.*, vol. 1, no. 4, pp. 373-386.

Slater, P.E. (1955) "Role differentiation in small groups" in *Small Groups*, pp. 498-515.

Slavson, S.R. (1966) "The phenomenology and dynamics of silence in psychotherapy groups", *Int. J. Group Psychotherapy*, vol. 16, no. 4, pp. 395-405.

Sohl. J. (1967) *The Lemon Eaters*, Simon and Schuster, N.Y.

Specht, H. (1969) "Disruptive tactics", *S. W.*, vol. 14, no. 2, pp. 5-15.

Spergel, I. (1966) *Street Gang Work, Theory and Practice*, Addison-Wesley, Mass.

Sprott, W.J.H. (1955) *The Problem of Self-Respect*, Fourth Charles Russell Memorial Lecture, University of Nottingham, p. 8.

Sprott, W.H. (1958) *Human Groups*, Penguin, London, pp. 160-166.

Standish, C.T. and Semrad, E.V. "Group psychotherapy with psychotics" *J. of Psychiatric Social Work*, vol. 20, no. 4, pp. 143-150.

Star, S.A., Williams, R.M. and Stouffer, S.A. (1958) "Negro infantry platoons in white companies" in *Readings in Social Psychology*, ed. MacCoby, Newcomb and Hartley; Holt, N.Y. p. 596.

Steinzor, B. (1950) "The spatial factor in face to face discussion groups", *J. Abnorm. Soc. Psychol.*, no. 45, pp. 552-555; also in *Small Groups*, etc. ed. Hare, Borgatta and Bales, 1955, Knopf, New York, pp. 348-352.

Stephen, F.F. and Mishler, E.G. (1952) "The distribution of participation in small groups; an exponential approximation", *Am Sociol. Rev.*, vol. 17, pp. 598-608.

Sernbach, O. (1947) "The dynamics of psychotherapy in the group", *J. Child Psychiatry*, vol. 1, pp. 91-112.

Stoller, F. (1968) "Accelerated interaction: a time-limited approach based on the brief intensive group", *Int. J. Group Psychotherapy,* vol. 18, pp. 220-235.

Stoller, F.H. (1968) "Marathon group therapy", in *Innovations in Group Psychotherapy,* ed. Gazda, G.M.; Thomas, Springfield, Ill., pp. 42-95.

Storr, A. (1968) *Human Aggression,* Atheneum, London 1968, pp. 56-57, and Penguin, London, 1968, pp. 82-83.

Strickler, M. and Allgeyer, J. (1967) "The crisis group: a new application of crisis theory", *S.W.,* vol. 12, no. 3, pp. 28-32.

Talland, G.A. (1955) "Task and interaction process: some characteristics of therapeutic group discussion", in *Small Groups,* pp. 456-463.

Thelen, H. and Dickerman, W. (1949) "Stereotypes and the growth of groups", *Educational Leadership,* vol. 6, no. 5, pp. 309-316.

Theodorson, G.A. (1953) "Elements in the progressive development of small groups", *Social Forces,* vol. 31, pp. 311-320.

Thibaut, J.W. and Kelley, H.H. (1959) *The Social Psychology of Groups,* Wiley, New York.

Thomas, E. and Fink, C.F. (1963) "Effects of group size", *Psychol. Bull.,* vol. 60, pp. 371-384.

Thompson, S. and Kahn, J.H. (1970) *The Group Process as a Helping Technique,* Pergamon, London, pp. 23-27.

Tuckman, W. (1965) "Development sequence in small groups", *Psychol. Bull.,* vol. 63, no. 6, pp. 384-399.

Verba, S. (1961) *Small Groups and Political Behaviour: a study of leadership,* Princeton Univ. Press, New Jersey, pp. 217-225.

Verstrate, D. (1959) *Social Group Work with Deaf-Blind Adults,* American Foundation for the Blind, New York.

Vigilante, J.L. (1972) "Ethnic affirmation, or Kiss me, I'm Italian" *S.W.,* vol. 17, no. 3, pp. 10-20.   -20.

Vinter, R. (1967) "The essential components of social group work practice", *Readings in Group Work Practice,* ed. Vinter, Campus Publishers, Michigan, pp. 8-38.

Vinter, R. (1967) "Program activities: an analysis of their effects on participant behaviour", in *Readings in Group Work Practice,* ed. Vinter, Campus Publishers, Michigan, pp. 95-109.

Wahrman, R., (1974) "Some observations on sensitivity training research", *S.G.B.,* vol. 5, no. 3, pp. 321-330.

Walker, L. and Irvine, E.E. (1968) *Group Work with the Inarticulate,* F.S.U. Paper No. 1, London.

Wasser, E. (1966) *Creative Approaches in Casework with the Aging,* F.S.A.A., New York, p. 88.

Weiner, H.J. (1971) "The trade union: a group approach to link community mental health with labour", *The Practice of Group Work,* ed. Schwartz, W and Zalba, S.R., Columbia University Press, New York, pp. 144-156.

Whitaker, D. Stock and Lieberman, M.A. (1965) *Psychotherapy through the Group Process,* Tavistock, London.

Whittaker, J. (1974) "Program activities: their selection and use in a therapeutic milieu", in Glasser, P., Vinter, R. and Sarri, R. eds. *Individual Change through Small Groups,* Free Press, N.Y., pp. 244-257.

Wilson, G. and Ryland, G. (1949) *Social Group Work Practice,* Houghton, Mifflin,

Boston, pp. 65-76.

Wissler, C. (1912) "Societies and associations in the Oglala Division of the Teton-Dakota', *Anthropological Papers of the American Museum of Natural History,* vol. XI, pt. 1, N.Y.

Wolfe, T. (1970) *Radical Chic and Mau-Mauing the Flak Catchers,* Farrar, Straus and Giroux, New York.

Zadrozny, J.T. (1959) *Dictionary of Social Science,* Public Affairs Press, Washington, p. 169.

INDEX